S0-CPR-775

NATHANIEL HAWTHORNE

After the Painting by Cephas G. Thomson, 1850

THE REBELLIOUS PURITAN

The REBELLIOUS PURITAN: Portrait of Mr. Hawthorne

by

LLOYD MORRIS

In the depths of every heart there is a tomb and a dungeon, though the lights, the music, and revelry above may cause us to forget their existence, and the buried ones, or prisoners, whom they hide.

The Haunted Mind.

New York
HARCOURT, BRACE AND COMPANY
1927

PRINTED IN THE U. S. A. BY
QUINN & BODEN COMPANY, INC.
RAHWAY, N. J.

To

GLENWAY WESCOTT

. . . *forsan et haec olim meminisse invabit.*

ACKNOWLEDGMENT

Other than Hawthorne's own *Notebooks,* the books most important as sources of documentary material for his biography are: Julian Hawthorne's *Nathaniel Hawthorne and His Wife* (1885: James R. Osgood and Co.); Rose Hawthorne Lathrop's *Memories of Hawthorne* (1897: Houghton Mifflin Co.); Horatio Bridge's *Personal Recollections of Nathaniel Hawthorne* (1893: Harper and Bros.); Caroline Ticknor's *Hawthorne and His Publisher* (1913: Houghton Mifflin Co.); George Parsons Lathrop's *A Study of Hawthorne* (1876: James R. Osgood and Co.). The correspondence between Hawthorne and Ticknor published in part in *Hawthorne and His Publisher* was published in full by the Carteret Club of Newark, New Jersey, in a limited edition for the members. Many of the letters, diaries, and other records from which I have quoted were first published in one or another of these books.

Hawthorne's *Notebooks* were edited by his widow, who exercised unlimited liberty in preparing the published text, especially as respects deletion and emendation. Similar liberty was exercised by Julian Hawthorne in editing the correspondence between his father and his mother, a portion of which was published by him in his biography of his parents. Through the courtesy of the Morgan Library I have had recourse to such of Hawthorne's manuscript *Notebooks* as are still extant. In my quotations from the *Notebooks* I have followed, whenever possible, the manuscript and not the published version. Through the courtesy of Mr. William K. Bixby I have had the privilege of using the original texts of Hawthorne's letters to his wife, heretofore printed only in an edition of sixty-one copies for the Society of Dofobs. The charm and beauty of these love letters are very great; their value to his biographer is inestimable, for they reveal Hawthorne in a new and intimate light.

I am faced by the impossibility of acknowledging specifically my indebtedness to the innumerable sources of material relating to Hawthorne's life. A fairly comprehensive list of these sources is contained in Nina E. Browne's *A Bibliography of Hawthorne* (1905: Houghton Mifflin Co.); in addition to those therein listed, there are the memoirs and the correspondence of Hawthorne's friends and associates among the New England group of writers.

My grateful thanks for their courteous kindness are due, and are offered, to Miss Belle Greene and Miss Thurston of the Morgan Library; to Mr. William K. Bixby; and to Miss Rebecca Manning, Doctor Clifford Smythe, Mr. James Oppenheim, Mr. George S. Hellman, and the Essex Institute of Salem, Massachusetts.

L. M.

CONTENTS

ILLUSTRATIONS

THE REBELLIOUS PURITAN

THE ANCESTRAL FOOTSTEP

(I)

DECOROUSLY, one morning in the spring of 1808, death crept into an old house near the Salem wharves. "Bold Daniel" Hathorne had bought the place when he retired from the quarter-deck, choosing it because it gave him the illusion of proximity to the sea. He had lived there stormily, but after his death a strict propriety had governed the life of his home. Within its quiet rooms circumstance and mortality seemed destitute of casualness, as if calculated elements of an austere design. The household consisted of three women and the children of one of them; Rachel, the widow of Daniel; her daughter Ruth, a virgin aged thirty; Elizabeth, wife of Daniel's son, Nathaniel, the mother of a boy and two girls.

It was to Elizabeth that bereavement was announced; her husband had died of a fever at Surinam, during one of the protracted voyages habitually undertaken by Salem captains.

She called her son from the adjoining room. The child, a slender, bright-haired lad of four, came running to her side.

"Natty, your father is dead."

(II)

In later years, Nathaniel's memory of that morning

never lost its sharpness. During a lonely childhood and youth he brooded upon the simple facts of his family's history, gleaned from the casual allusions of his elders to events long past and people long deceased, or from the stories which they told him. Gradually he wove the fabric of the past, a texture somber as an ancient tapestry from which the brightness has faded, the figures of his ancestors forming an arrested procession in its obscurity. In this procession, as he became familiar with it, every figure had its story and every story had its meaning; the stories of his grandfather, and his grandfather's grandfather, and that remote ancestor's father; together their stories made a single story which also had its meaning. Of his own father Nathaniel had no recollection, but he knew that unremembered figure better than any other. For despite death, his father seemed to live, a ghostly lover, in the chamber where his mother had shut herself away and to which she admitted no visitors.

As he grew older, Nathaniel tried to understand the meaning of her seclusion, which no member of the family ever questioned. He tried to realize her thoughts and feelings on that morning when she told him of his father's death. He thought that he knew her story as she knew it; in his childhood it seemed a sad story, and later he perceived its irony. But only later still did he learn that she had spent her life in the service of a phantom; she had believed the phantom to be her husband, but it was not; she had given her life for that of a man who had never lived. Then he began to ponder her long immolation, and it seemed to him selfish and a little cruel. And, remembering the story he had made in his childhood, he knew it now not only as she had known it, but in another way as well.

HAWTHORNE'S BIRTHPLACE

In the northwest chamber of this house at 27 Union St., Salem, Hawthorne was born on July 4, 1804

(III)

The married life of his parents had been brief. A few years only, in which short periods of union alternated with longer ones of separation. In his mother's memory it must have possessed the quality, not of a continuous experience, but of a sequence of intense moments punctuating the tedious monotony of existence. If she reflected upon it in the early hours of her grief, it was probably not of the termination, but of the content of her marriage that she thought. Possibly she lingered among the memories of courtship, as fragile and precious as the bits of carved jade which her husband had brought home from the distant east. . . .

The gardens of old Captain Hathorne and of her father, Richard Manning, adjoined. A limited, formal intercourse had long been maintained by the two families. But the slender young shipmaster, enjoying the vacant intervals between voyages, soon found this insufficient, for he had fallen in love with his neighbor's grave and beautiful daughter. Nathaniel imagined the episode of his father's courtship; an affair of stilted, reticent notes, of sober flowers shyly offered and modestly accepted, of walks along decorous, elm-shaded streets. Like all the Hathornes, Captain Nathaniel had been severe and reserved; his sedateness was that of a man disciplined, from early youth, to responsibility and command. His taciturnity and the serious cast of his mind had impressed the sensitive girl; their love, flowering in a gentle silence, had seemed to her more perfect because of the delicacy of its absentions.

The Hathornes had been settled in Salem for nearly two centuries. Despite their declining prosperity, their prestige was still sufficient to establish their affairs in the concern of their neighbors. Dark legends of their early misadventures were revived and related to the Mannings. Anecdotes illustrative of the inflexibility of their character, the harshness of their temperament, and the eccentricity of their behavior were brought like gifts into the Manning home. Nothing of consequence could be asserted against the Hathornes except the deterioration of their fortunes. In a community which made moral probity a condition of existence, they had always been notable for their undeviating austerity. It was, perhaps, their composed, arrogant indifference to the interests and the opinion of Salem that had cost them, in all but every generation, the friendship though not the respect of their townsmen. Salem's view of Elizabeth Manning's marriage had been that of old Captain Knights, who, meeting Mr. Manning on the street, had drawled reflectively, "I hear your darter is going to marry the son of Captain Hathorne?"

"I believe she is," Mr. Manning had replied.

"I knowed him," the old Captain had continued, "I knowed the old man, and he was the sternest man that ever walked a deck!"

A few brief years; many long absences; then the idyll ended, leaving Elizabeth with her memories, her grief and her three children. It had made little difference to her, so her son reflected in after years, that similar losses had been suffered and survived by generations of Salem women to whom the tropical seas were the source of desolation as often as the source of fortune. In the early period of her widowhood nothing had been capable of dispelling her apathy.

In later years, whenever he revived the memory of that morning, Nathaniel recalled that the garden had stirred vaguely with the intimations of a meager New England spring. A resurrection and a life had been implied by that agitation, even as it was promised by the faith of his ancestors. After leaving childhood behind him, he pondered this promise. His father lived on in death as he had not lived in life; his mother, who still lived, seemed dead to all life. Was this the meaning of the promise? Or was its meaning to be found only in the solace of his mother's memories, more consoling to her than the life she had renounced?

(IV)

Shortly after her widowhood, Elizabeth removed to the Manning home, the grounds of which extended from Herbert Street to Union, where they adjoined the Hathorne garden. Two of Elizabeth's brothers resided there, one of whom had undertaken to provide for her children and herself, since her husband's death had left her with inadequate resources.

The two houses and plot of land between them, with its apple trees and currant bushes, encompassed Nathaniel's early years. His sister Ebe, two years his senior, was his companion; his younger sister, Louisa, was an infant when their mother became a widow. An enduring melancholy pervaded the Manning house, for the uncles were often away and Elizabeth maintained a rigorous seclusion. She left the house scarcely ever, and passed her days in the darkened solitude of her room. The house seemed to be inhabited by a gravely beautiful ghost, whose insubstantial existence, although remote from the routine of domestic life, dominated the household by an unacknowledged tyranny. It seemed as if, in that comfortable New England dwelling, there were being celebrated a secret rite of perpetual vigil and lamentation. The children saw their mother only briefly, when she came to them in their rooms; into her room, where she sat engrossed by her memories and her pieties, they were never permitted to penetrate. Her meals were served to her there, and the dining room, because of her invariable absence from the family table, echoed with the silent obstinacy of her grief. As time passed her intercourse with her children and the members of her family slackened. Her contact with the world outside her home gradually diminished and finally ceased. She was content, at last, in her isolation. In this desolate anti-life her rebellious heart achieved an austere, comfortless peace.

Nathaniel, a vivacious child, romps in the shaded grass plot that separates the silent houses of his relatives. In his ninth year an accident befalls him. While playing, he is struck on the foot by a ball, and from this injury there develops a serious lameness. He has already begun to attend school, a new one lately opened by Doctor Worcester, a scholar whose passion is lexicography. But the lameness interrupts his attendance, and Doctor Worcester comes every evening to the Manning home to continue the lessons.

At eleven, Nathaniel is a grave and gentle lad, condemned by his lameness to a continuously recumbent position; he lies in front of the fire in the parlor and reads all the books he can secure. Among them, he reads Shakespeare, Milton, Thomson and Rousseau. His first purchase, with money given to him by a relative, is *The Faërie Queene*. It opens a new world of enchantment and wonder. He reads Froissart's *Chronicles* and Clarendon's *History*, and is transported far from the bleak little parlor into a world of pageantry. In other hours he reads *The Newgate Calendar* and enters a world of violence. On Sundays he is permitted to cross the garden on his crutches, and spends the afternoon in the home of his grandmother Hathorne, crouching over a copy of *Pilgrim's Progress*; he has read it many times, but finds it forever new. He is extravagantly fond of cats. He has a pet cat for which, in idle moments, he builds houses of books, imprisoning her within the walls of his expanding culture. His disability isolates him from all companionship with boys of his own years.

Later in life Nathaniel realized that it was during this period of disability and convalescence that he had acquired an intimate knowledge of the annals of his family. Gradually, as he brooded upon the stories that he had been told, the past assumed a reality more convincing than his familiar environment. As he grew older his awareness of kinship with its figures, now no longer shadowy, became so intimate, his imagination of them so vivid, that he could not pass the burying-ground in Charter Street without seeing before him the somber procession of his ancestors. And on Sundays, when he attended service in the old First Church, it seemed to him that the present suddenly vanished, leaving him to take his place among five generations of stern, black-browed men who, like himself, had come there to propitiate an inexorable God.

Occasionally, in spring, he was taken to the top of Gallows Hill, where the witches had been put to death. It was glossy with dark green wood-wax and destitute of any other vegetation. Sometimes he fancied that the dust of those martyrs to superstition anciently bur-

HAWTHORNE HOUSE AT 12 HERBERT ST., SALEM

ied there had blasted the earth with a curse of perpetual barrenness. Lying in the sunshine and looking down upon the wooden-roofed town, he saw, instead of the Salem that lay stretched below him, the little first settlement with its peaked roofs set in patches of green. For that quaint village, whence the fortunes of his family had sprung, he felt both affection and hostility. Even in youth he was absorbed by its possession of himself. Nothing, he fancied, would be capable of breaking the spell of that possession, enforced by the continuity of two centuries of antecedent life that had flowed into his. Wherever the future might find him, he knew that it would be to Salem that he would return in spirit, as to the source of his being; he would return, perhaps involuntarily, under the compulsion of a heritage as inevitable as destiny itself.

Whenever he summoned up that earlier Salem, so unlike the commonplace town in which he lived, the apparitions of his ancestors confronted him across the gulf of time.

(V)

The first settlement; the early Salem . . .

A cluster of houses, roughly built, huddling on the rocky shore of a bay; open to icy eastern gales and within sound of the incessant pounding of the surf. Around the houses a few acres of cleared land, planted to Indian corn, meager in its promise of fruitfulness. To the west a marsh, green with water moss; beyond this the ominous twilight of the wilderness. A trail, as yet scarcely a path, leads out across the marsh into the forest. It begins in the center of the tiny settlement, in front of a small, low-roofed house built, like the others, of rough-hewn timber. This is the meeting-house. It lacks a spire and bells, the dignity of richly stained windows, the quiet beauty of ancient carvings in stone and wood. But to the little congregation that gathers within it, it enshrines the presence of God.

Nathaniel's ancestor joined the settlement in 1637. William Hathorne had emigrated from Wiltshire at the age of twenty-three. He came to Massachusetts as a planter, one of the venturesome company brought by John Winthrop in 1630. He settled in the town of Dorchester, where he held grants of land, prospered, and was twice elected deputy to the Colonial Assembly. The town of Salem, learning of his excellent citizenship, offered him a grant of land as an inducement to transfer his residence. William Hathorne's sagacity approved the compliment; he accepted the land and moved to Salem.

He rose to eminence in the community and the colony. Energy and righteousness collaborated in his success. "Grave, bearded, sable-cloaked and steeple-crowned," William Hathorne successively held most of the offices within the colony's gift. For nearly a quarter of a century he was Speaker of the Assembly; he was frequently a magistrate; he served as commissioner of marriages and as tax-collector; he was chosen captain of the first military organization to be founded in Salem and in due time was commissioned major. These occupations did not deplete his energy. He planned the formation of a great company to undertake a monopoly of the trade in furs. He made frequent journeys into the wilderness; to trade with the Indians, to ratify treaties with them, to subjugate them, and, when necessary, to kill them. He took with him upon these excursions a Bible as well as his sword and blunderbuss; for his own spiritual satisfaction and, no doubt, for the edification of the redskins. Occasionally he preached in Salem and the neighboring towns as well, and his exhortations to piety were memorable for their vehemence. Even secular literature engaged his attention, for he imported from England an early edition of Sir Philip Sidney's *Arcadia,* and admired it sufficiently to preserve it for his children.

Severe and uncompromising in his private life, Major Hathorne's discharge of his official duties won him the confidence and admiration of his fellow-townsmen. In his lifetime the settlement became a town; the log houses gave way to substantial dwellings with massive central chimneys and many gables; the woodland receded; the marsh was bridged with stout oak logs; the trail became a street. William Hathorne continued to prosper. He married, and his family increased with his fortune. He was equally eminent as merchant, warrior, and official.

In his fifty-ninth year, Major Hathorne's colonial patriotism impelled him to covert, but sturdy, defiance of his king. In the previous year, Charles II had sent a commission of inquiry to the colony. Upon its return it presented a report which induced the king to issue orders to the General Court of Massachusetts for the appearance in London of Governor Bellingham, William Hathorne and others. The General Court declined to obey the king's mandate. Then, under an anagram of his own name, Major Hathorne wrote to Secretary Morrice in London, defending the colonial government against the accusations of the Royal Commission of Inquiry, and justifying the disobedience of the General Court to His Majesty's commands. He reminded Mr. Morrice of the causes leading to the settlement of Massachusetts, and of the provisions of the charter which guaranteed the colony full direction of its own religious affairs. "If the wall of the civil government be pulled down," he prophesied, "the wild boar will soon destroy the Lord's vineyard. . . . There are not wanting many sectaries and profane persons that are sprung up among themselves, who do long for such an opportunity."

Major Hathorne's pious zeal, his terror of the perils of heresy, were expressed more emphatically in his magisterial sentences upon itinerant preachers of unauthorized doctrines and other wild boars who threatened the Puritan vineyard. These sentences were invariably severe, but never more so than when the delinquents belonged to the dangerous sect of Quakers. He ordered five women of that sect to be stripped to the waist, bound to the tails of carts, and lashed by the constable as they were dragged through Salem, Boston, and Dedham. This, he hoped, would prove an example to all sinners. Justice, with him, was an austere and exacting virtue; sin, a necessary preoccupation. At seventy years, he ordered the execution of a fellow-townsman for the crime of shooting an Indian. Three years later, a vigorous and martial figure, he led the opposition to Randolph. Within the year he died. With rewards and honors appropriate to his undeviating rectitude, he went confidently to meet the implacable God he had helped to create.

(VI)

When his father died, in 1681, John Hathorne was forty years of age. He had married Ruth, the daughter of Lieutenant George Gardner, and she had borne him three children. He occupied a seat in the Colonial Assembly; he held the rank of colonel in the military forces; he was a reputable and prosperous merchant. John Hathorne had achieved two of the aims permitted to Puritan ambition: a position of prominence in the affairs of the community, and a competence adequate to his station in life. He coveted an appointment to the bench.

The Salem of John Hathorne's maturity was a comfortable and pious town. The wilderness no longer threatened its existence; it was surrounded, now, by tidy hamlets and productive farms. Along the coast, as far as Portsmouth, similar towns succeeded one another, complacent in a frugal prosperity, rejoicing the eyes of God-fearing men, not offending those of the God they feared. The pioneers had suffered, toiled and died. They had begun the task of subduing the wilderness to the needs of the race; their successors continued it and subdued the sea as well; to agriculture there was now added a precarious but thriving trade with England. The novelty, the insecurity, the questionable stir of adventure had disappeared from colonial life. The new generation was less sturdy but more anxious than the old, more austere in the habit of its life, and more accessible to the importunity of sin. Righteousness was no longer an ideal to be approximated, but an accomplishment to be practised, in conduct. The detection of sin, usually in other people, had become an imperative moral obligation. Salem possessed the gallows, the pillory, the whipping-post, the stocks, and the cage. These were in frequent demand for the punishment of people who mistakenly assumed that the doctrine of religious liberty comprehended the liberty to differ, in matters of religion, with those who professed it.

The ten years following his father's death were marked by no important changes in the fortunes of John Hathorne. His wife presented him with a fourth child, a son, whom they named Joseph. Then, in the winter of 1692, as a suitable reward of his impeccable life and conscientious service, he received his appointment as judge. Almost immediately there occurred a series of events which terrorized the community.

A group of young girls and married women had been meeting at the home of Doctor Samuel Parris for the purpose of practising divination under the tuition of the minister's Indian servant, Tituba. The minister countenanced this questionable recreation, permitting his little daughter and young niece to join it. Suddenly a mysterious malady broke out among those who had indulged in it. They were racked by violent contortions and afflicted, in the meeting-house or on the street, by irresistible incentives to impiety. Their conduct became a public scandal. The town physician, consulted about their ailment, expressed the opinion that they had been bewitched; medical science afforded no relief. Doctor Parris, having ventured one Sabbath to implore divine mercy upon the afflicted females, had been interrupted during the very supplication by ribald indications of their affliction. He now summoned the clergymen of the vicinity to meet at his house for a day of fasting, prayer, and deliberation. The behavior of the women and girls upon this occasion was so monstrous as to leave no possible doubt in the minds of the ministers. It appeared certain that the afflicted ones were the victims of a sinister possession by evil spirits. To ferret out the witches was the next step.

The afflicted ones were questioned judicially, and the names of several women were extracted from them. Three of these women were brought before John Hathorne and Jonathan Curwen, sitting as examining magistrates, and were bound over for trial. Their examination was followed by that of two aged women, Martha Corey and Rebecca Nurse, both of hitherto saintly life, and that of a five-year-old child, Dorcas Good. By this time terror dominated the countryside. Rumor swept everywhere, attaching itself indiscriminately, now to this person, now to that. The slightest accusation was equivalent to indictment; nobody was safe from accusation. Peace and contentment had disappeared. Even the magistrates were susceptible to the general contagion of fear. Tales were circulated of aged folk who sped forth at night upon broomsticks to attend black masses in near-by forests, of children who impishly tortured their playmates in the dark of night, of reputable citizens who perpetrated crimes upon the bodies of their neighbors. There were those who confessed.

Rebecca Nurse, wife of Francis Nurse, was a grandmother. A lifetime of piety and toil had been blessed with family and fortune. In their extreme age Rebecca and Francis sat by their fireside contented with their lot, cherishing the love of their children and the friendship of their neighbors. Into their domestic peace the dread accusation came stealthily. Ann Putnam, a twelve-year-old child, and Abigail Williams, the minister's niece, testified that Rebecca had bewitched them. Twoscore of her neighbors signed a paper affirming that Rebecca had had no commerce with spirits and had practised no black arts. But this was of no avail. Rebecca was taken into custody and brought before Justice Hathorne for examination.

When she appeared before Justice Hathorne, she was instructed to stand with arms outstretched, in such fashion that her aged body was unsupported by chair or table. Francis, her husband, pleaded that he might be permitted to hold her by the hand, but his request was denied. Rebecca asked him to wipe the tears from her eyes, then asked Justice Hathorne whether she might not lean upon her husband, for she feared that she would faint. But Justice Hathorne replied that, since she had had sufficient strength to torture her two accusers, she should now have strength enough to stand alone. The two girls who had accused her were unable to endure her presence. When her defiant eyes met theirs they suffered torture, and one cried aloud and was seized with a fit. Rebecca quietly protested her innocence. Her husband murmured a complaint against the cruelty of the proceedings, and was commanded by Justice Hathorne to be silent, lest he be ejected from the room.

"Goody Nurse, here is now Ann Putnam, the child, and Abigail Williams complains of your hurting them," Justice Hathorne charged. "What do you say to it?"

"I can say before my Eternal Father that I am innocent, and God will clear my innocency."

"You do know whether you are guilty," Justice Hathorne continued, "and have familiarity with the Devil; and now when you are here present to see such a thing as these testify—a black man whispering in your ear, and devils about you—what do you say to it?"

"It is all false. I am clear."

"Is it not an unaccountable thing," Justice Hathorne asked, "that when you are examined, these persons are afflicted?"

"I have nobody to look to but God," Rebecca replied.

Despite her protestations of innocence, Rebecca was held for trial before the special court convened by the Governor, Sir William Phips, upon the advice of Doctor Increase Mather, to try the alleged witches. The court met at Salem to try no less than fifty people who were held in custody on the charge of having trafficked with the Devil. Rebecca was brought once again before Justice Hathorne and his colleagues. A jury twice de-

clared her innocent, but the court was not satisfied. She was interrogated a third time, and failed to reply to a question about the meaning of a phrase which it was alleged she had uttered in a previous examination. This time the jury declared her guilty. She was sentenced to death by hanging, and after the sentence had been read she turned toward Justice Hathorne and, looking fixedly upon him with old eyes that were now tearless, she solemnly cursed him and his posterity to the last generation.

A few weeks afterward a dolorous procession wound its way from the Salem jail toward Gallows Hill where, in the presence of an agitated crowd, the witches were put to death. One after another were hanged until, when it came the turn of old Giles Corey, the fury of the people exploded in violence. Seizing the old man from his jailors, they stretched him upon the ground and laid heavy stones upon him, one by one, until he died. That evening the people dispersed to their homes in high contentment.

After these events, ten more years of life remained to John Hathorne. Honors accumulated to him, but his fortunes declined. He was appointed justice of the Supreme Court of the colony, and held that office with dignity for seven years. Two of his children died, and his money dwindled away in a series of unsuccessful ventures. He was forced, at the last, to borrow money from his remaining children, and lacked the means to repay these loans. In his seventy-seventh year he died, embittered by his reverses, and his body was laid away in the Charter Street burying-ground. In the days of his greatest prosperity, he had purchased a wide tract of land in the northern forests, in what later was to become the state of Maine. But after his death, his heirs discovered that the title to this vast tract of wilderness had disappeared, unaccountably. And his descendants, disappointed of their inheritance, attributed their loss to the curse laid upon them by Rebecca Nurse.

(VII)

John Hathorne was succeeded by his son Joseph, the child of his middle age. His other sons, inheriting somewhat of their grandsire's hardihood, had followed the sea and engaged in the growing commerce with England. Unlike his brothers, Joseph did not crave adventure and the hazards of commerce. A timorous, home-loving man, he had few ambitions and no aspirations. He bought a farm in the vicinity of Salem, married Sarah, the daughter of Captain William Bowditch, and was content to abandon the claims of his predecessors to leadership in the colony's affairs. Public concerns did not engage his attention; he was enslaved by no dreams of power and prestige; no passionate conviction of superiority impelled him to achievement. "Farmer Joseph" he was called by his neighbors, and to Nathaniel, in his boyhood, the name portrayed the man. Joseph was satisfied with his crops, his cattle, and his growing family. He led an uneventful, almost humble, life, and with him the Hathorne name lapsed from the gentry into an undistinguished mediocrity. In the square house which he built amidst his rocky acres he died at an advanced age, surrounded by his family, and left behind him no memorials to accomplishment or to failure.

Joseph's youngest son, Daniel, like his paternal uncles, followed the sea. A robust man, blue-eyed and ruddy, he was of a violent, morose disposition and easily excited to passion or to wrath. After a wild youth, he fell in love. The object of his affections was a young woman of Boston named Mary Runnel. He courted her by lending her the folio copy of the *Arcadia* which his great-grandfather had imported from England, drawing her attention to the amatory lyrics by noting in the margin such injunctions as "Pray, mistris, read this!" and "Lucke upon this as if I my on selfe spacke it!" Mary returned his affection and his book, the latter with equally appropriate annotations, but the affair ended unhappily and Mary died shortly afterward. In the course of time Daniel recovered from this disappointment and married Rachel Phelps. He carried on the enterprise of trading, as a merchant captain, with the Indies, China, Africa, and Brazil. During the War of Independence Daniel became a privateer and his ship was the source of some losses to British commerce. He figured in a naval engagement off the coast of Portugal and put a British troopship to flight, earning for this exploit the sobriquet of "Bold Daniel." In due course of time he retired from the sea, bought a house convenient to the wharves of Salem, and was succeeded by his son Nathaniel in what had now come to be the family profession. "From father to son, for above a hundred years, they followed the sea; a gray-headed

DANIEL HAWTHORNE

shipmaster, in each generation, retiring from the quarter-deck to the homestead, while a boy of fourteen took the hereditary place before the mast, confronting the salt spray and the gale which had blustered against his sire and grandsire. The boy, also in due time, passed from the forecastle to the cabin, spent a tempestuous manhood, and returned from his world-wanderings to grow old, and die, and mingle his dust with the natal earth."

But, as Nathaniel learned in his boyhood, the Hathornes did not invariably come home to die. His father did not, but died miserably of a fever at Surinam. And his Uncle John had embarked upon a voyage, at the beginning of the War of 1812, and had never been heard from thereafter. John's mother, until the day of her death, believed that he still lived. And to the boy Nathaniel this uncle seemed to lead a ghostly existence, for the sad old lady was constantly hearing of people who answered to the description of her son, in one or another part of the world, and lived in the anticipation of his imminent return.

(VIII)

As Nathaniel brooded upon the lives led by his ancestors, the conviction grew upon him that his line was set apart, though not only by the indelible stain of the witch's curse, to which every misfortune was traditionally ascribed. Through the mist of their hazardous exploits, cruelties, renunciations and their diminishing fortune, he became aware of their common temperament. From that earliest hardy ancestor whose weapons had been the Bible, blunderbuss, and sword, to the father whom he could not recall, they had been armed for conflict always. It was their fortune to be engaged in contest. They strove with the wilderness, with the sea, with sin, with the stubborn soil, with adversity. Even their obdurate faith suggested a combat with God. Nathaniel did not know whether, to his ancestors, their God had been a lover to be possessed or an enemy to be vanquished. He thought that their perception of the hostility of circumstance to their projects had resigned them to isolation. Their reserve, their arrogance, and their indifference emphasized their acceptance and contempt. They found comfort in solitude and their native town had become, for them, little more than a familiar but alien asylum in which to await death. In every generation but one the story had been repeated; a conviction of superiority, an ambition for distinction, the bitterness of essential failure. In their melancholy they sought to overcome adversity by pride or indifference; it was their distinction to have been marked by God for obscurity and misfortune; they strove to outwit destiny, but esteemed their failure more honorable than another's success. Nathaniel saw his ancestors always alienated from the common fortunes of men, as though to be a Hathorne were a kind of doom, and he wondered what they would say to the last scion of their line, could they but communicate with him.

It was his father, whose absence, commemorated by his mother's seclusion, was more ponderable than physical presence, who turned Nathaniel's thoughts toward the sea. As he lay before the fire in the Manning parlor the dull clamor from near-by wharves wove itself into his day-dreams. Or from an upper window he would see the harbor and a ship outward bound, and a puff of wind from the east filled his nostrils with the

HAWTHORNE'S RESIDENCE AT RAYMOND, MAINE

bitter, salty odor of the Atlantic. At such times, if his mother were present, he would murmur, "I'm going away to sea some time, and I'll never come back again!"

(IX)

Ultimately he did go away, but not to sea. At Raymond, in Maine, his uncle Robert Manning owned a tract of land. Originally this tract had been the property of Justice Hathorne, but because of the mysterious disappearance of the deeds his heirs had been unable to establish their claims to it, and it had passed, after many years, into the hands of the Mannings. Robert Manning had built a comfortable home at Raymond, a house that would have been unremarked in decorous Essex County, but which seemed pretentious on the edge of the wilderness and was therefore called Manning's Folly. Across a little brook and opposite his own dwelling, Robert had built a similar house for his sister, which she had not yet occupied. It was pleasantly situated with a garden around it and beyond the garden an apple-orchard, and Elizabeth's brother urged her to install her family there. To this home, therefore, the Hathornes migrated in the autumn of 1818.

The Manning property was situated on the edge of a virgin forest. On a headland thrusting out into Lake Sebago there was a tiny settlement; the two homes, a mill and store, a few casual houses. To the northwest, low hills receded toward the distant White Mountains; to the east and north lay unfrequented ponds and dense woods. Limited as had been the resources of Nathaniel's life at Salem, at Raymond they were still further restricted. There were a few boys in the vicinity whom he came to know; there were his sisters, with whom he sometimes fished and tramped; but mostly he went his way alone. He angled for trout in the little brook or, lying in the sunshine on a flat rock above the lake, idly waited for the pickerel to bite. He swam, and ranged the woods with a fowling-piece, and picked up an easy acquaintance with the settlers who inhabited scattered clearings along the lake. In winter he skated alone on the lake and, often finding himself far from home at dusk, took refuge in a cabin where the half of a tree smoldered upon the hearth. Then, after stoking up the fire, he would sit under the huge chimney, gazing at the stars through the aperture in which the flames danced noisily. On stormy days he turned to books; Bunyan was a perennial favorite and Shakespeare and Spenser, but he read as well the popular writers of romance and fantasy.

On idle afternoons, lying in the sunlight on his favorite rock, he speculated about the future, seeking to imagine a life into which he might project himself as convincingly as he projected himself into the past. But the past bound him, and he could construct no image of his future except in terms of the lives of his father and grandfather. Even in these northern woods the sea was present always to his imagination; in the murmuring of the pines he heard an echo of the surf, and when the hills were muffled in mist the lake became a gray Atlantic. He saw himself following the traditional profession of the Hathornes, a career which would finally satisfy his eager curiosity about life and people and places. He would voyage in remote seas and trade in ports that were drowsy with the perfume of spices; he would barter with men whose skins were lemon-colored or brown or burnished black; he would walk the quarter-deck, night after night, under the Southern Cross, as his ship drove on toward the Horn; he would have sharp scrapes with pirates; he would visit the Dutch Indies, where dancers practiced curious rites before gruesome idols. . . . In the stories that he invented for the amusement of his sisters he multiplied his adventures in distant lands. But the stories came to an identical conclusion; when his ship tied up to the Salem wharf, his family would discover that he had unaccountably failed to return.

Not until much later did it occur to Nathaniel that the melancholy conclusion of these stories probably affected his mother's decision to send him back to Salem to prepare for college. Just after his fifteenth birthday he returned to the Manning home on Herbert Street, and was entered in a day school. The sudden curtailment of his liberty made Salem seem even less agreeable than his memories of it. His heart was still in Raymond, and the recollection of idle, careless days there induced a fit of depression and distaste for his native town. "I do not know what to do with myself here," he wrote to his sister Louisa. "I shall never be contented here, I am sure. I now go to a five-dollar school—I, that have been to a ten-dollar one. 'O Lucifer, son of the morning, how art thou fallen!' " In this letter he remarks that he has read *Waverley*, *The Mysteries of Udolpho*, *The Adventures of Ferdinand Count Fathom*, *Roderick Random* and the first volume of the *Arabian Nights*. He is "full of scraps of poetry," cannot keep it out of his brain, and produces, for her sisterly inspection, some dreary verses lamenting the passing of genius. These, he informs her, are his rhymes if not precisely his thoughts, and bids her tell Elizabeth that she is "not the only one of the family whose works have appeared in the papers." But, as if overcome with sudden embarrassment, he enjoins Louisa to show the letter to nobody but their mother.

He applied himself seriously to his studies, and read eagerly all the fiction and poetry he could obtain. He indulged his taste for writing by issuing four numbers of a paper entitled *The Spectator,* composed entirely of his own contributions. He was withdrawn from school, and his final preparation for college was entrusted to Benjamin Oliver, a lawyer of the town. Meanwhile, he was made to spend a portion of his time in the office of his uncle William Manning, who owned stage-coach lines serving the New England territory. Another letter to Louisa gently chides her for her ingratitude in not having sent him some examples of her verse. He has, he tells her, recently bought *The Lord of the Isles,* which he likes as well as any of Scott's poems. He has read Hogg's *Tales, Caleb Williams, St. Leon* and *Mandeville;* he admires Godwin's novels and intends to read all of them. "I shall read *The Abbot,* by the author of *Waverley,* as soon as I can hire it. I have read all of Scott's novels except that. I wish I had not, that I might have the pleasure of reading them again. Next to these I like *Caleb Williams.* I have almost given up writing poetry. No man can be a Poet and a book-keeper at the same time. I do find this place most 'dismal,' and have taken to chewing tobacco with all my might, which, I think, raises my spirits. . . . I do not think I shall ever go to college. I can scarcely bear the thought of living upon Uncle Robert for four years longer. How happy I should be to be able to say, 'I am Lord of myself'!"

A few months later he writes to his mother: "I dreamed the other night that I was walking by the Sebago; and when I awoke was so angry at finding it all a delusion that I gave Uncle Robert (who sleeps with me) a most horrible kick. I don't read so much now as I did, because I am more taken up in studying. I am quite reconciled to going to college, since I am to spend the vacations with you. Yet four years of the best part of my life is a great deal to throw away. I have not yet concluded what profession I shall have. The being a minister is of course out of the question. I should not think that even you could desire me to choose so dull a way of life. Oh, no, mother, I was not born to vegetate forever in one place, and to live and die as calm and tranquil as—a puddle of water. As to lawyers, there are so many of them already, that one half of them (upon a moderate calculation) are in a state of actual starvation. A physician, then, seems to be 'Hobson's choice'; but yet I should not like to live by the diseases and infirmities of my fellow creatures. And it would weigh very heavily on my conscience, in the course of my practice, if I should chance to send any unlucky patient 'ad inferum,' which being interpreted is, 'to the realms below.' Oh that I was rich enough to live without a profession! What do you think of my becoming an author, and relying for my support upon my pen? I think the illegibility of my handwriting is very author-like. How proud you would feel to see my works praised by the reviewers, as equal to the proudest of the scribbling sons of John Bull. But authors are always poor devils, and therefore

Satan may take them. I am in the same predicament as the honest gentleman in *Espriella's Letters:*

"'I am an Englishman, and naked I stand here
A-musing in my mind what garment I shall wear.'"

(x)

When in later life Nathaniel recollected the four years spent at Bowdoin College in Brunswick, he revived an impression of inward excitement and outward placidity. His life at Bowdoin, as he recalled it, might well have been composed of two independent existences, so slender seemed the connection between its external events and its intimate significance.

It had begun with a long trip by stage-coach from Boston, during which he struck up an acquaintance with two New Hampshire lads, Franklin Pierce and Jonathan Cilley, also on their way to Bowdoin; they had later become his intimate friends. Then the little town of Brunswick; a ragged village, remote from the highways of travel, with dusty unshaded streets, a tavern, a church, and a handful of commonplace dwellings on the borders of the college grounds. The college itself; a few unlovely buildings into which an earnest faculty herded about one hundred students and attempted to infect them with the contagion of culture. In his studies Nathaniel had found it possible to indulge his preferences. He had disliked mathematics and philosophy, neglected them, and had not been ashamed of his frequent failures in recitation. He had distinguished himself in Latin and in English composition. In other branches he had lapsed into a comfortable mediocrity, and had displayed only one idiosyncrasy, a steadfast refusal to declaim in chapel, as had been required of all students. Admonitions, reproofs, and fines imposed by an outraged faculty had been without avail. In his later life in England, when the making of addresses had become a part of his official

BOWDOIN COLLEGE, AS IT WAS IN HAWTHORNE'S DAY

duties as American consul, Nathaniel remembered painfully his early dislike of public speaking and its cause. Once in Salem he had gone upon the schoolroom platform to declaim and had been loudly ridiculed by some older schoolmates. His mortification had been so extreme that for nearly half a century afterward he had been incapable of mounting a platform and facing an audience; and never in his life could he do so with a sense of pleasure and ease. But at college his delinquency in declamation had been punished at graduation; although he ranked eighteenth in a class of thirty-

CAPTAIN NATHANIEL HAWTHORNE

eight, he had been denied a part in the Commencement exercises, failing to win the privilege of "speaking in public upon the stage."

He had been indolent in his studies and he had not been amenable to the severe discipline imposed upon the students by the sensitive conscience of President William Allen. Card-playing for stakes and the drinking of wines or spirits were forbidden; he had indulged in both at the comfortable tavern conducted by respectable Miss Ward. On one occasion, at the end of his freshman year, all the card-players had been discovered and summoned to appear before the President; one had been expelled, two suspended, and the remaining delinquents, Nathaniel among them, had been fined and their misconduct reported to their families by President Allen. In his letter to Madam Hathorne, the President had injudiciously remarked that perhaps Nathaniel "might not have gamed, were it not for the influence of a student whom we have dismissed from the college." Nathaniel's comment upon this had been pointed. "I was fully as willing to play as the person he suspects of having enticed me," he had informed his sister, "and would have been influenced by no one. I have a great mind to commence playing again, merely to show him that I scorn to be seduced by another." But the incident had not been lacking in effect. "I have involved myself in no 'foolish scrape,' as you say all my friends suppose," he had written to his sister, "but ever since my misfortune I have been as steady as a signpost and as sober as a deacon, have been in no 'blows' this term, nor drank any kind of 'wine or strong drink.' So that your comparison of me to the 'prodigious son' will hold good in nothing, except that I shall probably return penniless, for I have had no money these six weeks."

He had attached to himself, as companions rather than as friends, Franklin Pierce and Jonathan Cilley. Pierce was the son of a distinguished Revolutionary general, and his martial proclivities induced him to organize a military company at Bowdoin, which Nathaniel joined. The three had likewise joined the Athenæum, the more radical of Bowdoin's two literary clubs, in the modest library of which, as Nathaniel always believed, he had spent the most productive hours of his college residence. He had met, but had not then become intimate with, a boy who was afterward destined to become a valuable friend; Henry Longfellow, who at fourteen was Bowdoin's youngest and most accomplished student. And, most importantly of all, he had found, in a youth named Horatio Bridge, an intimate companion and confidant with whom to share the troubled excitement of his inward life.

(XI)

Until, in his seventeenth year, he met Horatio Bridge, Nathaniel had formed no intimate relationships whatever. His two years of invalidism and subsequent year of residence in Maine had removed him from all contact with boys of his own age. His childhood and adolescence had been spent in an atmosphere almost exclusively feminine, dominated by the morbid sensibility of his mother. The household had been, as though under quarantine, isolated from all contact with the world. Within the house every member of the family maintained an all but complete solitude. They were obsessed by the past, and had told him the tragic history of his family as a preparation for life. Its melancholy significance had been emphasized by their pride, embittered by an increasing adversity that testified to the efficacy of the curse that had been put upon them. He had therefore come to regard the world as hostile and contaminating; but his fear of it, nourished by every element of his environment, had only quickened his curiosity. This curiosity was further stimulated by his reading, which had familiarized him with the picture of life achieved in poetry and romance. He was eager for knowledge, but apprehensive of experience. At seventeen he was unsophisticated and exceptionally impressionable. He was sensitive, reticent, and abnormally introspective. He was painfully lonely, but scarcely realized it, for solitude had come to seem an inevitable condition of his existence.

Then, as it seemed to him at the time, a miracle had occurred. He had been introduced to Bridge one evening, and had been confused by the excitement with which the introduction was acknowledged. During the whole evening Bridge had never left his side; when others joined them, he became abruptly silent but never took his eyes from Nathaniel's face; when the gathering dispersed, Bridge had insisted upon making an appointment for the following day. His extraordinary attraction for this new acquaintance had embarrassed Nathaniel. He knew that his classmates considered him handsome; he was aware that his face was not without beauty and his body not without grace; but no one had ever sought as positively as had Bridge to win his regard. For Bridge had not attempted to conceal his admiration; as their acquaintance ripened into intimacy Nathaniel learned what it is to be loved. In the beginning of their association he had been embarrassed by Bridge's ingenuous expression of affection. Every shy, wistful glance and every casual gesture was an avowal. Bridge's eyes sparkled when Nathaniel addressed him, and his voice took on unaccustomed tones of tenderness when he replied. Nathaniel's habitual reserve was intensified by his embarrassment; afterward he realized that to Bridge he must have seemed discouragingly remote and indifferent. But Bridge, with a prophetic intuition of Nathaniel's necessity, had persisted imperturbably until his overtures met with success. For notwithstanding his apparent hostility, Nathaniel was lonely in his inaccessibility, and he suffered in his nostalgia for the companion he had never possessed. He was grateful for Bridge's patient confidence in the birth of their friendship, and accepted with reticent pleasure Bridge's romantic devotion.

It was chiefly with Bridge that Nathaniel wandered in the countryside about Brunswick. The college stood at the edge of a wide tract of pine forest where footpaths wound through miles of fragrant shade, and a brook loitered on its way to the Androscoggin River. The two companions shot pigeons and gray squirrels in the woods and fished the little brook for trout. On spring days they often strolled over the fields and along the river to the falls, and lingered to watch the pine logs from distant forests plunge over the brink and tumble into the foaming pool beneath. Another frequented walk took them to Maquoit Bay, a remote inlet of Casco, where the air held a faintly perceptible tang of salt and a dilapidated wharf and an occasional desolate lumber-sloop reminded Nathaniel of the seacoast. In the long evening twilight, after tea, they often tramped the deserted road along the river, and it was on these evening strolls that Nathaniel became most communicative. Darkness seemed a promise of secrecy that impelled him to confidences, and one night he confided to Bridge his desire to become a writer. To this tentative Bridge responded with enthusiasm, prophesying success and fame for Nathaniel as a writer of fiction. Of his conviction Bridge was able to give no rational account, but he reiterated his prophecy at every opportunity, and never with greater emphasis than when Nathaniel objected that he would never succeed in pleasing the public sufficiently to be supported in a literary career.

Nevertheless the encouragement so liberally given cheered Nathaniel, and hardened his wavering desire into firmness of purpose. He did not share Bridge's conviction, nor did he have any exceptional faith in his own abilities. To doubt was as natural to him as to believe was necessary. He considered himself excluded from the world and uninfluenced by its purposes and activities. But incommunicable even to Bridge and unacknowledged to himself he cherished a craving for fame and an ambition to achieve it; he wished to be isolated from the world, yet to affect it profoundly. He did not realize that this had been the ambition of his ancestors. Such as it was, it was sufficient to persuade him to resume the practice of writing.

In the summer of 1825 Nathaniel departed from Bowdoin; a slender, dark-haired youth whose eyes and sensitive lips and creamy skin produced the effect of beauty. He had profited by four years of college, having employed his time in acquiring, indolently and without effort, an acquaintance with literature and an ability to live among men. He had drawn to himself two friends and one intimate companion. He had, secretly and with trepidation, sketched out the draft of a novel and begun the labor of composition. And he had satisfied the expectations of his family; perhaps too well. The commendation of an uncle having preceded him from Brunswick, he wrote to his sister in an effort to modify their excessive ambition for him: "The family had before conceived much too high an opinion of my talents, and had probably formed expectations which I shall never realize. I have thought much upon the subject, and have finally come to the conclusion that I shall never make a distinguished figure in the world, and all I hope or wish is to plod along with the multitude. I do not say this for the purpose of drawing any flattery from you, but merely to set mother and the rest of you right upon a point where your partiality has led you astray. I did hope that Uncle

Robert's opinion of me was nearer to the truth, as his deportment toward me never expressed a very high estimation of my abilities."

What he hoped for was freedom to gratify his own ambition, not that of his family.

THE HAUNTED MIND

(I)

NATHANIEL returned to Salem and the old Manning house on Herbert Street. After his fifteenth year he had had little home life; the image of home attracted him, and his anticipations of domesticity were not without eagerness despite their moderation. The household that awaited him was almost precisely like that in which his childhood had been passed. His mother, after nearly two decades of widowhood, had not relaxed her isolation. She received none of her husband's relatives and met the members of her own family only infrequently. She never left the house, and seldom quitted her room. His elder sister, Elizabeth, was now a handsome girl of twenty-three. A masculine inflexibility of character made her seem more stable than she was; her sensibility was excessive and often precipitated stormy outbursts of emotion. Like her mother, Elizabeth was a recluse. She kept to her room throughout the day, began her day at dusk and made midnight her noontime. She read widely, and on rare daylight excursions she took long walks in the country. Salem gossip, exceptionally sensitive to the peculiarities of the Hathornes, affirmed that Elizabeth's seclusion was the consequence of a disappointment in love. If this were true she never admitted it, but as time passed her wit grew more caustic, the discipline of her routine became more rigorous, and an intolerance of all contacts hardened upon her like a shell. The younger sister, Maria Louisa, was verging upon womanhood. She lacked the austere, unyielding character possessed by her mother and sister. Unlike them, she was amiable and affectionate, fun-loving, and in a shy way eager for life. But the stern example of her mother and sister discouraged her. In the silence of that household it would have seemed a perversity to respond gaily to any experience. Louisa's seclusion, although reluctant, was all but complete. An old aunt, virginally fragile, pottered about the garden under a black hood; an elderly butterfly; a silent, ominous symbol of the household life. . . .

The addition of a man to this eccentric nunnery effected few changes in a routine of which the only common habit was to have no habits in common. Madam Hathorne was gratified by the presence of her son. Notwithstanding the lack of convincing evidence, her stubborn pride made her consider Nathaniel a genius. Pride was the only emotion capable of being aroused by a restless world that continued its incursions upon her despite her repudiation of it. Such other emotions as she still suffered referred only to the distant past. They were emotions no longer; what remained to her was the memories of ancient passions, desires and enmities which once had stirred into life and were now consecrated by their history. These, like her old-fashioned costumes, she wore with dignified indifference, as a priest wears the prescribed vestments; they had long since become the familiar garments of her established ritual. But her pride lived on, consuming its intensity in her contempt for the people of Salem, in a silent assertion of her superiority to them; and its scornful incandescence furnished the only warmth that she drew from life. An element of her pride was her love for her children; a bleak sentiment, forbidding and reticent, that disguised her lonely yearning for the affection it was inadequate to stimulate and incapable of receiving.

Nathaniel occupied a room under the eaves whose single window admitted the frugal afternoon sunlight and afforded him a view of the traffic of streets adjacent to the wharves. Here he began spending his days, gradually drifting into habits of isolation. His door was locked against casual interruption, but this was an unnecessary precaution, since nobody indicated any disposition to intrude upon his privacy. He spent the days in composition, and read in the evenings. He seldom went out by daylight, unless to bring home books from the Athenæum or to make an infrequent excursion afoot through the countryside or along the shore. Every evening he went walking, heedless of weather, and returned to eat a bowl of thick chocolate and bread, or a dish of fruit, and to read in his upper chamber. His mother and sisters ate their meals in their rooms; his were commonly brought to his door and left there to await his convenience. There were few opportunities for intercourse within the household, and although its members occasionally met one another by appointment Nathaniel scarcely ever saw his mother and sisters. "We do not even *live* at our house!" he said, in describing existence in Herbert Street.

Nathaniel had no friends in Salem and but few acquaintances. Hardly twenty people in the town, he thought, were aware of his existence. He frequented only the Athenæum, bringing home innumerable books; volumes of fiction which he examined with the patient care of an ambitious apprentice, and publications relating to the early history of Massachusetts. He was completely cut off from contact with Salem society. An earlier generation of Salem shipmasters had sent their fleets to the Orient, Africa, and South America. They had accumulated considerable fortunes, and had celebrated success by constructing substantial mansions whose hospitable gardens and graceful "captain's walks" commemorated both the uses and the origin of wealth. A thin stream of luxury had been diffused in the sober little town that had always prided itself upon retaining the simplicity of its earliest traditions. With the incidence of luxury a society had crystallized, a group of families living in comfort, aspiring to elegance, and cultivating the tradition of ancestry in a community which had not previously found it necessary to distinguish between genealogical values and biological facts.

Into this circumspect society Nathaniel did not penetrate. Neither the dinner-parties nor the daughters of Chestnut Street were graced by his attendance. Probably both exercised some attraction for him, for he was not destitute of social ambitions. But his eagerness was thwarted by poverty, diffidence, and pride. His pride was an inheritance. During three generations it had been injured and aggrieved. It had nourished its resentment upon the decline of the family fortunes and the disappearance of the family prestige. In Nathaniel it had become arrogance without assurance. The family conviction of superiority was, in Nathaniel, accompanied by a clear perception of the mediocrity of the situation into which the family had sunk, and of its actual inability to establish its claims. The Herbert Street household seemed very like that of a degraded and forgotten aristocracy; its members had withdrawn from a world which denied them their ancient prerogatives. Throughout his life Nathaniel was uncertain about questions of caste, and inconsistent in dealing with them. His associates were usually people who, from his own point of view, were his social inferiors. His preference was for the companionship of unpretentious, if not humble folk; possibly it furnished a compensation for his uneasy arrogance. His attitude toward people whom he considered his superiors in caste was resentful; he gratified the resentment by recording in his notebooks, with evident satisfaction, any adverse criticism made possible by their conduct.

During the twelve years of residence in Salem that succeeded his graduation from college, Nathaniel met only three men with whom he came to associate freely. All of them began life in somewhat humble circumstances. William B. Pike, who became a valued friend, was the son of a Salem carpenter. Pike adopted the paternal trade and the paternal religion as well, and during his youth was a zealous preacher of Methodism. Somewhat later in life he renounced the doctrines of

"THE HOUSE OF THE SEVEN GABLES"

This is the John Turner house at 54 Turner St., Salem

Wesley for those of Swedenborg, entered political life, and was ultimately appointed Collector of the Port of Salem. In one of his notebooks, Nathaniel described Pike as a "shortish man, very stoutly built, with a short neck—an apoplectic frame. . . . His face is dark and sallow,—ugly, but with a pleasant, kindly as well as strong and thoughtful expression." Pike's sturdy, phlegmatic figure did not suggest his eager, inarticulate mind, which was given to speculation upon abstruse metaphysical problems. He had a fund of shrewd common sense and wit. This, at a time when the natural wisdom of a natural man was considered a prime intellectual commodity, gave him some local reputation as a philosopher. Pike was an enthusiastic collector of local anecdotes and traditions. To Nathaniel, who was exploring the early history of Salem, Pike's stories constituted a windfall. Gradually, Nathaniel became attached to this simple, serious man whose devotion to him was equalled by a respectful admiration.

His two other friendships of the period were associated with an old, many-gabled house on Turner Street, not far from the Manning home and near the bay, a house then the property of a distant cousin, Miss Susan Ingersoll. Miss Ingersoll was a descendant of "Farmer Joseph" Hathorne; she had inherited the Hathorne pride of family, and was an unfailing source of information about family legends and traditions. She was a stately middle-aged lady who, as Nathaniel noted with some amusement, was not only proud, but proud of being proud. She held court in her dim, ancient house, surrounded by relics of the past; delicate old glass, homely pewter, and bits of ivory and porcelain brought home from the Orient by her father; she mused on times and people whose only life was in her recollection. With her lived a young man named Horace Conolly who was understood to be her nephew, and who ultimately became her heir and adopted her name. Conolly's parentage was unknown to Salem, and various rumors were in circulation concerning his relationship to Miss Ingersoll. When Nathaniel first met him, Conolly was rector of St. Matthew's in South Boston; later he resigned from the ministry and turned to the practice of law, gave up the law for medicine and discarded that in turn. He was eccentric, ill-tempered and vain; but he was also intelligent and witty. He was fond of cards and of liquor; these tastes Nathaniel shared, and he frequented the evening parties which Conolly held in the kitchen of the old Turner Street house. Nathaniel's third Salem friend, David Roberts, was likewise a friend of Conolly. Roberts was the son of a prosperous mechanic; he had graduated from Harvard, studied law, and when Nathaniel first knew him had embarked upon a political career which shortly afterward brought him to the State Legislature. The convivial evenings in Turner Street, the society of Conolly and Roberts, and the conversation of Pike were Nathaniel's principal diversions during the early years of his Salem residence.

Meanwhile, Nathaniel's energy went into his writing. When he became lonely or discouraged, as he often did, his recourse was his correspondence with Bridge, or their occasional meetings in Boston. And Bridge, whatever

NATHANIEL HAWTHORNE

From the portrait painted by
Charles Osgood in 1840

the complications of his own career, was never too busy to respond with affectionate encouragement.

(II)

His energies were bent upon his writing. And, imperceptibly, time consumed itself, the afternoon sunshine thinning and departing earlier from his window, the east wind complaining in the elm boughs as summer slipped into autumn and autumn faded into winter. It was good to have before one long, empty stretches of time. It was good to feel the confidence of power, the urgency of talent; to know the elation that accompanies the discovery of a perfect image, the subtle excitement of finding a single inevitable word. He was learning that by weaving words into a pattern (but how carefully, humbly, lovingly!) the writer constructs an image of reality.

Of reality? . . . Even now, as in his childhood, he often doubted the reality of the actual. The Salem of his ancestors, agitated by dark passions and obscure compulsions, was more convincingly real to him than the Salem outside his window. His contact with the world of the past was intimate and absorbing, but with the world in which he lived his connection was scarcely casual. Day by day, as he brooded upon that melancholy world of the past, it acquired greater potency; its gloomy mysteries gradually became clearer to his understanding; there were moments of intense perception when he took his station in it, witnessing, as in a ghostly procession, the evil and the good of its experience illustrated by the lives of its people. He pondered the circumstances of this vicarious existence, probing every episode until it yielded its significance, its fullest intensity of emotion.

But to recreate this experience in words; to make the insubstantial image of it embody the meaning; to make the impact of that meaning produce emotion in a reader! . . . "Sometimes my ideas were like precious stones under the earth, requiring toil to dig them up, and care to polish and brighten them; but often a delicious stream of thought would gush out upon the page at once, like water sparkling up suddenly in the desert; and when it had passed, I gnawed my pen hopelessly, or blundered on with cold and miserable toil, as if there were a wall of ice between me and my subject." It was good, when darkness came, to leave his room and wander about in the open air. After having dreamed for so many hours among fantasies he saw the real world as a fantasy also, a thing of shadows and indefinite masses, opaque and impenetrable. He strode for miles across the sea-meadows, or clambered over the rocky coast in the teeth of a gale, listening to the pounding of the surf below, its surge mechanically repeating the burden of his thoughts.

(III)

He finished his book at last. *Seven Tales of My Native Land.* Tales of the New England past through which his meditations drifted so familiarly. Had he not learned from Scott to seek the materials of fiction in the history of his people? Had it not been said, over and over again, that American writers should look to their own land for their subjects? He had turned to the only subject that he knew; the experiences that he had inherited from the past. He was a little proud of his achievement, a little jubilant in his discovery of this new material, and he confidently anticipated an inevitable success.

But success, so confidently expected, revealed an unaccountable disposition to delay its arrival. None of the publishers to whom Nathaniel submitted the precious manuscript were willing to undertake its publication, and various polite evasions accompanied its invariable return. It was even suggested that publication might be arranged if the author agreed to advance half the cost of an edition and give bond for the remainder, besides assuring the publisher of a profit independent of possible sales. When books by celebrated English authors could be pirated so inexpensively, why should any publisher meddle with an American book, especially by an unknown writer, excepting at the writer's risk?

Nathaniel finally discovered in Salem a young printer named Ferdinand Andrews who appeared to be willing to undertake the risk of publishing his book. Arrangements were made with him; time passed; publication made no headway. Andrews was prolific in excuses, Nathaniel deficient in patience. His exasperation mounted, and finally he made a peremptory demand upon Andrews for the return of the manuscript. This aroused the printer to a belated realization of his responsibilities. Ashamed of his unfulfilled promises,

Andrews explained that the delay had been caused by lack of capital, and offered to proceed immediately with publication. But Nathaniel, although aware that he had been too harsh in his censures, remained inexorable. The manuscript was therefore returned to him. In a mood of savage desperation he burned it in the kitchen stove.

(IV)

The novel that Nathaniel had sketched out while at college engaged his attention during the dreary pilgrimages of the *Seven Tales*. He set to work upon it and brought it to completion, drawing upon his memories of Brunswick and its environs for the scene, and upon his inventive skill for the melodramatic story. Upon the hero, a scholarly young recluse, he draped the attributes of character and temperament which he believed to be peculiar to himself. Did Nathaniel employ a romantic portrait of himself only because he did not yet know other people as well as he thought he knew himself? Or was this portrait the expression of "the yearning of a soul, formed by Nature in a peculiar mold, for communion with those to whom it bore a resemblance, yet of whom it was not?" Fanshawe "deemed himself unconnected with the world, unconcerned in its feelings, and uninfluenced by it in any of his pursuits. In this respect he probably deceived himself. If his innermost heart could have been laid open, there would have been discovered that dream of undying fame which, dream as it is, is more powerful than a thousand realities. But, at any rate, he had seemed, to others and to himself, a solitary being, upon whom the hopes and fears of ordinary men were ineffectual." Fanshawe was an image of the incurable loneliness of Nathaniel's mind.

Profiting by the experience of his efforts to place the *Seven Tales,* Nathaniel arranged to publish the novel at his own expense, and anonymously. At a cost to him of one hundred dollars, *Fanshawe* was published by Marsh and Capen of Boston in 1828. It failed, completely and immitigably.

Not long afterward Nathaniel came to realize that the book had deserved no greater success than it had received. He was ashamed of the book itself, as well as of its failure. He therefore called in and destroyed all the copies remaining in the publishers' stock, with the intention of assuring it a permanent oblivion. It did not occur to him that the destruction of an anonymous book by its unknown author indicated conceit rather than shame. He still believed in the "dream of undying fame" and was taking precautions against future encounters with an embarrassing error.

(v)

Although, like its predecessor, *Fanshawe* nourished the stove in Herbert Street, it accomplished more important results than the *Seven Tales.* It attracted the attention of Samuel G. Goodrich, who somewhat later achieved celebrity as "Peter Parley." Goodrich, having learned the author's name, began a correspondence with

Nathaniel. He had lately inaugurated the publication of an annual, *The Boston Token,* and to this receptacle for miscellaneous literary products he invited Nathaniel to contribute. Nathaniel was delighted by this opportunity. During the course of their correspondence he sent Goodrich a group of stories as specimens of his work, and intimated his desire to collect them in a volume of *Provincial Tales* for which, with Goodrich's assistance, he hoped to find a publisher. Goodrich promised his influence in this project, expressed the opinion that *Fanshawe* had not been exploited properly, and offered Nathaniel thirty-five dollars for the privilege of printing one of the stories, *The Gentle Boy,* in *The Token.* Four months later Nathaniel forwarded two more stories. "You can insert them," he told Goodrich, "(if you think them worthy a place in your publication) as by the author of *Provincial Tales,*—such being the title I propose giving my volume. I can conceive no objection to your designating them in this manner, even if my tales should not be published as soon as *The Token,* or, indeed, if they never see the light at all. An unpublished book is not more obscure than many that creep into the world, and your readers will suppose that the *Provincial Tales* are among the latter."

Goodrich was unsuccessful in his attempts to find a publisher for the book, and Nathaniel, abandoning the project for the time, permitted him the use of any that he chose to print in *The Token* of 1832. Goodrich chose four stories, informing Nathaniel that since they were to be published anonymously, "no objection arises from having so many pages by one author, particularly as they are as good, if not better, than anything else I get."

(VI)

During the following few years Nathaniel continued his contributions to *The Token* and began contributing to other publications. After abandoning the projected volume of historical tales he turned to other subjects, finding his material in the common aspects of village life that he observed in Salem and the characteristic incidents and scenes of his occasional journeys. It was his custom to leave Salem "once a year, or thereabouts" for an "excursion of a few weeks" during which he "enjoyed as much of life as other people do in the whole year's round." In this way he visited Martha's Vineyard, took a jaunt through Connecticut, and traveled through New York. In 1831 he traveled through New Hampshire with his uncle Samuel Manning, visiting the Shaker colony at Canterbury. The Mannings controlled several stage-coach services, and Nathaniel availed himself of the facilities which these afforded him to become familiar with the New England countryside as far north as the White Mountains.

Once again he planned the publication of a book, in which he proposed to make use of the materials gathered upon these modest excursions into the world. *The Story Teller* was to recount the adventures of an itinerant teller of tales and an eccentric preacher on their journeys afield in New England. Nathaniel designed this book to exploit the two kinds of material with which he had been working; the sketch of rural life, and the historical tales to be told by the story-teller. In the person of the wandering narrator he again drew a portrait of himself:

"I was a youth of gay and happy temperament," the narrator confesses, "with an incorrigible levity of spirit, of no vicious propensities, sensible enough, but wayward and fanciful. What a character was this to be brought in contact with the stern old Pilgrim spirit of my guardian! We were at variance upon a thousand points; but our chief and final dispute arose from the pertinacity with which he insisted on my adopting a particular profession; while I, being heir to a moderate competence, had avowed my purpose of keeping aloof from the regular business of life. This would have been a dangerous resolution anywhere in the world; it was fatal in New England. There is a grossness in the conceptions of my countrymen; they will not be convinced that any good thing may consist with what they call idleness; they can anticipate nothing but evil of a young man who neither studies physic, law, nor gospel, nor opens a store, nor takes to farming, but manifests an incomprehensible disposition to be satisfied with what his father left him. The principle is excellent in its general influence, but most miserable in its effect on the few that violate it. I had a quick sensitiveness to public opinion, and felt as if it ranked me with the tavern haunters and town paupers—with the drunken poet who hawked his own Fourth of July odes, and the broken soldier who had been good for nothing since the last war."

Pressure was, in fact, being brought to bear upon Nathaniel to relinquish the unprofitable career of literature for a more remunerative occupation. His way of life had incurred the disapproval of his practical Manning relatives. His mother and sisters "were in those days almost absolutely obedient to him" and it did not occur to them to distract their young genius with discouraging importunities. But the Manning uncles felt no such tender compunctions. The young man had been out of college for more than five years, during which he had accomplished nothing; he spent his time locked in his room, emerging only for solitary walks or disreputable drinking parties with other irresponsible young men; he associated, in wayside taverns, with low company; he appeared to have no comprehension of his obligation, as an American, to get on in the world. At various times Nathaniel contemplated embarking upon a mercantile career by entering the employ of his uncles. At one time this was a fixed purpose with him. He continued to postpone taking action upon it, partly through a repugnance to commercial employment, partly through a lingering expectation of eventual success as a writer, and partly through an inertia always natural to him.

He completed the opening chapters of *The Story Teller* and confided them to Goodrich, who submitted them to *The New England Magazine*. A change of editorial direction was taking place, the new editors welcomed the contribution, and it was published in the first two issues produced by them. Four months afterward Park Benjamin assumed control of the magazine and Nathaniel contributed, with but one exception, to every issue from November, 1834, to December, 1836, when the magazine was merged with another publication and its office transferred to New York. At this time the magazine was in arrears of payment and Nathaniel ceased contributing, but Benjamin begged for "a mass of manuscript in his possession and it was scornfully bestowed." "Thus," Nathaniel remarked, "has this man, who would be considered a Mæcenas, taken from a penniless writer material incomparably better than any his own brain can supply." The breach was healed, however, during the course of the year.

Recognition, in any substantial sense, had not yet come to Nathaniel. It was perhaps the more dilatory because of his carefully guarded anonymity, which prevented his readers from identifying much of his work and attributing it to one man. As a result of his apprenticeship to Scott he had proposed to become known as "the author of *The Gentle Boy*" or another of his tales; he had succeeded only in remaining unknown. In 1833 Park Benjamin, reviewing *The Token* of the following year, referred to him as "the most pleasing writer of fanciful prose, except Irving, in the country." And Henry Chorley, reviewing the same publication in the *Athenaeum* of London, quoted from his stories and declared that every one possessed "singularity enough to recommend it to the reader." This, after ten years of writing and some five years of increasingly frequent publication, was Nathaniel's principal reward.

(VII)

Nathaniel had formed the habit of keeping a journal. In it he recorded suggestions for plots, most of which he never employed, scraps of unusual information that he had come upon in his miscellaneous reading, and detailed descriptions of what he had observed during his walks and rides about the countryside. In these descriptions he satisfied his eager, perhaps unconscious, curiosity about reality. His walks and drives yielded him very little more than views of a familiar landscape under changing seasons, or casual encounters with common rural types; he filled his notebooks with an accumulation of the comparatively unimportant data of observation. These detailed records exercised a delicate process of selection, and they taught Nathaniel to reproduce in words the distinctive attributes of whatever he attempted to describe. But this precision of representation was the result not so much of deliberate intention as of an unusual susceptibility to impressions. A condition of perception rather than an esthetic aim determined the character of his records. The accumulation of impressions recorded, differing in quality but not in kind, indicates both the urgency of his curiosity and the meagerness of the world which offered itself to his observation.

Nathaniel's preoccupation with the past aggravated his curiosity about the external world. He brooded upon his possession by a world of fantasy. That fantasy often seemed more real to him than reality itself he considered a painful symptom of some mysterious disequilibrium of his mind. It was as though he had renounced life in the real world to immerse himself in a world of phantoms, and could now return only with difficulty. He speculated about the problem of destiny; had he actually stepped out of the natural order of life by so readily adopting the habit of seclusion? Was it possible that, by taking a step aside from the natural order, a man forever lost his place within that order? What are the consequences of tampering with predestined order by making whimsical and violent departures from it? This question, suggested by his personal experience, soon assumed the importance of a central theme in his stories.

Meanwhile he was making an effort to reintegrate himself in the real world, to subject his mind and his perceptions to its discipline, and, by doing this, to exorcise the compelling fantasy of his imaginative life. Society, in any general sense, he considered closed to him; ten years of alienation from the common interests of men had resulted in a conviction of his incapacity to begin sharing them. Since participation in life now appeared impossible, he regarded observation of it as his only recourse. "The most desirable mode of existence," he wrote, "might be that of a spiritualized Paul Pry, hovering invisible round man and woman, witnessing their deeds, searching into their hearts, borrowing brightness from their felicity and shade from their sorrow, and retaining no emotion peculiar to himself." Were there not, particularly for a writer, advantages in detachment?

At other times, however, he bitterly resented his

isolation from the common fortunes of life. He considered the content of his existence inadequate, and felt burdened by its emptiness. Observation could never be a satisfactory substitute for experience, and when he contemplated his own existence it seemed to him destitute of all experiences. The years were passing; he had not yet begun to live; he saw no way in which life might be commenced. When he looked in his mirror he was shocked by the thought that his pale beauty and youthful grace would gradually decay; he dreaded their loss, and often felt that an early death would be infinitely preferable. His very beauty seemed a reproach to his life; it was made for love, and although he had been beloved, he had never known what it is to love. In such moods the pangs of loneliness were sharp, and they gave rise to overwhelming depression.

(VIII)

The year 1836 was destined to prove one of the turning points in Nathaniel's career. It opened, not very auspiciously, with his determination to add to his income by means of some regular employment. He applied to Goodrich, who procured for him the editorial direction on an unimportant monthly, *The American Magazine of Useful and Entertaining Knowledge,* published in Boston by the Bewick Company. Goodrich had some financial interest in the company. The magazine combined miscellaneous information with illustrations; the editor's annual salary was five hundred dollars, and he was expected to write or compile the whole of every issue.

If Nathaniel did not welcome the change from his former irresponsible isolation in Salem, his friends greeted it enthusiastically. Bridge, now in Havana, remarked that "nothing has given me so much pleasure for many a day as the intelligence concerning your late engagement in active and responsible business. I have always known that whenever you should exert yourself in earnest, that you could command respectability and independence and fame. As for your present situation, I do not regard it as so much in itself—though it seems tolerably good to begin with—as I do for its being the introduction to other and better employment. Besides, it is no small point gained to get you out of Salem. . . . There is a peculiar dullness about Salem,—a heavy atmosphere which no literary man can breathe. You are now fairly embarked with other literary men, and if you can't sail with any other, I'll be damned." And Franklin Pierce, writing from Washington, cordially congratulated the new editor.

Bridge's optimistic predictions were not, however, fulfilled. The position involved a fatiguing amount of hack-work in compilation and rewriting, and in this Nathaniel was assisted by his sister Elizabeth. It wearied him and he complained of his weariness to Bridge, who wrote complimenting him upon his initial issue. As if in caution, Bridge added, "I fear that you may tire of your present situation too soon; but I think there is no danger of your wanting literary employment long in the future. You are in for it, and are known." Nathaniel's weariness was aggravated by the discovery that the magazine had become insolvent before the larger portion of his salary had been paid. In reply to a letter in which he had attempted to collect what was due him, he received notice that the company had made an assignment in favor of its creditors. He retained his connection until the publication of the August number, which contained illustrations so deplorable that he felt called upon to disclaim responsibility for their appearance. Shortly afterward he resigned his position and returned to Salem.

His financial difficulties in this venture resulted in some exasperation with Goodrich, whom he held personally responsible, and with whom he refused to have any communication for some little time. This was smoothed over and Goodrich offered him the task of compiling *Peter Parley's Universal History on the Basis of Geography*, for which his payment was to be one hundred dollars. With the assistance, once again, of Elizabeth, to whom he gave the money, Nathaniel undertook the task, finishing it early in September. Goodrich, in acknowledging receipt of the manuscript, remarked: "I like the History pretty well—I shall make it do." The history was published in 1837 in two duodecimo volumes of more than three hundred and seventy pages each, and during the many years that it remained in print is said to have achieved a circulation of more than one million copies. Nathaniel did not consider himself overpaid, for in December, when Goodrich offered him the task of writing a similar volume on "the manners, customs and civilities of all countries" for the sum of three hundred dollars, he declined.

In addition to producing seven numbers of the magazine and the two volumes of the *Universal History*, Nathaniel had found time to contribute eight tales to *The Token* for 1837. For these eight stories he received one hundred and eight dollars, and his contributions formed a third part of the contents of the volume. Its publication led to the first breach of his anonymity, for Park Benjamin printed a paragraph in *The American Monthly Magazine* which praised him under his own name (he had begun spelling it Hawthorne some years before), termed him the equal of Washington Irving, and urged him to collect his "various tales and essays into one volume."

Nathaniel's comment upon this not inconsiderable eulogy was confided to his notebook. "In this dismal chamber," he noted while in Salem, "FAME was won."

(IX)

Nevertheless Nathaniel was extremely dejected, and overcome with a sense of failure and hopelessness. He realized that he had not gained a reputation or a position in the world. While he had been sitting in his room overlooking the harborside streets of Salem his friends had forged ahead in the world. Pierce had been elected Senator from New Hampshire; Cilley had been elected to Congress; Longfellow, whom he knew only slightly, had been appointed professor at Harvard and had begun to establish a reputation as a writer. Nathaniel brooded upon the discrepancy between his situation and theirs. So dismal were his reflections that he began to dream that he was still at college, had been

HENRY W. LONGFELLOW

there unaccountably long, had failed utterly to keep pace with his contemporaries and, in his dream, met them with a shame and depression that he could not shake off when he recalled it in his waking life.

Bridge wrote to him:—"*The Token* is out, and I suppose you are getting your book ready for publication. What is the plan of operations? who the publishers, and when the time that you will be known by name as well as your writings are? I hope to God that you will put your name upon the title page, and come before the world at once and on your own responsibility. You could not fail to make a noise, and an honorable name, and something beside. I've been thinking how singularly you stand among the writers of the day; known by name to very few, and yet your writings admired more than any others with which they are ushered forth. One reason of this is that you scatter your strength by fighting under various banners. . . . Write to me soon, if it will not interfere with your book that is to come out. Don't flinch, nor delay to publish. Should there be any trouble in a pecuniary way with the publishers, let me know, and I can and will raise the needful with great pleasure."

Nathaniel was struck by the irony of Bridge's happy references to a forthcoming book. True, there was a book; when had there not been one? But the new volume, an expanded version of *Provincial Tales*, seemed destined to go the way of its three stillborn predecessors. No publisher was to be found. The same old excuses reappeared like aged actors pathetically assuming juvenile rôles. Of what avail was Bridge's advice, or

Park Benjamin's flattering suggestion, that he collect his stories in a volume? Of what practical value were their prophecies of success should he do so?

Nathaniel replied to Bridge's letter, confessing his miserable despondency. He appreciated Bridge's dependable, affectionate concern for his welfare, and was cheered by Bridge's unwavering faith in his destiny, but he declined Bridge's offer to assume financial responsibility for the book. Bridge's reply came quickly. "I have a thousand things to say to you," Bridge wrote, "but can't say more than a hundredth part of them. You have the blues again. Don't give up to them, for God's sake and your own and mine and everybody's. Brighter days will come, and that within six months. It is lucky that you didn't quarrel with Goodrich, he being a practical man who can serve you."

Why should Bridge think that better days were coming within six months? Why should he regard it as fortunate that Nathaniel had not quarreled with Goodrich? Nathaniel replied with a letter in which he permitted his depression free rein. "I'm a doomed man," he said, "and over I must go!"

A few days later Bridge wrote again. "I have just received your last, and do not like its tone at all. There is a kind of desperate coolness in it that seems dangerous. I fear that you are too good a subject for suicide, and that some day you will end your mortal woes on your own responsibility."

Two weeks later came a letter from Goodrich. "I have seen Mr. Howes, who says he can give a definite answer Saturday. . . . He seems pretty confident that he shall make the arrangement with a man who has capital, and will edit the book. I think your selection of the tales nearly right."

As soon as he heard that the book had been accepted, Nathaniel informed Bridge of the good news and, in the exuberance of his gratitude to Goodrich, mentioned his intention of dedicating the book to him. He was surprised, a few days later, by Bridge's unqualified disapproval of this intention. "I fear you will hurt yourself by puffing Goodrich *undeservedly*—for there is no doubt in my mind of his selfishness in regard to your work and yourself. I am perfectly aware that he has taken a good deal of interest in you, but when did he ever do anything for you without a quid pro quo? The magazine was given to you for $100 less than it should have been. *The Token* was saved by your writing. . . . And now he proposes to publish your book because he thinks it will be honorable and lucrative to be your publisher now and hereafter, and perhaps because he dares not lose your aid in *The Token.* Unless you are already committed, do not mar your *first* book by hoisting Goodrich into favor."

Not until the book was in press did Nathaniel learn why Bridge had discouraged the dedication to Goodrich. Immediately after receiving Nathaniel's first despairing letter, Bridge had sought to ascertain from Goodrich why Nathaniel had been unable to secure a publisher for his book. Goodrich had replied that arrangements could be made for the publication of an edition, if Bridge would furnish a guarantee of two hundred and fifty dollars. Bridge, stipulating only that all knowledge of the transaction be concealed from Nathaniel, had immediately furnished the required guarantee.

The excitement of projected publication served only temporarily to distract Nathaniel's mind. His depression returned. He made some desultory efforts to secure an editorial position, but met with no success. He was doubtful of the success of his book, and distressed by his lack of confidence in his future. Bridge, as usual, tried to encourage him:

". . . Whether your book will sell extensively may be doubtful; but that is of small importance in the first one you publish. At all events, keep up your spirits till the result is ascertained; and, my word for it, there is more honor and emolument in store for you, from your writings, than you imagine. The bane of your life has been self-distrust. This has kept you back for many years; which, if you had improved by publishing, would long ago have given you what you must now wait a short time for. It may be for the best, but I doubt it.

"I have been trying to think what you are so miserable for. Although you have not much property, you have good health and powers of writing which have made, and can still make, you independent.

"Suppose you get 'but $300 per annum' for your writings. You can, with economy, live upon that, though it would be a tight squeeze. You have no family dependent upon you, and why should you 'borrow trouble'?"

Early in March, 1837, *Twice-Told Tales* appeared, over its author's name. "I hope Longfellow will review the book, for I think him a man of good taste and kindly feelings," Bridge had said. Nathaniel therefore sent Longfellow a copy of the book immediately upon publication, with a note expressing his regret that they had not become more intimately acquainted at college and his felicitations upon Longfellow's literary achievement and appointment to Harvard. Despite the publisher's assurance that the book was receiving a favorable press, Nathaniel thought the newspapers cold to it. But within a month Goodrich reported favorably upon sales, and told Bridge, whom he met in Boston, that the book had already satisfied the guaranty, having sold between six and seven hundred copies.

It was clear, both to Nathaniel and his friends, that the publication of this volume would not solve the problem of securing a regular livelihood. Pierce and Bridge regarded a complete change of environment as essential to him, and Nathaniel himself had begun to long for any occupation which would remove him from the loneliness of his life in Salem. At this juncture Pierce suggested to Nathaniel the possibility of his joining, as historian, the exploring expedition being organized by J. N. Reynolds, which the Navy Department intended to send to the Antarctic Ocean. Nathaniel at once expressed his willingness to accept the post, and an active correspondence ensued. As time passed Nathaniel's eagerness increased; partly, perhaps, because of his old unsatisfied craving for travel, and partly also because the position carried with it a salary of fifteen hundred dollars. It did not occur to any one concerned that, from the point of view of an increasing contact with society, the polar regions would offer few advantages over Salem. Pierce and Cilley brought their influence to bear upon the Navy Department in Nathaniel's behalf, and Bridge canvassed his political friends. Finally the delegations from Maine and New Hampshire were induced to support Nathaniel's candidacy, but success became doubtful because of disagreements which arose between Reynolds and the Navy Department, and ultimately the projected expedition was abandoned. As the chances for his appointment diminished, Nathaniel's depression returned. Bridge, who was living alone in his family home at Augusta, where he had invested his fortune in an ambitious water-power development, invited Nathaniel to spend the summer with him. "It is no use for you to feel blue," he wrote. "I tell you that you will be in a good situation next winter, instead of 'under a sod.' Pierce is interested for you, and can make some arrangement, I know. An editorship or clerkship at Washington he can and will obtain. So courage, and *au diable* with your sods! I have something to say to you upon marriage, and about Goodrich, and a thousand other things."

In July Nathaniel went to visit Bridge at Augusta, but before leaving Salem, he wrote once again to Longfellow, who had cordially acknowledged his book with praise and overtures to friendship.

"By some witchcraft or other—for I really cannot assign any reasonable why and wherefore—I have been carried apart from the main current of life and find it impossible to get back again. Since we last met, which you remember was in Sawtell's room, where you read a farewell poem to the relics of the class,—ever since that time I have secluded myself from society; and yet I never meant any such thing, nor dreamed what sort of life I was going to lead. I have made a captive of myself, and put me in a dungeon, and now I cannot find the key to let myself out,—and if the door were open, I should be almost afraid to come out. You tell me that you have met with troubles and changes. I know not what these may have been, but I can assure you that trouble is the next best thing to enjoyment, and that there is no fate in this world so horrible as to have no share in either its joys or sorrows. For the last ten years I have not lived, but only dreamed of living. It may be true that there have been some unsubstantial pleasures here in the shade, which I might have missed in the sunshine, but you cannot conceive how devoid of satisfaction all my retrospects are. I have laid up no treasure of pleasant remembrances against old age; but there is some comfort in thinking that future years can hardly fail to be more varied and therefore more tolerable than the past.

"You give me more credit than I deserve in supposing that I have led a studious life. I have indeed turned over a good many books, but in so desultory a way that it cannot be called study, nor has it left me the fruits of study. As to my literary efforts, I do not think much of them, neither is it worth while to be ashamed of them. They would have been better, I trust, if written under more favorable circumstances. I have had no external excitement—no consciousness that the public would like what I wrote, nor much hope nor passionate desire that they should do so. Nevertheless, having nothing else to be ambitious of, I have been considerably interested in literature; and if my writings had made any decided impression, I should have been stimulated to further exertions; but there has been no warmth of approbation, so that I have always written with benumbed fingers. I have another great difficulty in the lack of materials; for I have seen so little of the world that I have nothing but thin air to concoct my stories of, and it is not easy to give a lifelike semblance to such shadowy stuff. Sometimes through a peephole I have caught a glimpse of the real world, and the two or three articles in which I have portrayed these glimpses please me better than the others.

"I have now, or shall soon have, a sharper spur to exertion, which I lacked at an earlier period; for I see little prospect but that I shall have to scribble for a living. But this troubles me much less than you would suppose. I can turn my pen to all sorts of drudgery, such as children's books, etc., and by and by I shall get some editorship that will answer my purpose. . . ."

Longfellow's extremely generous review of the book was published in the *North American Review* for July. It gave Nathaniel more pleasure than he had hoped for. "I have today," he wrote in acknowledgment, "received and read with huge delight your review of Hawthorne's *Twice-Told Tales*. I frankly own that I was not without hopes that you would do this kind office for the book; though I could not have anticipated how very kindly it would be done. Whether or no the public will agree to the praise which you bestow on me, there are at least five persons who think you the most sagacious critic on earth, viz., my mother and two sisters, my old maiden aunt, and finally the strongest believer of the whole five, my own self."

(x)

The month of July was passed in Augusta, at Bridge's home. Bridge's French teacher, Monsieur Schaeffer, was residing in the house and attracted Nathaniel by his intelligence, his vivacity and the pathetic courage with which he spent his days in "teaching French to blockheads who sneer at him." In many pages of his notebook Nathaniel recorded his scrupulous and perplexed attempts to analyze the character of this curious expatriate who, after a day of stifled bitterness, would return to the house to sing, to discuss philosophy and literature, to express his hatred for the Yankees. The month was passed in quiet diversions; conversations with Bridge and the eccentric Monsieur Schaeffer, walks and drives in the near-by country, and dinners in roadside taverns, where Nathaniel made elaborate notes of trivial episodes and, as "hints for characters," recorded the personal peculiarities of patrons and attendants. Toward the end of the month he met, for the first time since their graduation, his old friend and classmate Jonathan Cilley, and committed to his notebook a shrewd analysis of Cilley's character; he thought Cilley a crafty man, who "deceives by truth." But he liked Cilley well, and early in August visited him at Thomaston, stopping the night at a tavern and indulging in a mild flirtation with the "frank, free, mirthful daughter of the landlady, about twenty-four years old" which made them both "feel rather melancholy" when they parted.

By the middle of August he had returned to Salem and once again taken up the habit of his life there. He rambled about the countryside, occasionally went to Boston to meet Bridge or Cilley, or to Cambridge to dine with Longfellow whose cellar was excellent, and continued his writing. He made connections with the *Knickerbocker Magazine* and with the *The Democratic Review*, a new periodical established by a gay and irresponsible young Irishman named John O'Sullivan, whose whimsical humor and incurable optimism endeared him to Nathaniel. He began now to sign his stories as by the author of *Twice-Told Tales*. As for any marked change in his circumstances or prospects, none was perceptible.

(XI)

In later years, after he had achieved celebrity, Nathaniel requested Bridge to burn all of his early letters. Bridge conscientiously complied with the request, thereby destroying the only complete and intimate record of Nathaniel's most desolate years. From Bridge's replies to this correspondence it appears that Nathaniel's despondency was sufficiently acute in 1836-7 to cause him on several occasions to threaten suicide. This despondency was not entirely due to his poverty, his failure to achieve success as a writer, and what he felt to be his unfavorable prospects. It was due as well to his sober judgment of the character of his life.

In college he had hoped for freedom to stand aloof from the world; he had been given that freedom, and the blessing had proved a curse. The barrenness of his existence oppressed him, and he considered himself condemned to a future of unendurable loneliness and solitude. Among all the elements of human happiness that he had renounced, it is probable that he regretted none more than love. He was technically chaste; his code of sexual morality was exceedingly strict; his desires had been aggravated by prolonged asceticism. The frustration of his sexual life must have played a large part in giving his mood of despondency a morbid, almost hysterical turn. And in the midst of his despondency it appears that he was preoccupied with the idea of matrimony.

Bridge wrote to him from Augusta: "I shall try your advice with regard to the women sometime when I am away from here, though I shall make a poor hand of it most certainly. I sometimes think seriously of matrimony for ten minutes together, and should perhaps perpetrate it if I did not like myself too well. My morals have improved exceedingly in the past year; your advice in a former letter was very efficient in this improvement. . . . I take advice from you kindly. It seems divested of the presumption and intermeddling spirit with which advice is usually tinctured. . . . But a little wickedness will not hurt one, especially if the sinner be of a retiring disposition. It stirs one up and makes him like the rest of the world." What was Nathaniel's advice "with regard to the women" which Bridge would try only when away from home? That the general tenor of his counsel was morally edifying is certain; was he, in this single instance, advocating sexual adventure? And was Bridge's remark about the beneficial influence of wickedness upon a retiring sinner an autobiographical reflection, or a sly gibe at Nathaniel's asceticism?

Nathaniel often came back to Salem from his annual journeys with tales about some humble maiden whom he had met, fancied, and perhaps talked with. Later he would put the maiden into a story. These "fancies," as his sister Elizabeth termed them, served no other than literary purposes. But in 1837 they appear to have taken a more serious turn. In April of that year, just after the publication of his book and when his friends were busily engaged in an attempt to secure his appointment to the Antarctic exploring expedition, Bridge wrote of these matters, but referred incidentally to Nathaniel's preoccupation with the idea of matrimony.

"Are you seriously thinking of getting married? If you are, nothing that I could say would avail to deter you. I am in doubt whether you would be more happy in this new mode of life than you are now. This I am sure of, that unless you are fortunate in your choice, you will be wretched in a tenfold degree. I confess that, personally, I have a strong desire to see you attain a high rank in literature. Hence my preference would be that you should take the voyage *if you can.* And after taking a turn round the world, and establishing a name that will be worth working for, if you choose to marry you can do it with more advantage than now."

Two weeks later, writing to Nathaniel of his interview with Goodrich and of the steps being taken in the matter of Nathaniel's appointment, Bridge inquired, "What has become of your matrimonial ideas? Are you in a good way to bring this about?" "I wish you would tell me whether you are in earnest about marrying," he remarked later. And in May, writing of Nathaniel's projected visit to him, Bridge observed, "I have something to say to you upon marriage and about Goodrich and a thousand other things."

One episode which occurred about this time is wrapped in mystery.[1] It appears that Nathaniel was taken by one of his friends to call, at her request, upon a lady of good family and excellent social position, whose interest had been aroused by what she had heard about the handsome and hermit-like young writer. The acquaintance established, the young lady favored him with her confidences, which he accepted with the interest appropriate to a confessor. He did not, however, favor the lady with similar confidences; and she, piqued by his refusal to do so, dramatically informed him of the injurious treatment which she alleged that

[1] This episode was first related by Julian Hawthorne in *Nathaniel Hawthorne and His Wife*, vol. I, pp. 167-175. Mr. Hawthorne states that Nathaniel's willingness to undertake a duel was later responsible for Cilley's acceptance of Graves's challenge, and hence indirectly for Cilley's death. He also asserts that this indirect responsibility weighed upon Nathaniel, and that his brooding upon it led him to compose *Fancy's Show Box*. In this, however, he is apparently in error, for *Fancy's Show Box* was first published in *The Token* for 1837, which was issued in the autumn of 1836, and Cilley did not meet his death until February 24, 1838. Bridge, who was in a position to know, denies that Cilley was influenced by Nathaniel's example. In recounting this episode, Julian Hawthorne conceals the names of the actors under the sobriquets of "Louis" and "Mary," and is indefinite as to the time of its occurrence. In reply to my request for additional information relating to this episode, Mr. Hawthorne refused all other details than those incorporated in his book.

she had received from the friend who had introduced them, apparently intending to provoke a quarrel between the two men. In this she succeeded only too well. Nathaniel, indignant and resentful, challenged the man at once. But his friend, aware of the lady's reputation for earlier ventures in similar mischief, declined the challenge and refuted the charge so convincingly as to make Nathaniel realize that he had been deceived. He was overcome with repentance for his unjustified precipitancy, and broke with the lady. But the episode wounded his vanity, for he realized that he had been made ridiculous.

It is probable that Nathaniel's preoccupation with the idea of matrimony was the result merely of his acute realization of his loneliness, and, subconsciously, of his long sexual frustration. There is no indication that he was in love with any woman; the bitter edge of his despondency may even have been due to the fact that he had not yet fallen in love and perhaps believed that the experience was, like so many others, to be denied to him. It is certain, however, that he wished to fall in love, that he regarded matrimony as a means of escape from the unendurable loneliness which threatened to continue throughout his future, and that he saw in it a means of reëstablishing himself in the common life of the world. But even in this vague project circumstances were hostile to him; his poverty and his lack of prospects made him incapable of assuming the burden of additional economic responsibilities. Finding himself apparently condemned to an indefinite continuance in a situation which had long been intolerable, he recurred more and more frequently to the idea of suicide.

ALLEGORIES OF THE HEART

(1)

On the edge of the Charter Street Burying Ground, most ancient of the Salem cemeteries, stood a square-fronted, three-storied, wooden house about a century old. Its small enclosed porch opened directly upon a shabby by-street, and the side windows of its parlor overlooked the moss-grown, sunken memorials to Puritan prestige. The house had an air of faded respectability; it was shabbily genteel. In 1837 it was occupied by Doctor Nathaniel Peabody and his family.

The Peabodys were of old Salem stock; the Doctor's forefathers were conveniently entombed within reach of his back yard fence. But the family had fallen upon meager days, and in the lifetime of the Doctor's children had migrated frequently under the spur of necessity. The Doctor was an irresolute, benign gentleman who cherished pronounced, but often inconsistent, convictions. He had, however, been consistent in his inadequacy to the struggle with circumstance that had fallen to his lot. His own incompetence never induced him to abate his high expectations of others, particularly the members of his family; his motives were excellent, but even his wife asserted that he had no knowledge of human nature. His benevolent severity made him a strict disciplinarian; with so extensive an experience of misfortune, he believed himself to be well equipped to undertake the successful direction of other lives. Hence his wife had found it necessary to teach school during the infancy and youth of their children; one son had run away to sea after quarreling with his father; another had married as early as possible and removed from Salem; and all three daughters were still unmarried.

The Charter Street house harbored two of the Doctor's daughters and a son, a bed-ridden invalid painfully awaiting death. The third and eldest daughter taught school in Boston and was a frequent visitor. All three daughters were remarkable women. The Doctor acknowledged that they fulfilled his expectations. Their mother, a cultivated and sentimental woman, believed them to be individually, though differently, perfect. And with affectionate enthusiasm they modestly attributed to one another the perfection to which they all aspired.

The eldest daughter, Elizabeth Palmer Peabody, was now thirty-three years old. She had begun her career as a teacher at sixteen, opening a school in the family home and taking her younger sisters as her first pupils. At eighteen she had met a young graduate of Harvard, Ralph Waldo Emerson, whom she induced to give her lessons in Greek. Such was his opinion of her attainments that he refused to accept payment for his instruction, for he thought that he could teach her nothing. When the Peabodys removed to Boston, Elizabeth opened a school there and read to her pupils de Gérando's essay on moral perfection and self-education. The idea that human life is an educational process having

FRANKLIN PIERCE

perfection as its aim appealed to her; she never found it necessary to scrutinize the degrees conferred by the school of experience. She became for a short time literary assistant to William Ellery Channing, the apostle of Unitarianism and leader in the cause of abolition. She had been an admirer of Bronson Alcott, and had taught for a while in his extraordinary Temple School, recording his "conversations" with his pupils in a little book published in Boston in 1835. She was the intimate friend of Margaret Fuller. Elizabeth Peabody was a studious woman. She was intellectually vigorous, and her moral zeal was indomitable. Her appetite for ideas was matched only by her capacity to assimilate them. She browsed omnivorously in the field of culture, and was unperturbed by an occasional cropping of intellectual cactus. She was on terms of intimacy with all the more radical thinkers of the day, and most of them considered her a superior votary of enlightenment. She loved reforms with an indiscriminate ardor, and since it was her conviction that every moral effort deserved her support, she led, in Boston, a busy life. Delighting in spiritual agitation of all kinds, she submitted to the full tide of Transcendental philosophy that was inundating New England, and emerged amply wreathed in the mystical doctrines which it was stirring to the surface.

Her younger sister, Mary, had an equivalent reputation for cultural accomplishment. She, too, taught school in the Salem home. Her public career began some years later, after her marriage to the educator Horace Mann. The most suggestive portrait of Mary Peabody is contained in a few sentences written by her sister Sophia after the birth of Mary's first child. "I suspect," Sophia then wrote, "that Mary's baby must have opened its mouth the moment it was born, and pronounced a School Report; for its mother's brain has had no other permanent idea in it for the last year. It will be a little incarnation of education systems—a human school." Mary was that kind of woman.

The third daughter of Doctor Peabody, Sophia Amelia, was twenty-six years old. As a consequence of improper medical attention in infancy, she suffered from violent headaches for which no cure had been discovered. Her mother assured her that she was a person of exceedingly sensitive nature, vivid imagination, confiding affection, with shattered nerves and precarious health. She was beloved by children, for her presence in the house, imposing a necessity for quiet, was the sole and successful admonition used by Mary in her classes. She was small, graceful, bird-like in her movements, and her smile was a "delicate sunshine." Her protracted invalidism made her consider herself still a child, and she possessed the ready enthusiasm, the naïve high spirits, the quick and often fallacious intuition of childhood.

Sophia's ill-health had not diminished her appetite for knowledge. She was conversant with French, Italian, German, Latin, Greek and Hebrew. She had studied painting and sculpture, and her paintings had been praised by Doughty and Washington Allston. She read, extensively, ardently and rapidly. In her twentieth year she recorded in her journal having read on one

THE NATHANIEL PEABODY HOUSE

Also known as the "Dr. Grimshawe" house, this was the scene of Hawthorne's courtship. The novel, *Dr. Grimshawe's Secret*, describes it. (53 Charter St., Salem)

rainy day de Gérando, Fénelon, St. Luke and Isaiah, Young, *The Spectator*, and four of Shakespeare's comedies, besides having sewed; there is no indication that the day's occupations were unusual.

In the Charter Street home Sophia had fitted up a studio on the third floor with characteristic prettiness, and in it she secluded herself, taking her meals apart from the family, reading, painting and meditating, but usually remaining accessible to the many visitors who frequented the house. She was a tender-hearted Stoic, capable of ecstatic emotion at the sight of a flower or a happy child, and disposed, in her meditations, to disguise unpleasant facts by diffusing a sentimental radiance about them. Thus she found compensation for fifteen years of physical misery in the "divine sentiment" which she inspired in children. She found ample proof of the divinity of human nature in the conviction that, by merely being true to it, we may accomplish all things. And she prayed with fervor, "Oh, let not the light within me be darkness!"

(II)

When Elizabeth Peabody returned to Salem in 1836, her attention had already been arrested by certain anonymously published stories, and after investigation she had determined that they were the work of one of the Misses Hawthorne. In her childhood the families had been neighbors, but the migratory habits of the Peabodys and the removal of the Hawthornes to Maine had interrupted their intercourse, and she had seen no member of the Hawthorne family since, as a little girl, she had played and studied with Elizabeth. Being an intrepid person with a hearty contempt for casual obstacles, Elizabeth Peabody determined to renew her acquaintance with the Hawthornes in spite of their habitual seclusion. She was a collector of interesting minds, and had the collector's zest for difficult and unique examples. She succeeded in meeting Louisa, who was the most accessible of the family, and in establishing a precarious acquaintance, but she learned nothing about the identity of the anonymous author until the spring of 1837 and the publication of *Twice-Told Tales*. Meanwhile she cultivated the friendly relation established with so much difficulty, and progressed sufficiently to borrow, after publication, Madam Hawthorne's copy of the *Tales* and to return it to her, handsomely bound, with an appreciatively flattering note. It was not, however, until the following year that she met Nathaniel and persuaded him to call with his two sisters in Charter Street.

They came one evening and found Elizabeth alone in the parlor, for Sophia had secluded herself in the studio. As soon as Elizabeth could do so, she ran upstairs to her sister.

"Oh, Sophia," she said, "you must get up and dress and come down. The Hawthornes are here, and you never saw anything so splendid as he is—he is handsomer than Lord Byron!"

Sophia laughed, and shook her head, and refused to come down. "If he has called once, he will do so again," she said.

So Elizabeth hastily returned to her guests, brought out the portfolio of Flaxman's illustrations for Dante which she had just received from Professor Felton of Harvard, and the evening was passed pleasantly in their examination. A barren little parlor, its ancient windows rattling dismally under the impact of a chilly east wind; in the pool of light about the center table four earnest, sensitive people eagerly turning the pages of a book of drawings. . . .

New England in the early days of "culture," with its solemn conversation and bleak effort to stimulate social intercourse! For the radically emancipated conscience recreation was a serious pursuit, and culture, especially in leisure moments, an exacting obligation. There existed a widespread desire to know and appreciate art which, like a gnarled apple tree in rocky soil, flourished in spite of deficient nourishment. There existed an optimistic belief in the value of unhindered speculation, of individual experience and opinion, together with a reluctance to examine their pronouncements too critically. Introspection, always a resource of the lonely mind in a monotonous society, had become a commendable enterprise. Had not Emerson announced that "the vision of genius comes by renouncing the too officious activity of the understanding, and giving leave and amplest privilege to the spontaneous sentiment?" New England responded to this suggestion with alacrity. To many fervent people all the high aspirations of the soul suddenly appeared to be realizable by conversation. Later, in the apogee of Margaret Fuller and Bronson Alcott, monologue gained favor as a medium, but at the moment it still seemed desirable to hear the spontaneous sentiments of more than one soul. In Boston a group of men and women had formed the habit of meeting at stated times for general discussion, and had come to be known as the Transcendental Club. At these meetings were to be found Emerson, the Orphic and discursive Alcott, Thoreau, the mystic poet Jones Very, Margaret Fuller in the full tide of her arrogant eloquence, Elizabeth Peabody, and George Ripley, who had just begun the publication of *Specimens of Foreign Standard Literature*. In Salem a similar group had been launched under the hospitable leadership of Miss Susan Burley, at whose home on Saturday evenings spontaneous sentiments were carefully kindled and warm discussions made the guests forget cold weather. To one of these meetings Elizabeth Peabody now caused Nathaniel to be invited. Somewhat to her surprise he came, and so pronounced was his agitation upon finding himself among unfamiliar people that "his face lost color and took on a warm paleness . . . he stood by a table, and, taking up some small object that lay upon it, he found his hand trembling so that he was obliged to lay it down."

But this morbid diffidence did not prevent Nathaniel from calling again at Charter Street, as Sophia had predicted. He came one evening about a week after his first visit, and this time he came alone. A few moments after his arrival Sophia came down, clad in a simple white wrapper, and sat on the sofa. As Elizabeth introduced him, he rose and looked at Sophia intently, more intently than he realized. Elizabeth continued their conversation, and from time to time Sophia interposed a remark in her low, sweet voice. Every time that she did so, Nathaniel looked at her again, with eyes that were hungry and preoccupied. Elizabeth, noticing this, was disturbed. "What if he should fall in love with Sophia!" she wondered, and the thought troubled her. For Sophia had always said that nothing would ever induce her to marry and inflict the care of an invalid upon her husband. When Nathaniel arose, abruptly, to take his leave, he promised to come and take Elizabeth to call upon his sisters.

"Won't you come too, Miss Sophia?" he asked.

"I never go out in the evening, Mr. Hawthorne," Sophia replied.

"I wish you would!" he said, in a low urgent tone. Sophia smiled and declined once more, and Nathaniel took his departure.

Sophia was troubled by an unfamiliar agitation. The evening had been, for her, a disturbing experience. She had known many men whose minds stimulated her own; she had been susceptible to the excitement produced by what she called Emerson's "soul beauty." But this evening had been strangely different. She was conscious of a subtle attraction exercised by Nathaniel, an attraction so powerful that, in instinctive self-defense, she had been forced to summon all her will to resist it. This power which she felt in him alarmed her. She did not understand its significance. She did not wish to experience its effect. She was able to feel only that she must combat it.

Little by little, as her admiration for the handsome

young author became articulate, she put her fear away. It became a secret source of pleasure to hear about him when her sister Mary, having gone walking with his sister Elizabeth, came home with such tidings as she had gathered by adroit inquiry. Occasionally he came to the house, never asking specially either for Mary or herself; she would contrive to see him, and sometimes she sent him home with flowers which his sister Elizabeth promptly appropriated, and when she heard this Sophia was surprised by her annoyance. She formed the habit of calling at Herbert Street in the course of her infrequent walks, and came to know Elizabeth Hawthorne. "I think I should love her very much. I believe it is extreme sensibility which makes her a hermitess," she reflected. And her pleasure in these little visits was increased when she learned that Nathaniel had been provoked at his failure to see her. Once he called, on a Saturday evening, to take Mary Peabody to Miss Burley's, and Sophia came downstairs to catch a glimpse of him. "He has a celestial expression which I do not like to lose," she confessed to her sister Elizabeth; and in his smile she found the innocence and purity of a child's soul. One afternoon he came while she was in the throes of a raging headache. She descended, "armed with a blue, odorous violet," saw him for a moment, passed a delightful night and, on the following day, felt "quite lark-like or like John of Bologna's Mercury." On another occasion he found her engaged in cleaning a picture, and later told her that he had invented a story in which this was to be the central episode. "To be the means, in any way, of calling forth one of his divine creations, is no small happiness, is it?" she asked Elizabeth, and added, "How I do long to read it!" A few days later, he called at noon, looking "brilliantly *ray-*

"THE GENTLE BOY"
A Drawing by Mrs. Hawthorne

onnant," and said, "*Your* story will be finished soon, Sophia—tomorrow or next day." "I was surprised," she told Elizabeth, "to have the story so appropriated, and I do long to see it."

While Nathaniel was writing her story, *Edward Randolph's Portrait,* Sophia was drawing an illustration for *The Gentle Boy,* a fanciful sketch of the child Ilbrahim. When she had completed it, she showed the drawing to Nathaniel, saying "I want to know if this looks like your Ilbrahim?" He sat down and looked attentively at the drawing, then up at her, and quietly answered, "He will never look otherwise to me!"

Somewhat later, she gave him a little forget-me-not that she had painted. One evening she was "lost in a siesta" when he called. "I was provoked," she admitted to Elizabeth, "that I should have to smooth my hair and dress, while he was being wasted downstairs. He looked extremely handsome, with sufficient sweetness in his face to supply the rest of the world with and still leave the ordinary share to himself. He took from his pocket the 'forget-me-not,' set in elegant style, beneath block crystal,—gold all over the back so that it is enshrined from every possible harm. He said he would leave it for inspection, and I have it on at this moment. 'It is beautiful, isn't it?' he said. He thought it too fine for himself to wear; but I am sure it is as modest as a brooch could be." Several days later Nathaniel came for his brooch, and when Sophia brought it to him he said, "If I did not like it so much, I could wear it better."

As the weather grew milder, Sophia began to accompany Nathaniel and her sister Mary to the club meetings at Miss Burley's. When she was with them Nathaniel was always "exquisitely agreeable, and talked a *great deal*, and looked serene and happy and exceedingly beautiful." Winter slipped quietly into spring; spring became summer before she was aware. Nathaniel was preparing for his annual journey into the world. In his notebook he remarked, "Ladurlad, in *The Curse of Kehama*, on visiting a certain celestial region, the fire in his heart and brain died away for a season, but was rekindled again on returning to earth. So may it be with me in my projected three months' seclusion from old associations."

When Nathaniel came to Charter Street to take leave of the Peabodys, he looked radiant. He told Sophia that he intended to tell nobody where he would be during the subsequent three months, not even his mother; that he proposed neither to write to any one nor to be written to. "He seems," she observed to Elizabeth, "to be determined to be let alone. . . . He looked the sun shining through a silver mist when he turned to say good-by. It is a most wonderful face. Mary asked him to write a journal while he was gone. He at first said he should not write anything, but finally concluded that it would serve very well for hints for future stories. I feel as if he were a born brother. I never, hardly, knew a person for whom I had such a full and at the same time perfectly quiet admiration. I do not care about seeing him often; but I delight to remember that *he is*, and that from time to time I shall have intercourse with him. I feel the most entire ease with him, as if I had always known him. He converses a great deal with me when you are not present,—just as he talks more to you when we are not present."

Nathaniel left Salem on July 23rd and returned on September 24th, having traveled through the Berkshires and the Green Mountains. He followed his usual custom of making elaborate notes of the incidents of his journey, but he did not set down among them his meditations upon the new experience that had come into his life. He had learned, at last, what it is to love. And the image of Sophia, so like his mother in her tender sensibility, her semi-invalidism, her seclusion from the world's activities, preoccupied his mind.

(III)

Nathaniel and Sophia became engaged toward the close of the year 1838, but the engagement was not made public, nor was it confided to the Hawthornes and the Peabodys. Nathaniel had been led by his sister Elizabeth to believe that their mother would disapprove of his marriage to anybody and would especially disapprove of Sophia because of her prolonged ill-health, and it had been intimated to him that disregard of his mother's wishes might endanger her life. In all the days of his courtship he had never spoken to his mother of Sophia, both because he wished to avoid her remonstrances and because he had never, since childhood, spoken to her of anything which importantly concerned him. She invited no confidences from him, and a habit of coldness had accumulated about their relation which neither of them desired to remove. But Elizabeth Hawthorne, cynically watching events from her abnormal solitude, loved her brother with an extreme and exigent passion. She was jealous of any influence to which he submitted, and the thought of his marriage and departure from home was intolerable to her. "He will never marry," she had said; "he will never *do* anything; he is an ideal person." She had been alarmed by his interest in Sophia Peabody. She disapproved of the unprecedented excursions into society in which he had indulged since first calling in Charter Street. And she had resolved to combat, while it was yet possible to do so, the forces which were slowly robbing her life of its central interest. Her expedient in ascribing her own views to Madam Hawthorne was entirely successful. When she learned of Madam Hawthorne's supposed disapproval, Sophia consented to a continuance of the engagement only upon the condition that marriage was to be contingent upon her complete recovery. "If God intends us to marry," she told Nathaniel, "He will let me be cured; if not, it will be a sign that it is not best." But when she called, as she sometimes did, in Herbert Street, she was aware of an indubitable chilliness in the atmosphere. And this gravely troubled her.

It was the fortunate issue of his love that made Nathaniel realize that the term of his seclusion had come to an end. He was aware now that he had exhausted the resources of solitude. His happiness increased rather than diminished the aversion with which he contemplated his separation from the common life. "I am tired of being an ornament!" he complained to Elizabeth Peabody. "I want a little piece of land of my own, big enough to stand upon, big enough to be buried in. I want something to do with this material world. If I could only make tables, I should feel myself more a man."

The intervention of Elizabeth Peabody and of Bridge secured him the fixed employment which he craved. The historian George Bancroft had been appointed Collector of the Port of Boston by President Van Buren.

Meeting him one night at the home of some friends, Elizabeth Peabody mentioned Nathaniel's desire for an active occupation. Bancroft remembered that Bridge, whom he knew well, had also mentioned Nathaniel's name, and in recommending him to the administration Bancroft alluded to Nathaniel's biographical sketch of his friend Cilley, contributed to *The Democratic Review* after Cilley's death in a political duel. This little essay was influential in securing from the new administration the position which Bancroft offered Nathaniel; an appointment as measurer in the Boston Custom House at an annual salary of fifteen hundred dollars. Nathaniel accepted the appointment, which took effect in January, 1839, and removed to Boston to take up his new duties.

He looked forward to them with eagerness and some humor. He anticipated a certain amount of leisure for his writing, and he fondly hoped that the discipline of a practical daily task would destroy the dominion of that unsubstantial and enthralling world which had preoccupied him for so many years. Besides, he was now armed with a compelling motive for the future; to the old dream of fame had succeeded the new dream of happiness; and to the prospect of his marriage he had now committed all his hopes. Writing to Longfellow of his appointment he remarked gaily: "I have no reason to doubt of my capacity to fulfill the duties; for I don't know what they are. They tell me that a considerable portion of my time will be unoccupied, the which I mean to employ in sketches of my new experience, under some such titles as follow: 'Scenes in Dock,'

SOPHIA PEABODY HAWTHORNE

From a Portrait Painted in 1846

'Voyages at Anchor,' 'Trials of a Tide-Waiter,' 'Romance of the Revenue Service,' together with an ethical work in two volumes on the subject of Duties; the first volume to treat of moral duties, and the second of duties imposed by the revenue laws, which I begin to consider the most important."

He entered upon his employment with characteristic conscientiousness. Within a few months Bancroft told Emerson that Nathaniel was "the most efficient and best of the Custom House officers." The novelty of his occupation exhilarated him. It brought him out-doors and into the daylight, and he was content to think of himself as essential to the busy traffic of the wharves. His life seemed to touch, however remotely, the romantic commerce of the seas, for which family traditions had prepared his interest. The daily routine of his office brought before him an interminable possession of sturdy men from all the sea-ways of the world, and he found them as brisk and shrewd as the folk with whom he had delighted to mingle during his journeys about the country, and often more quaint or colorful. He filled his journal with detailed notes of the day's labor; glimpses of the unloading of ships; impressions of the shifting color of the harbor; sketches of sailors at work, and of the piled merchandise that burdened the wharves—"ponderous, evil-smelling, inelegant necessaries of life." Because, contrary to his expectations, he found no leisure for creative activity, he recorded the outward circumstances of his life with more than customary accuracy. He had sought the world of fact as a promised land; his observation exhausted it painfully and all but uselessly. There was something pathetic in his inexorable necessity for ruminating the commonplace.

At the end of six months he began to weary of a too exclusively factual world. "I do not mean to imply that I am unhappy or discontented," he told Sophia, "for this is not the case. My life only is a burden in the same way that it is to every toilsome man; and mine is a healthy weariness, such as needs only a night's sleep to remove it. But from henceforth forever I shall be entitled to call the sons of toil my brethren, and shall know how to sympathize with them, seeing that I have likewise risen at the dawn, and borne the fervor of the midday sun, nor turned my heavy footsteps homeward till eventide. Years hence, perhaps, the experience that my heart is acquiring now will flow out in truth and wisdom."

After a year disillusion had been added to weariness. To submerge himself completely in reality had been his hope. But as the material world began to take possession of him, as the the world of imaginative creation receded, he became aware of a restless discontent. "Your husband has been measuring coal all day, on board of a black little British schooner, in a dismal dock at the north end of the city," he reported to Sophia in describing a typical day of what he termed his outward life. "Most of the time he paced the deck to keep himself warm; for the wind (northeast, I believe it was) blew up through the dock as if it had been the pipe of a pair of bellows. The vessel lying deep between two wharves, there was no more delightful prospect, on the right hand and on the left, than the posts and timbers, half immersed in the water, and covered with ice, which the rising and falling of successive tides had left upon them, so that they looked like immense icicles. Across the water, however, not more than half a mile off, appeared the Bunker Hill Monument; and, what interested me considerably more, a church steeple, whereby I was enabled to measure the march of the weary hours. Sometimes your husband descended into the dirty little cabin of the schooner, and warmed himself by a red-hot stove, among biscuit-barrels, pots and kettles, sea chests and innumerable lumber of all sorts—my olfactories, meanwhile, being greatly refreshed by the odor of a pipe, which the captain, or some one of his crew, was smoking. But at last came the sunset, with delicate clouds, and a purple light upon the islands, and your husband blessed it, because it was the hour of his release, and so came home to talk with his dearest wife."

Shortly afterward he begins to pray that within a year he "may find some way of escaping from this unblest Custom House; for it is a very grievous thralldom." He is trying to return to his writing during the long, lonely evenings, but "with a sense as if all the noblest part of man had been left out of my composition, or had decayed out of it since my nature was given in my own keeping." But his habit of weighing experience in terms of its moral values prevailed, and he attempted to ascertain the benefits of this one, now becoming so tedious. He tries to reassure Sophia by telling her that "her husband," as he calls himself, is not unhappy. "It is only once in a while that the image and desire of a better and happier life makes him feel the iron of his chain; for, after all, a human spirit may find no insufficiency of food fit for it, even in the Custom House. And, with such materials as these, I do think and feel and learn things that are worth knowing, and which I should not know unless I had learned them there, so that the present portion of my life shall not be quite left out of the sum of my real existence. . . . It is good for me, on many accounts, that my life has had this passage in it. Thou canst not think how much more I know than I did a year ago—what a stronger sense of power I have to act as a man among men—what worldly wisdom I have gained, and wisdom also that is not altogether of this world. And when I quit the earthly cavern where I am now buried, nothing will cling to me that ought to be left behind. Men will not perceive, I trust, by my look, or the tenor of my thoughts and feelings, that I have been a custom house officer."

Notwithstanding these possible advantages, Nathaniel could no longer subdue his dissatisfaction with the despotism of the material world. As the spring advanced, he traced the footprints of May upon the islands, watching their tints of green gradually deepening into graver beauty. His spirit protested against confinement in his "darksome dungeon at the Custom House," which seemed to him "a sin—a murder of the joyful young day,—a quenching of the sunshine." When he regains his freedom, he muses, he will once more enjoy all things with the fresh simplicity of childhood; he will renew his youth. "I will go forth and stand in a summer shower, and all the worldly dust that has collected on me shall be washed away at once, and my heart will be like a bank of fresh flowers for my Dove to rest upon." Watching carefully the chance incidents of the day, he finds many that "in future years, when I am again busy at the loom of fiction, I could weave in; but my fancy is rendered so torpid by my ungenial way of life, that I cannot sketch off the scenes and portraits that interest me." He is convinced that "Christian's burden consisted of coal; and no wonder he felt so much relieved, when it fell off and rolled into the sepulcher." By contrast with the perpetual coal, "salt is white and pure,—there is something holy about salt."

His own burden was shortly to fall from his shoulders. In March, 1841, the Democratic administration was to go out of office. Nathaniel, either because he anticipated decapitation at the hands of the Whigs, or because his weariness was no longer to be borne, resigned his office at the beginning of the year. It was after his resignation that he reached his final verdict upon the experience. "It pleased thy husband to think that he also had a part to act in the material and tangible business of this life, and that a part of all this industry could not have gone on without his presence. Nevertheless, my belovedest, pride not thyself too much on thy husband's activity and utilitarianism; he is naturally an idler, and doubtless soon will be pestering thee with bewailments at being compelled to earn his bread by taking some little share in the toils of mortal men."

The two years had been productive of a very little

creative work. He had published one story, and had written three small volumes of tales for children, drawn from episodes of New England history, and together forming the series *Grandfather's Chair*. These had been projected before his entry into the government service, for in writing to Longfellow four years before, he had mentioned turning to the writing of children's books as a source of possible income. The suggestion had originated in the success of the Peter Parley books, and the encouragement had come from Elizabeth Peabody, who was professionally interested in this kind of literature and published Nathaniel's little volumes.

That Nathaniel had felt little incentive to write is not remarkable. His production during the preceding few years had been, for him, unusually rapid; his preoccupation with the business of his office had been exacting; his courtship absorbed whatever remained of the creative spirit. He acknowledged to Sophia that the secret, inward life which nourished his imagination now had its only incitement in her and its most ample fulfillment in their relation. It was a profound awareness of the integrity of this inward life and its separateness from the occupations of his days that made him avow that "any sort of bodily and earthly torment may serve to make us sensible that we have a soul that is not within the jurisdiction of such shadowy demons,—it separates the immortal within us from the mortal." But he had come to distrust its too arrogant exclusiveness, and fear its dominion over him, and he felt the need of supplementing it by an active, crowded career in the material world. He suffered because of this divided allegiance which compelled him, submitting to whichever mood prevailed, to exorcise one world by abandoning himself to the other. Ultimately he perceived the necessity of preserving intact that inward life, and he regarded the tedious hours of his employment as an incubus upon the free career of his spirit. He was incapable of considering his employment the satisfaction of an economic necessity; he was unable to regard the practical business of life as itself an end. He sought to determine in what ways the outward life had served the inward, and came to the conclusion that the inward life had not been served.

(IV)

Elizabeth Peabody had quarters at 19 West Street, and after the death of her invalid brother in 1840 her family abandoned Salem and joined her there. In the West Street rooms Doctor Peabody opened a homeopathic drug shop, Mrs. Peabody conducted a circulating library and bookshop, and Elizabeth entered the publishing business by issuing Nathaniel's books for children and a new magazine, *The Dial*, which Margaret Fuller edited as the organ of Transcendentalism.

The West Street house became the unofficial center of Transcendentalism, Margaret Fuller conducted her "conversations" there to small and serious audiences of admiring women who were perversely flattered by her contempt for them, which she made no effort to conceal, and attracted by her reputation for satire and scholarship. Margaret's ambition in holding these weekly meetings was "to pass in review the departments of thought and knowledge, and endeavor to place them in due relation to one another in our minds. To systematize thought, and give a precision and clearness in which our sex are deficient. . . . To ascertain . . . how we may make best use of our means for building up the life of thought upon the life of action." It was characteristic of Margaret, and of New England culture, that she should undertake the functions of a university. "The circle I meet interests me," she told a friend after the meetings had got under way. "So devoutly thoughtful seems their spirit that, from the very first, I took my proper place, and never had the feeling I dreaded, of display, of a paid Corinne. I feel, as I would, truly a teacher and a guide. . . . But I am never driven home for ammunition; never put to any expense; never truly called out. What I have is always enough." What Margaret had was always enough; even when the question under discussion was "What Is Life?" She held thirteen "conversations" on Greek mythology, and thirteen on the fine arts; most of these were monologues, and twenty-five earnest ladies of Boston presumably acquired a thorough understanding of both subjects by the end of the winter. . . .

Eternities, immensities and infinitudes were the familiar gods of the West Street rooms, and what with homeopathy, books, lectures and a magazine, Elizabeth Peabody justified her reputation for always "supplying some want that had first to be created." Emerson and Thoreau were frequent visitors from Concord, Dwight and Ripley dropped in from time to time, Alcott came and discussed the universe with whoever would listen to him, and occasionally Jones Very, troubled by a return to mundane life after a long indulgence in ecstasy, read his verses aloud to a carefully chosen audience. His visits to Sophia brought Nathaniel into frequent association with the apostles of Transcendentalism, and this contact provided him with a foundation for the criticism of their ideas which he was later to embody in his romances. He was not attracted to many of the people whom he met in West Street. "I was invited to dine at Mr. Bancroft's yesterday with Miss Margaret Fuller," he told Sophia one day, "but Providence had given me some other business to do, for which I was very thankful." And another time he reported that Jones Very had come to see him, adding "you know that he is somewhat unconscionable in the length of his calls." But he listened to them attentively, and his skepticism pushed their theories to the startling conclusions which they were apt, through sheer excess of optimistic zeal, to neglect. But, on the whole, the rarefied atmosphere of West Street depressed him; he wearied of the incessant talk that echoed through the Peabody house; and often he was embarrassed by the depredations practised by culture on courtship.

(v)

It was only in his letters to Sophia and in their meetings that Nathaniel found expression for his inward life. After a day spent in the coal-dust of the steaming docks, among "thick-pated, stubborn, contentious men," he assured her that his "real innermost soul . . . has not ceased to exist, as I might sometimes suspect, but is nourished and kept alive through you." There was a touch of reverence in his love for her as the source of all that he considered worthy and lucid in his spirit. "I always feel as if your letters were too sacred to be read in the midst of people," he told her half-playfully, "and (you will smile) I never read them without first washing my hands."

"It is very singular," he told her, "(but I do not suppose I can express it) that, while I love you dearly, and while I am so conscious of the deep embrace of our spirits, still I have an awe of you that I never felt for anybody else. Awe is not the word either, because it might imply something stern in you; whereas—but you must make it out for yourself. I do wish I could put this into words,—not so much for your satisfaction (because I believe you will understand) as for my own. I suppose I should have pretty much the same feeling if an angel were to come down from heaven and be my dearest friend,—only the angel could not have the tenderest of human natures too, the sense of which is mingled with this sentiment. Perhaps it is because, in meeting you, I really meet a spirit, whereas the obstructions of earth have prevented such a meeting in every other case. But I leave the mystery here. Some time or other it may be made plainer to me. But methinks it converts my love into religion."

His mind dwelt always upon the prospect of their union, and often he felt that it had already been approved, as when he wrote: "I am tired this evening, as usual, with my day's toil; and my head wants its pillow—and my soul yearns for the friend whom God has given it—whose soul He has married to my soul. Ah, my dearest, how that thought thrills me! We *are* married! I felt it long ago; and sometimes, when I was seeking for some fondest word, it has been on my lips to call you—'Wife'! I hardly know what restrained me from speaking it—unless a dread (for *that* would have been an infinite pang to me) of feeling you shrink back, and thereby discovering that there was yet a deep place in your soul which did not know me. Mine own Dove, need I fear it now? Are we not married? God knows we are. Often, I have silently given myself to you, and received you for my portion of human love and happiness, and have prayed Him to consecrate and bless the union. Yes—we *are* married, and as God himself has joined us, we may trust never to be separated, neither in Heaven nor on earth. . . . My beloved, why should we be silent to one another—why should our lips be silent any longer on this subject? The world might, as yet, misjudge us; and therefore we will not speak to the world; but why should we not commune together about all our hopes earthly and external, as well as our faith of inward and eternal union?"

Into the web of his passion for her was woven the realization that now, for the first time in his thirty-six years, he had been admitted to life. And often, in his letters to Sophia, he contrasted his present felicity with the frigidity and emptiness of his past. This was always the case when he returned to Salem, and took up once again the familiar thread of existence in Herbert Street.

"Here sits thy husband in his old accustomed chamber," he wrote to her upon one such occasion, "where he used to sit in years gone by, before his soul became acquainted with thine. Here I have written many tales,—many that have been burned to ashes,—many that doubtless deserved the same fate. This deserves to be called a haunted chamber, for thousands upon thousands of visions have appeared to me in it; and some few of them have become visible to the world. If ever I should have a biographer, he ought to make great mention of this chamber in my memoirs, because so much of my lonely youth was wasted here, and here my mind and character were formed, and here I have been glad and hopeful, and here I have been despondent, and here I sat a long, long time waiting patiently for the world to know me, and sometimes wondering why it did not know me sooner, or whether it would ever know me at all—at least, till I were in my grave. And sometimes (for I had no wife then to keep my heart warm) it seemed as if I were already in the grave, with only life enough to be chilled and benumbed. But oftener I was happy—at least, as happy as I then knew how to be, or was aware of the possibility of being. By and by, the world found me out in my lonely chamber, and called me forth—not, indeed, with a loud roar of acclamation, but rather with a still, small voice; and forth I went, but found nothing in the world that I thought preferable to my old solitude, till at length a certain Dove was revealed to me, in the shadow of a seclusion as deep as my own had been. And I drew nearer and nearer to the Dove, and opened my bosom to her, and she floated into it, and closed her wings there—and there she nestles, now and forever, keeping my heart warm and renewing my life with her own. So now I begin to understand why I was imprisoned so many years in this lonely chamber, and why I could never break the viewless bolts and bars; for if I had sooner made my escape into the world, I should have grown hard and rough, and been covered with earthly dust, and my heart would have become callous by rude encounters with the multitude; so that I should have been unfit to shelter a heavenly Dove in my arms. But living in solitude till the fullness of time was come, I still kept the dew of my youth and the freshness of my heart, and had these to offer to my Dove. . . . Ownest, in the times that I have been speaking of, I used to think that I could imagine all passions, all feelings, all states of the heart and mind; but how little did I know what it is to be mingled with another's being! Thou only hast taught me that I have a heart—thou only hast thrown a light deep downward, and upward, into my soul. Thou only hast revealed me to myself; for without thy aid, my best knowledge of myself would have been merely to know my own shadow—to watch it flickering on the wall, and mistake its fantasies for my own real actions. Indeed, we are but shadows—we are not endowed with real life, and all that seems most real about us is but the thinnest substance of a dream—till the heart is touched. That touch creates us—then we begin to be—thereby we are beings of reality, and inheritors of eternity. Now dost thou comprehend what thou hast done for me?"

(VI)

All unconsciously Nathaniel set forth the effect upon him of this "creating touch" in a letter to Sophia in which he attempted to define the mingling of awe with passion in his emotion toward her. While writing the letter, he fell asleep, and dreamed a dream that, to him, was incomprehensible. And upon waking, he wrote it into his letter, and asked Sophia to interpret it.

"I dreamed," he told her, "that I had been sleeping a whole year in the open air, and that while I slept, the grass grew around me. It seemed, in my dream, that the bed-clothes which actually covered me were spread beneath me; and when I awoke (in my dream) I snatched them up, and the earth under them looked black, as if it had been burnt,—one square place, exactly the size of the bed-clothes. Yet there were grass and herbage scattered over this burnt space, looking as fresh and bright and dewy as if the summer rain and the summer sun had been cherishing them all the time. Interpret this for me, my Dove—but do not draw any somber omens from it. What is signified by my nap of a whole year (it made me grieve to think that I had lost so much of eternity)?—and what was the fire that blasted the spot of earth which I occupied, while the grass flourished all around?—and what comfort am I to draw from the fresh herbage amid the burnt space? But it is a silly dream, and you cannot make any sense out of it."

How Sophia may have interpreted the dream is unknown. But its meaning seems evident. He looked back upon his hermit life in Salem as a dream; he felt that Sophia was leading him toward reality. The year's sleep, in his dream, was the period of this too-concentrated and too-prolonged introversion. During this period he had not made himself "unfit to shelter a heavenly Dove" in his arms; he had kept the dew of his youth and the freshness of his heart, and had these to offer his Dove; he had, in fact, led a life of absolute chastity. The fire was the repressed sexuality which, while it prevented a generous product of grass, gave a delicate freshness to what little had actually flourished; for the libido, withdrawn from outer application, had gone into his work; burning is sometimes employed as a means of enriching soil. He regretted the long period of his seclusion; he had lost "so much of eternity," not of time. His awakening came through his engagement to Sophia and his acceptance of a position in the working world; more through the prospect of marriage, with its disciplining realities of relationship and responsibility, than through his employment in the Custom House. Sophia was, for him, the source of his inward life, the symbol of his contact with the hidden world of his creative spirit. But she was also, to him, the most important object in a real and external world; she was a real woman with whom he must have a real relationship, involving genuine extraversion. If she meant to him the source of a rich inner life, she also meant the partial abandonment of an exclusive preoccupation with that life. She meant to him a departure from the citadel of his inward experience, and this forced departure produced a conflict which, while ultimately helpful to his art, momentarily impeded his creative expression. And to the long delay of his marriage, and the consequent protraction of this conflict without the decisive issue which union with her alone could bring, is probably due his silence of several years.

MARGARET FULLER

From the Original Painting by Chappel

A MODERN ARCADIA

(1)

IN the summer of 1840, while Margaret Fuller and Elizabeth Peabody were launching the first issue of *The Dial*, Doctor George Ripley and his wife were boarding at a dairy farm in the town of West Roxbury, nine miles out from Boston. It was an agreeable spot, secluded despite its nearness to the city, with broad meadows stretching down to the pretty Charles River and thick pine woods at no great distance from the house. The house was a simple, comfortable homestead. Its eastern windows overlooked green meadows and a little brook which gave the farm its name. It was shaded by a beautiful sycamore; a great elm was close to it; two terraced embankments planted with shrubs and flower beds separated it from the meadow; there were many mulberry and spruce trees about. A pleasant retreat, in a setting of gently rolling country; and the Ripleys thought it an admirable refuge from the perturbations of Boston.

The Ripleys were members of the Transcendental Club. Both were ardent converts to the new idealistic doctrines. Both, having looked at the world in which they were living, perceived innumerable opportunities for improving it. George Ripley had served for fourteen years as minister to a Unitarian parish in Boston. He was pious, scholarly and earnest. Success had been predicted for him from the moment of his graduation from Harvard, and a prudent marriage had increased his chances. But the prediction had not been fulfilled. Ripley's quiet virtues had not excited the world, nor had they agitated or increased his flock. He was erudite and zealous, but not eloquent and persuasive; his sermons edified, but did not inspire. Margaret Fuller remarked of Ripley that "his mind, though that of a captain, is not that of a conqueror." He considered himself an unsuccessful clergyman. For a long time he had been convinced that existing social conditions produced a fundamental incompatibility between Christian doctrine and Christian life. He observed with disquiet a discrepancy between Sabbath profession and weekday behavior. This distressed him, but it failed to agitate his flock when he spoke of it, and their apathy increased his sense of failure. He dreamed of a reorganized and ameliorated society, and he longed to make some application to life of the new philosophy.

After his vacation at Brook Farm Ripley's discontent with his ministry and with society reached a climax. He wrote a letter to his parishioners outlining his position, and for once he stirred them to action, for they immediately accepted his resignation. He now determined to make some practical application of his social theories, and selected the dairy farm at West Roxbury for the theater of this enterprise. Mr. Ripley had been educated at the Harvard School of Divinity. Therefore he neglected to ascertain what products, other than milk and experiments, the farm might be expected to supply.

When the Transcendental Club resumed its meetings, Ripley disturbed their habitual serenity by inviting the members to join him in the experiment of applying to life the doctrines which they so ardently professed. The members of the club were, by temperament, reformers. In theory they were profoundly dissatisfied with a society content to live by ideals less remote and exacting than theirs. They were ostentatiously at home in the infinite, and their nostalgia for that convenient abode always increased when their meditations were interrupted by finite, material problems. They were therefore hospitable to Ripley's ideas, but distressed by his desire to act upon them. The rhetoric of Ripley's prospectus was admirably Transcendental; it left his purposes so vague that they harmonized with the other furniture of the infinite and eternal. Among other reforms he proposed to "insure a more natural union between intellectual and manual labor than now exists; to combine the thinker and the worker . . . in the same individual;" and "to prepare a society of liberal, intelligent and cultivated persons, whose relations with each other would permit a more wholesome and simple life than can be led amidst the pressure of our competitive institutions." Writing to Emerson, Ripley asserted that "to accomplish these objects, we propose to take a small tract of land which, under skillful husbandry, uniting the garden and the farm, will be adequate to the subsistence of the families; and to connect with this a school or college, in which the most complete instruction shall be given, from the first rudiments to the highest culture." What Transcendentalist could resist an opportunity to give instruction, particularly in the highest culture?

The composure of the members of the Club was disturbed, however, when it became known that Ripley had prepared a plan in which they were invited to participate. This plan contemplated the formation of a joint-stock company, the stock to be guaranteed by the real-estate which it was proposed to purchase, and the shareholders to be guaranteed a fixed interest on their investments. It was eminently characteristic of the New England temperament to effect the regeneration of society by means of a joint-stock company. The response of the club members to this project was equally characteristic. They assented warmly to the ideal, but they politely declined the invitation. The New England temperament bestows sympathy upon any worthy cause, but carefully avoids all hazardous investments. Emerson, when replying to Ripley's invitation, frankly admitted that he considered investments in Concord more secure than investments in Brook Farm. It was only four years afterward that he asserted the philosophical objections that "no society can be as large as one man" and that "union must be ideal in actual individualism."

Discussion of the projected community was frequently to be heard in Elizabeth Peabody's rooms during the winter; the plan, in its idealistic purpose and Utopian promise, commended itself to her zeal for reform. Unperturbed by the coolness of the Transcendentalists, Ripley had proceeded with his scheme. By midwinter he had decided to rent or buy Brook Farm and, with such adherents as might be gathered, establish the community in the spring. It was at this time that he became acquainted with Nathaniel who, having lately resigned from the Custom House, was casting about for a permanent situation.

To Ripley's optimistic vision of a regenerated society Nathaniel was capable, at best, of giving only qualified assent. Society in the abstract concerned him very little. His was not the temperament of a reformer, and he had no interest and but small sympathy with reform in any sphere. In so far as he possessed any philosophy, he was in agreement with some of the beliefs commonly held by the Transcendentalists, but the temper of his mind was skeptical and habitually he reached his conclusions by observing life rather than by absorbing doctrine. Neither his temperament nor his opinions predisposed him to active participation in a regenerative experiment conducted by a group of radical theorists.

He became involved in the projected Utopia for reasons of personal convenience. The community, as Ripley described it, appeared to promise that combination of material tasks with leisure for creative work which he had so long been seeking. In the new community there were to be available separate cottages for the occupancy of individual families; this promised necessary seclusion in the midst of an agreeable society. The economic burdens of family life were to be alleviated by various coöperative arrangements, and the problem of securing a permanent source of income was to be solved by coöperative agriculture. Nathaniel was now thirty-seven years old and Sophia twenty-nine; they had been engaged for two years, and were anxious to marry. In Ripley's projected community Nathaniel saw a congenial means to that happy consummation. He therefore invested in the enterprise his total savings from his Custom House salary, a sum of one thousand dollars. He made this investment believing that he had reserved the right to withdraw it should he later become dissatisfied with the venture and decide to leave the community.

He was not moved to this course by any profound attachment to the ideals declared by Ripley, or by any violent contagion from the social dissatisfaction then agitating all Transcendentalists. Doubtless the writer and investigator of moral phenomena, the "spiritualized Paul Pry," anticipated with interest observing the conduct of the impassioned dreamers who were to be his associates. To the observer of life no spectacle could have seemed more remunerative than this attempt to discard a time-worn social system and erect a Utopia in the civilized suburbs of Boston. But these motives were purely accessory to Nathaniel's purpose. He enrolled himself in the colony for exclusively practical reasons.

Ripley later confessed that when Nathaniel's accession to the colony was announced, he felt as if a miracle had happened, or "as if the heavens would presently be opened and we should see Jacob's ladder before us. But we never came nearer to having *that,* than our old ladder in the barn, from floor to hayloft."

Scarcely a year before Nathaniel had written, in unconscious prophecy, "when I shall be again free . . . I will go forth and stand in a summer shower." He had made a miscalculation only in the nature of the weather.

(II)

Nathaniel arrived at Brook Farm on the twelfth of April in the midst of a driving snowstorm. He had been preceded by a small and devoted band that had accompanied Ripley to West Roxbury and taken possession of the farmhouse and barn. Valiantly, in the hostile circumstances of a New England spring, they had begun to usher in the millennium. Cheerfully and confidently they attempted to furnish in collaborative zeal what they individually lacked in agricultural experience. For the millennium, as they immediately learned, depended far more upon the milking stool and manure pile than upon ecstatic appreciations of "Nature."

"Here is thy poor husband in a polar Paradise!" Nathaniel wrote to Sophia on the day after his arrival. "I know not how to interpret this aspect of Nature—whether it be of good or evil omen to our enterprise. But I reflect that the Plymouth pilgrims arrived in the midst of storm and stept ashore upon mountain snowdrifts; and nevertheless they prospered, and became a great people,—and doubtless it will be the same with us. I laud my stars, however, that thou wilt not have thy first impressions of our future home from such a day as this. Thou wouldst shiver all thy life afterwards, and never realize that there could be bright skies, and green hills and meadows, and trees heavy with foliage where now the whole scene is a great snowbank, and the sky full of snow likewise. . . .

"Belovedest, I have not yet taken my first lesson in agriculture, as thou mayst well suppose—except that I went to see our cows foddered yesterday afternoon. We have eight of our own, and the number is now increased by a transcendental heifer, belonging to Miss Margaret Fuller. She is very fractious, I believe, and apt to kick over the milk pail. Thou knowest best, whether in these traits of character, she resembles her mistress. Thy husband intends to convert himself into a milkmaid this evening, but I pray heaven that Mr. Ripley may be moved to assign him the kindliest cow in the herd, otherwise he will perform his duty with fear and trembling."

Notwithstanding his valorous intentions, Nathaniel did not establish a reciprocal relation with the cows until four days after his arrival; whether Mr. Ripley was afraid to trust them to his hands or him to their horns he never learned. But on the first morning of his stay he was invited, before breakfast, to the barnyard, where he was set to work chopping hay for the cattle. He labored with such "righteous vehemence," as Ripley called it, that within ten minutes he had broken the machine. He then brought wood and replenished the fires, and consumed at breakfast a "huge mound of buckwheat cakes." His enthusiasm for rural occupations expressed itself in an undisciplined muscular energy which seemed likely to prove destructive of equipment and prejudicial to the peace of the livestock. Ripley, observing this, offered him a pitchfork—probably the most indestructible of implements—and set him to work on a manure pile, where he could do no possible damage. He ruefully named the manure pile his "gold mine," and it engaged his unremitting attention until the early days of June. His other occupations included chopping wood, turning the grindstone, planting vegetables, milking the cows, and the usual "chores." He wore a blue smock made by his sister Louisa, a "tremendous pair of cowhide boots with soles two inches thick," and considered himself a "complete farmer."

Nathaniel embarked upon life at Brook Farm in a spirit of holiday enjoyment, as though he were engaged in a delightful game. In his first letter to Sophia he expressed his satisfaction with his "brethren in affliction." "Could you see us sitting round our table at mealtimes," he told her, "before the great kitchen fire, you would call it a cheerful sight." The Hive, as the farmhouse was named, echoed with gay chatter. Its inmates arose at half-past four, breakfasted at half-past six, dined at half-past twelve, and usually retired at half-past nine. The whole fraternity assembled at meals; and, as Nathaniel informed his sister, "such a delectable way of life has never been seen on earth since the days of the early Christians."

The community seemed to him a veritable Arcadia. "I shall make an excellent husbandman,—" he told Sophia on the second day of his residence, "I feel the original Adam reviving within me." And some days later, after four clergymen had added themselves to the group, he had already adopted the vocabulary of Brook Farm's contempt for a competitive world. "I cannot too highly applaud," he wrote, "the readiness with which these four gentlemen in black have thrown aside all the fopperies and flummeries which have their origin in a false state of society. When I last saw them, they looked as heroically regardless of the stains and soils incident to our profession as thy husband did when he emerged from the gold mine. . . ."

A notable conversion! Here was the sensitive, fastidious recluse, odorous of manure, dripping with sweat, vigorously plying a pitchfork, and listening to the classical allusions made by an awkward clergyman who was helping him load a wagon with fertilizer.

(III)

In the evening Nathaniel enjoyed sitting in the wide, old-fashioned center hall of the Hive, holding a book before his face but turning its pages only infrequently. For, as he acknowledged, it was truly his nature "to be a mere spectator both of sport and serious business." He found the study of his fellow colonists an excellent entertainment. In matters of labor, he discovered, the community was aggressively democratic; but once out of the fields, the members of the fraternity divided naturally into two groups, the intellectually superior and the agriculturally experienced. Among the brethren there were some simple folk, supposedly unlettered, to whom the words of Emerson or Channing or Theodore Parker had come as the gospel of a new dispensation. They had listened, had come away refreshed by the cheerfulness with which these anarchic sages had uttered their startling doctrines, and had found their way to Brook Farm. Usually they proved to be the most productive workers. Among them, Nathaniel discovered, there flourished an extraordinary though confused idealism. Minot Pratt, who became Ripley's chief adviser in matters of practical agriculture, took pains to rescue all the flowers uprooted during the morning's plowing, and faithfully replanted them by the roadside. William Allen, a young farmer from Vermont, delighted in patiently directing the energy of his intellectual superiors into productive channels. Frank Farley, who had had some farming experience in the west, was a marvel of eager docility; he was mildly mad, and many of the colonists shunned him; Nathaniel pitied him, and made him the companion of his walks.

Nearly all the intellectually superior members of the community, Nathaniel soon learned, were in some way eccentric. There was George Bradford, who became his best friend at the Farm. Bradford had studied for the ministry at Harvard, but had never taken a parish. On the occasion of his first sermon his professor had remarked, "Your discourse, Mr. Bradford, is marked by the absence of every qualification which a good sermon ought to have." The remark had been fatal; Bradford thereafter was afflicted by self-distrust. He took up teaching. He would remain in one place for a year, become dissatisfied with the results of his work, resign, migrate to a new place, and commence again with undiminished ardor. He was painfully conscientious; Nathaniel thought that Bradford's conscientiousness was like an itch, keeping him always uneasy and inclined to scratch. He was, among other things, an expert in market-gardening. At the farm he taught literature and German in the school attached to the colony, labored faithfully in the barnyard or fields, and at night discussed philosophy with any disputant that offered.

There was Charles Newcomb, who was a boarder but not an active worker at the Farm. Newcomb was slight, awkward, anaemic and exceedingly sensitive. Emerson had announced him as a genius, and the brethren tried to forgive him for being a nuisance. He was a mystic, and asserted the value of a purely contemplative life by sitting by the hour under a tree in communion with nature. He was given to loudly reciting the litany in the middle of the night, which disturbed the sleep of his more active neighbors. His room was decorated with pictures of the saints whom he particularly admired; having seen Fanny Ellsler dance in Boston, he hung her portrait between those of Ignatius Loyola and Francis Xavier, although he had previously denounced her as a "vile creature." Once he had insisted upon changing his seat at table because of the "profound exactions" made by the eyes of the lady opposite him; he was incorruptibly ascetic.

There was John Dwight, whose devotion to music was so inspiring that at one time he had the whole community engaged in studying the masses of Mozart and Haydn. He taught Latin and music with fervor, detested farm work and avoided it whenever possible, and, like many another Transcendentalist, habitually mistook the indefinite for the infinite. Having studied divinity and abandoned it, he disliked all religious observances. One Sunday Ripley and Theodore Parker, walking across the fields, saw Dwight painfully at work. "There," said Ripley, "is your accomplished friend. He would hoe corn all day Sunday if I would let him, but all Massachusetts could not make him do it on Monday."

There was Warren Burton, another retired clergyman, whose passions were nature-study, phrenology and the doctrines of Swedenborg, and whose appetite for conversation upon any of these subjects exhausted the patience of all his listeners. There were the two Curtis brothers, Burrill and George William, who were students in the Brook Farm school, but who passed their evenings at the Hive urging the more sedate members of the community to take part in charades, or dance, or take moonlight rides on the river. There was Charles A. Dana, who was called "The Professor" because he taught German and Greek, and whose consistent skepticism toward all things, including the Farm and its ideals, assured a lively discussion of any topic broached in his presence.

Amusement was resolutely cultivated by the fraternity when the day's work had been finished, and conversation formed the principal diversion. It ranged from the execrable punning that was prevalent at table, to the impromptu debates often organized by Ripley, and the occasional discourses pronounced by such eminent visitors as Emerson, Alcott and Margaret Fuller.

Margaret recorded one "general conversation" which she opened, "upon Education, in its largest sense, and on what we can do for ourselves and others." "I took my usual ground," she said. "The aim is perfection; patience the road. The present object is to give ourselves and others a tolerable chance. Let us not be too ambitious in our hopes as to immediate results. Our lives should be considered as a tendency, an approximation only. Parents and teachers expect to do too much. They are not legislators, but only interpreters to the next generation. Soon, very soon, does the parent become merely the elder brother of his child;—a little wiser, it is to be hoped. . . . The people showed a good deal of the *sans-culotte* tendency in their manners,—throwing themselves on the floor, yawning, and going out when they had heard enough. Yet as the majority differ from me, to begin with—that being the reason this subject was chosen,—they showed, on the whole, more respect and interest than I had expected. As I am accustomed to deference, however, and need it for the boldness and animation which my part requires, I did not speak with as much force as usual."

A day or two later, Margaret held another conversation; this time on "Impulse." "The reason for choosing this subject," she recorded, "is the great tendency here to advocate spontaneousness at the expense of reflection. It was a much better conversation than the one before. None yawned, for none came, this time, from mere curiosity. There were about thirty-five present, which is a large enough circle. Many engaged in the talk. I defended Nature, as I always do;—the spirit ascending through, not superseding, nature. But in the scale of Sense, Intellect, Spirit, I advocated tonight the claims of Intellect, because those present were rather disposed to postpone them. On the nature of Beauty we had good talk."

After her first visit to the Farm, Margaret returned frequently. To Mrs. Ripley, Margaret had objected that her position at the Farm would be too uncertain, as she could do no work. Mrs. Ripley had replied that the members of the colony "would all like to work for a genius; they would not like to have this service claimed from them, but would like to render it of their own accord." "Yes," said Margaret, "but where would be my repose, when they were always to be judging whether I was worth it or not. It would be the same position the clergyman is in, or the wandering beggar with his harp. Each day you must prove yourself anew. You are not in immediate relations with material things." Her objections were, however, finally overcome. And when she visited the Farm Margaret received the deferential treatment which she exacted; pastilles were burned in her room before her arrival to perfume it, and her morning coffee was brought to her bedside in the only decorated china cup which the community possessed.

The discourses of Margaret and her colleagues were by no means the only intellectual diversion available at the Farm. On Sunday afternoons Mr. Ripley expounded Kant and Spinoza in the Hive parlor; a class without an instructor read the *Divine Comedy* aloud in Italian; there was a considerable preoccupation with Shakespeare that resulted in several readings and performances. The whole estate resounded with incessant talk and fermented in a tumult of ideas. Life also had its lighter aspects. Marianne Ripley's school, domiciled in a cottage across the road, harbored a flock of young people who preferred jollity to metaphysics and morals. They mingled on fairly equal terms with the older members of the community, and their custom of drifting through the rooms at the Hive every evening imported an element of gaiety into the Transcendental atmosphere.

The long evenings at the Hive were not unprofitable to a patient observer who sat silently watching, with a courteous but cool detachment, the characteristic behavior of his partners in Arcadia. After visiting Nathaniel at the Farm, Sophia told him that "notwithstanding your exquisite courtesy and conformableness and geniality there, I could see very plainly that you were not leading your ideal life. Never upon the face of any mortal was there such a divine expression of sweetness and kindliness as I saw upon yours during the various transactions and witticisms of the excellent fraternity. Yet it was also the expression of a witness and hearer rather than of comradeship." From comradeship Nathaniel knew that the substance of his temperament precluded him. He could watch with sympathy the gaiety of young people to whom life was a perpetual frolic. He could listen to optimistic prophecies of a society reborn with a perception of the eternal comedy of aspiration. He could ponder the meaning of such terms as reform, change, civilization and equality. He could appreciate the beauty of a dream and the courage of its dreamer. But he could discover in no dream, however beautiful, the final remedy of all the untoward circumstances that afflict life. And he could give his faith exclusively to no one aspiration, however worthy. "The peril in our new way of life," he reflected, "was not lest we should fail in becoming practical agriculturists, but that we should probably cease to be anything else."

In the progress of his reflection upon his own life, and in his meditation upon what he saw, there began the growth of an enduring disenchantment, the abdication of a romantic illusion, the confirmation of a skepticism which made him thenceforward content merely to question without affirming and to learn without believing. To Brook Farm was due his perception of the ultimate relativity which pervades all life.

(IV)

"It is an endless surprise to me how much work there is to be done in the world," Nathaniel told Sophia some ten days after his arrival at the Farm, "but, thank God, I am able to do my share of it, and my ability increases daily." A few days later he took a trip into Boston to see her, came away in a heavy storm, caught cold, and was secretly pleased with an excuse to abstain from work for a few days. Spring came late, the ground was damp and the sky sullen, winter's chill was in the air, and the prospect of a day with Carlyle on *Heroes* was preferable to that of a struggle with the "gold mine." But although when May Day came, only one flower had been found on the domain, and that an anemone, "a poor, pale shivering little flower that had crept under a stone wall for shelter," the world of nature testified its faith in the renascent spring. For wasps' nests were discovered in the bedrooms at the Hive, and the insect tenants, reviving when the world still seemed asleep, taught the fraternity that "a rural life is not one of unbroken quiet and serenity."

Nathaniel went walking with Frank Farley, and was astonished that there could be found such seclusion at so short a distance from a great city. "Many spots seem hardly to have been visited for ages," he told Sophia, "—not since John Eliot preached to the Indians here. If we were to travel a thousand miles, we could not escape the world more completely than we can here." A few days later he returned to work, on a hill-side, under the clear blue sky. "Sometimes it almost seemed as if I were at work in the sky itself, though the material in which I wrought was the ore from our gold mine. Nevertheless, there is nothing so unseemly and disagreeable in this sort of toil as thou wouldst think. It defiles the hands, but not the soul. This gold ore is a pure and wholesome substance, else our Mother Nature would not devour it so readily, and derive so much nourishment from it, and return such a rich abundance of good grain and roots in requital of it." Far from expressing the conventional Transcendental piety toward nature, Nathaniel was seeking to keep up his flagging spirits. "I do not believe I should be so patient here if I were not engaged in a righteous and heaven-blessed way of life," he told Sophia, and the avowal implies more than it expresses; "when I was in the Custom House and then at Salem I was not half so patient. . . ."

A scant month later, at the beginning of June, his mood had changed. "I have been too busy to write a long letter by this opportunity," he informed Sophia, "for I think this present life of mine gives me an antipathy to pen and ink even more than my Custom House experience did. . . . In the midst of toil, or after a hard day's work in the gold mine, my soul obstinately refuses to be poured out on paper. That abominable gold mine! Thank God, we anticipate getting rid of its treasures in the course of two or three days. Of all hateful places that is the worst, and I shall never comfort myself for having spent so many days of blessed sunshine there. It is my opinion, dearest, that a man's soul may be buried and perish under a dung-heap, or in a furrow of the field, just as well as under a pile of money."

Two months more, and disenchantment was complete. "Joyful thought! in a little more than a fortnight thy husband will be free from his bondage,—free to think of his Dove,—free to enjoy Nature,—free to think and feel! I do not think that a greater weight will then be removed from me than when Christian's burden fell off at the foot of the Cross. Even my Custom House experience was not such a thralldom and weariness; my mind and heart were freer. Oh belovedest, labor is the curse of the world, and nobody can meddle with it without becoming proportionably brutified! Dost thou think it a praiseworthy matter that I have spent five golden months in providing food for cows and horses? Dearest, it is not so."

Leisure was in sight, but he felt that it would be long before he could make good use of it, either for enjoyment or for literary work. He had planned to absent himself from the Farm in order to visit his mother and sisters in Salem. Their demands to see him had become imperative. They had never approved of his experiment. The stubborn Hawthorne pride was revolted by the picture of a Hawthorne toiling, like the coarsest of farmhands, among the beasts of the field. Madam Hawthorne groaned over it, and vehemently wished that Nathaniel would return; Louisa continually urged him not to overwork; Elizabeth directed the shafts of her satire against the Farm and all connected with it. "What is the use of burning your brains out in the sun when you can do anything better with them?" they asked, and plaintively, as the weeks went by and still he did not return, they reminded him of the pain which his absence caused them. "Mother apostrophizes your picture because you do not come home," Louisa wrote him; "she takes up a lamentation because you stay away so long and work so hard." It had been a great deal better, they thought, and far more pleasant, when he had been at the Custom House, and came home every fortnight. A fortnight was quite long enough to stay away. But nine weeks of absence! "Mother is very vehement about it!" In all this complaint there was more than mere wounded pride of family; more, even, than an unremitting solicitude for his welfare and happiness. For they now realized that he had deserted them, that he had left the quiet Salem house perhaps forever, and their jealous, exacting love was desperately striving to bind him to them once more; protesting, as they knew but would not acknowledge, against inevitable defeat.

Partly in affectionate pity for them, he had planned to return to Salem for a week. But there were compelling personal reasons which made the projected visit opportune. Brook Farm had come to seem a Bedlam of unsubstantial opinions and irresponsible visions, detached from the world and existing in a private and slightly ridiculous vacuum. Once more Nathaniel felt that he was losing touch with the actual world. "I was beginning to lose the sense of what kind of a world it was, among innumerable schemes of what it might be or ought to be," he wrote long afterward. And he was convinced that "no sagacious man will long retain his sagacity, if he live exclusively among reformers and progressive people, without periodically returning into the settled system of things, to correct himself by a new observation from that old standpoint." He was aware of a pressing need to think over his experiences.

He required, most importantly, an opportunity to master the swift disillusion that had overtaken him. While the experiment had been only a project Nathaniel had amused himself with a romantic dream of the "spiritualization of labor." The days spent in the fields were to have been the ritual of a new worship of nature, and from communion so intimate a new and rich wisdom was to have been gained. Pausing at his labors on the hillside, and looking upward at the sky, he had hoped to "catch glimpses into the far-off soul of truth." This had been the dream; the reality had been disconcerting. Occasionally, when he had casually looked up from his work, he had seemed to catch nature unawares, to perceive some novel and unwonted aspect of a familiar earth and sky, as though the universe, taken by surprise, had failed to don its customary mask. But this was all. The riches of the "gold mine," so constantly turned over, had never been refined into thought. It seemed to him that his thoughts were becoming cloddish. His labor symbolized no purpose higher than its own, and left him weary and dull at the day's end. He had come to feel that intellectual activity is incompatible with any large amount of physical exertion. He knew now that the yeoman and the artist are forever divorced. With that knowledge had come the conviction that his dream of a divided life was an illusion no less impossible of realization than any of the vagaries uttered at the Farm.

Inexorable practical difficulties appeared now to attend his original project of locating at the Farm after his marriage. It seemed unlikely that Ripley would be able to acquire the Farm as a permanent site. "We must form other plans for ourselves;" he wrote to Sophia in a mood of discouragement, "for I see few or no signs that Providence proposes to give us a home here. I am weary, weary, thrice weary, of waiting so many ages. Yet what can be done? Whatever may be thy husband's gifts, he has not hitherto shown a single one that may avail to gather gold. I confess that I have strong hopes of good from this arrangement with Monroe; but when I look at the scanty avails of my past literary efforts, I do not feel authorized to expect much from the future. Well, we shall see. Other persons have bought large estates and built splendid mansions with such little books as I mean to write; so that perhaps it is not unreasonable to hope that mine may enable me to build a little cottage, or, at least, to buy or hire one. But I am becoming more and more convinced that we must not lean upon this community. Whatever is to be done must be done by thy husband's own individual strength. Most beloved, I shall not remain here through the winter, unless with an absolute certainty that there will be a house ready for us in the spring. Otherwise, I shall return to Boston,—still, however, considering myself an associate of the community, so that we may take advantage of any more favorable aspect of affairs. Dearest, how much depends upon these little books! Methinks if anything could draw out my whole strength, it would be the motives that now press upon me. Yet, after all, I must keep these considerations out of my mind, because an external pressure always disturbs instead of assisting me."

(v)

Once back in Salem he resumed, almost automatically, the habit of his old life. "Dearest, I have been out only once, in the daytime, since my arrival," he informed Sophia. "How immediately and irrecoverably (if thou didst not keep me out of the abyss) should I relapse into the way of life in which I spent my youth! If it were not for my Dove, this present world would see no more of me forever. The sunshine would never fall on me, no more than on a ghost. Once in a while people might discern my figure gliding stealthily through the dim evening,—that would be all. I should be only a shadow of the night; it is thou that givest me reality and makest all things real for me. If, in the interval since I quitted this lonely old chamber, I had found no woman (and thou wast the only possible one) to impart reality and significance to life, I should have come back hither ere now, with a feeling that all was a dream and a mockery."

He began thinking about his life at the Farm and suddenly perceived that the whole experience had been, for him, an unnatural one, with something of the quality of a waking dream. He could not bring himself to believe in its reality. "But really," he told Sophia, "I should judge it to be twenty years since I left Brook Farm; and I take this to be one proof that my life there was an unnatural and unsuitable, and therefore an unreal one. It already looks like a dream behind me. The real Me was never an associate of the community; there has been a spectral Appearance there, sounding the horn at daybreak, and milking the cows, and hoeing potatoes, and raking hay, toiling in the sun, and doing me the honor to assume my name. But be thou not deceived, Dove of my heart. This specter was not myself."

It now struck him with peculiar force that, although

the community at the Farm had been founded as a protest against competitive society, it sought to gain an advantage over that society by competitive methods. The members rose before dawn in order that they might produce more milk, or vegetables, and have them in the market stalls of Boston at an earlier hour than the products of their neighbors. Was this not because, as respected society at large, the community stood in a position of new hostility rather than new brotherhood? Was it not true that membership in any minority implies estrangement from the world?

And this estrangement from the broad, deep current of life; was it, after all, to be called good? You undertook it, and accepted the consequences, if you had a vision of a world reformed, of a new and perfect life. But, granting that you had this inspiration, would not a too exclusive devotion to it ultimately make you an ineffective servant in its cause? Would not the cultivation of a noble ideal bring a man to a nobler life only if it did not lead him aside from the normal course of his true development? Was it not foolish to suppose that the realization of any ideal, however noble, could bring about a final remedy of circumstances, making life perfect? And was not this folly, this concentration of effort upon a single purpose, the failing of all reformers?

Nathaniel recalled some phrases of Mr. Emerson's: "Whoso would be a man must be a nonconformist. . . . Nothing is at last sacred but the integrity of our own mind. . . . If I am the devil's child, I will live then from the devil. . . . No law can be sacred to me but that of my nature." This was exciting doctrine. It made you the center and final arbiter of your world. It made you self-reliant and self-responsible. It freed you from the accumulated burden of the past. But Mr. Emerson also said that Nature is forever revealing an inevitable order. He said that to acquire wisdom and power you must submit yourself to the order of Nature; to the "beautiful necessity," or strict consequences which flow from every least event. How were you to reconcile these conflicting doctrines? If you became a nonconformist, how were you to be certain that you had submitted yourself to Nature's inevitable order? How could you know that you had not set yourself in opposition to that order, placing yourself outside the path of your destined development, perhaps never to return? If you relinquished the past completely, did you not also relinquish the essence of culture? If you isolated yourself to that extent, might not the noblest part of you be ineffectual? Nathaniel recalled his own long, ineffectual years of isolation. . . .

If you accepted the alternative counsel, and submitted to the slowly evolving order of Nature, in so far as you could discover it, did you not cease to be a nonconformist? To apprehend the order of Nature you must study the past and the present; these two points would reveal the direction of the future. The past is not sacred; the present is not sacred, for it too will change. Was it not the part of wisdom merely to seek the direction of that change and submit to it; to keep aloof from all exigent reforms and rely upon the slow processes of Nature?

Might it not even be true that the only constant principle of life is change? Do we not live in a universe so arranged that our only certainty is a perception of its inconstancy? No springtime ever returns; no two are ever precisely alike. Times change, and people change, and our hearts change also, though we might wish for this single inflexibility amidst so much fluctuation. Mr. Emerson had suggested this; he had said that "*if we are true* . . . our crimes may be the lively stones out of which we shall construct the temple of the true God." What he seemed to mean is that there is no such thing as evil. "No evil is pure, nor hell itself without its extreme satisfactions." He appeared to imply that what seems at any moment to be most thoroughly evil will ultimately be found to contain good, and that what appears to be good will prove to be so.

What, then, is sin; and what is evil? To perceive the path of our appointed destiny is difficult; if we step aside from what appears to be the moral order, is it not possible that we shall come upon a nobler morality? May not the soul be saved through what appears to be sin; not through repentance, but through consistent adherence to the sin? And, conversely, may not consistent devotion to an ideal that appears to be noble bring us, in the end, to evil? Is sin, then, only an element in experience by means of which we progress to a higher development? Is sin the ultimate instrument of our perfectibility?

Nathaniel supposed that there were no final solutions to these problems. To perceive them clearly; to observe life closely; to project the problems into life and deduce conclusions from what observation revealed; this was all one could do. At every point one was thrown back upon reality, upon the warm, rich substance of life. And this perhaps was for the best. For systems of society harden and decay; ideals which once carried conviction finally become mere conventions supported by force; only life itself, ceaselessly changing, reveals its permanence in its inconstancy. And no solutions, however acceptable to one's convictions or to the moment, could claim finality before that change. Surely it was best to realize this, to be content with one's doubts, to make them, as it were, a form of faith. . . .

(VI)

Nathaniel returned to the Farm, and it seemed to him that he had been absent from it for half a lifetime, so utterly had he grown apart from the spirit and manners of the place. He was received with the greatest kindliness by his associates, and began slowly to adapt himself to the life of the queer community. The fields and woods, copper and russet in the autumn sunshine, seemed beautiful once more, and he was the better able to enjoy their beauty because he was no longer obliged to toil in stubborn furrows. He had come back as a boarder, not a worker, and had determined to spend the remainder of his stay in the production of another book of stories for children.

He found that he could do little writing. He lacked the sense of absolute seclusion which had always been essential to his power of creation. Although nobody intruded into his room, he could not be quiet. Nothing was settled at the Farm; everything was but in process of arrangement; and though he seemed to have little to do with anything but his own thoughts, Nathaniel could not escape the atmosphere of activity. He felt that he could only observe and think, and content himself with catching glimpses of ideas that might be worked upon afterward. Meanwhile he knew that he would see his associates from a new point of view and would soon determine whether or not to retire from the enterprise. Shortly after his return he was elected a trustee of the estate, and chairman of the Committee of Finance. This office required him to undertake supervision of the financial affairs of the Farm, and drew him still further away from his work. He informed Ripley that his acceptance of these offices did not imply a permanent residence at the Farm.

He remained through the winter, completing the *Biographical Stories for Children* and preparing for the publisher, James Monroe, a new and enlarged edition of *Twice-Told Tales.* The greater portion of his time he spent in long solitary walks, along the Needham Road, to Cow Island, to Dedham and to Newton, observing the deepening colors of the autumn.

Late in September the community held a picnic in the woods, in honor of the birthday of one of the children, and Nathaniel recorded a picture of it as typical of Brook Farm in holiday mood. "I strolled out, after dinner, with Mr. Bradford, and in a lonesome glade we met the apparition of an Indian chief, dressed in appropriate costume of blanket, feathers and paint, and armed with a musket. Almost at the same time, a young gypsy fortune-teller came from among the trees and proposed to tell my fortune. While she was doing this, the goddess Diana (known on earth as Miss Ellen Slade) let fly an arrow, and hit me smartly in the hand. The fortune-teller and goddess were in fine contrast, Diana being a blonde, fair, quiet, with a moderate composure; and the gypsy, Ora Gannett, a bright, vivacious, dark-haired, richly-complexioned damsel,—both of them very pretty, at least pretty enough to make fifteen years enchanting. Accompanied by these denizens of the wild wood, we went onward, and came to a company of fantastic figures, arranged in a ring for a dance or a game. There was a Swiss girl, an Indian squaw, a negro of the Jim Crow order, one or two foresters, and several people in Christian attire, besides children of all ages. Then followed childish games, in which the grown people took part with mirth enough,—while I, whose nature it is to be a mere spectator both of sport and serious business, lay under the trees and looked on. Meanwhile Mr. Emerson, and Miss Fuller, who arrived an hour or two before, came forth into the little glade where we were assembled. Here followed much talk. The ceremonies of the day concluded with a cold collation of cakes and fruit. All was pleasant enough—an excellent piece of work,—'would 't were done!' It has left a fantastic impression upon my memory, this mingling of wild and fabulous characters with real and homely ones, in the secluded nook of the woods. I remember them, with the sunlight breaking through overshadowing branches, and they appearing and disappearing confusedly,—perhaps starting out of the earth; as if the everyday laws of nature were suspended for this particular occasion. There were the children, too, laughing and sporting about, as if they were at home among such strange shapes,—and anon bursting into loud uproar of lamentation, when the rude gambols of the merry archers chanced to overturn them. And apart, with a shrewd, Yankee observation of the scene, stands our friend Orange, a thickset, sturdy figure, enjoying the fun well enough, yet rather laughing with a perception of its nonsensicalness than at all entering into the spirit of the thing."

The last record of Nathaniel's residence at the Farm was made in October. "Fringed gentians,—I found the last, probably, that will be seen this year, growing on the margin of the brook." Thus ended the incident of his membership in the Transcendental Utopia. It had begun with a vigorous attack upon the manure pile; it concluded with a solitary view of the waning season's last flowers.

(VII)

"Belovedest," Nathaniel wrote from Salem in February, 1842—"Belovedest, I have thought much of thy parting injunction to tell my mother and sisters that thou art her daughter and their sister. I do not think that thou canst estimate what a difficult task thou didst propose to me—not that any awful and tremendous effect would be produced by the disclosure; but because of the strange reserve, in regard to matters of feeling, that has always existed among us. We are conscious of one another's feelings, always; but there seems to be a tacit law, that our deepest heart-concernments are not to be spoken of. I cannot take my heart in my hand and show it to them. There is a feeling within me (though I know it is a foolish one) as if it would be as indecorous to do so, as to display to them the naked breast. And they are in the same state as myself. None, I think, but delicate and sensitive persons could have got into such a position; but doubtless this incapacity of free communion, in the hour of especial need, is meant by Providence as a retribution for something wrong in our early intercourse. . . .

"I tell thee these things, in order that my Dove, into whose infinite depths the sunshine falls continually, may perceive what a cloudy veil stretches over the abyss of my nature. Thou wilt not think that it is caprice or stubbornness that has made me hitherto resist thy wishes. Neither, I think, is it a love of secrecy and darkness. I am glad to think that God sees through my heart; and if any angel has power to penetrate into it, he is welcome to know everything that is there. Yes, and so may any mortal, who is capable of full sympathy, and therefore worthy to come into my depths. But he must find his own way there. I can neither guide him nor enlighten him. It is this involuntary reserve, I suppose, that has given the objectivity to my writings. And when people think that I am pouring myself out in a tale or story, I am merely telling what is common to human nature, not what is peculiar to myself. I sympathize with them—not they with me."

(VIII)

Nathaniel had definitely determined not to cast his fortunes with those of Brook Farm. And, poor though he was, with no assured future before him, he had determined upon marrying immediately. Sophia had completely recovered from her lifelong illness. The future lay before them with the uncertainty and the happiness of hope. Their friend Elizabeth Hoar, the betrothed of Mr. Emerson's brother, had found them a house in Concord. All was ready for the marriage so long awaited; it remained only to tell Madam Hawthorne of the engagement so long concealed. Early in June Nathaniel went to Salem to inform his mother and sisters.

"Sweetest, scarcely had I arrived here," he wrote from Salem, "when our mother came out of her chamber, looking better and more cheerful than I have seen her this some time, and inquired about the health and well-being of my Dove, very kindly, too. Then was thy husband's heart much lightened; for I knew that almost every agitating circumstance of her life had hitherto cost her a fit of sickness, and I knew not but it might be so now. Foolish me, to doubt that my mother's love could be wise, like all other genuine love! And foolish again, to have doubted my Dove's instinct,—whom, henceforth (if never before) I take for my unerring guide and counsellor in all matters of the heart and soul. . . . Now I am happier than my naughtiness deserves. It seems that our mother had seen how things were, a long time ago; at first her heart was troubled, because she knew that much of outward as well as inward fitness was requisite to secure thy foolish husband's peace; but, gradually and quietly, God has taught her that all is good, and so, thou dearest wife, we shall have her fullest blessing and concurrence. My sisters, too, begin to sympathize as they ought; and all is well. God be praised! I thank Him on my knees, and pray Him to make me worthy of thee and of the happiness thou bringest me."

One month later, on July 9, 1842, the marriage took place, very quietly, in the West Street home of the Peabodys.

THE NEW ADAM AND EVE

(1)

At the suggestion of Elizabeth Hoar and the Emersons, Nathaniel had rented the old parsonage at Concord, left vacant by the death of its nonagenarian proprietor, Doctor Ezra Ripley.

The house had been built by Doctor Ripley's predecessor, Doctor William Emerson, who had watched the opening engagement of the Revolution taking place beneath his study window. Theology had brought Doctor Ripley to the pastorate, but matrimony had brought him to the Manse. He had married Doctor Emerson's widow, adopted her numerous family, and for sixty years maintained the priestly character of her dwelling.

To Nathaniel and Sophia the old Manse was as familiar as the unvisited home of an intimate friend. George Bradford, Nathaniel's companion at Brook Farm, had often stopped there when visiting his sister, Sarah, the wife of old Doctor Ripley's son and heir. Mr. Emerson himself had come to reside with his step-grandfather after resigning his Boston pastorate, and had composed his essay on Nature in the little study. As Nathaniel said, Mr. Emerson had watched "the Assyrian dawn and Paphian sunset and moonrise" from the summit of the eastern hill.

A square, two-storied, gable-roofed building, the

Manse stood in ample grounds bordering the languid Concord River. It was set far back from the highway, at the end of an avenue of balm-of-Gilead trees. Time and weather had stained its white walls a sober gray. It was shrouded in woodbine and shaded by ancient trees. At the back of the house the grounds descended gently to the river through a venerable orchard. There were apple trees, scraggy and goat-like; peach trees with gummy, rotted branches; pear and quince and cherry trees that yielded chiefly bitter fruit. A puritanical orchard, sadly but implacably fertile. The margin of the river was a tangle of flags and rushes where blue pickerel-weed and flaming cardinal-flowers seemed to utter impieties. Elder and ash and aspen boughs hung over the water, and its surface was stained with white pond-lilies and yellow water lilies.

The Manse contained an accumulation of ancient furniture: "high-backed, short-legged, rheumatic chairs, small old tables, bedsteads with lofty posts, stately chests of drawers, looking glasses in antique black frames." The wooden panels and beams, long innocent of paint, were drearily brown. A melancholy echo of forgotten sermons haunted the deserted rooms. Age brooded heavily over the Manse. Other wedded couples had come to it upon their honeymoons, children had been born there and come to maturity, men and women had grown old and died in its chambers. The unchanging ritual of life had been accomplished many times within its walls. But to Nathaniel and Sophia it seemed to accent the future, not the past. Its remoteness from the village, its seclusion from the traffic of the highway, its tranquillity fulfilled their expectations of a new Eden. Like Eden, as they might have remembered but probably did not, it possessed a tradition of sanctity. . . .

(II)

They began to make plans for the adornment of their home. As they examined one room after another, Sophia's eagerness to experiment in decoration became insistent. With cheerful paint and wallpaper, some new furniture, a gay carpet and the inevitable wedding-gift bric-a-brac, she transformed the old clergyman's bedchamber on the lower floor into a parlor. "The shade of our departed host will never haunt it," Nathaniel prophesied, "for its aspect has been changed as completely as the scenery of a theater. Probably the ghost gave one peep into it, uttered a groan, and vanished forever."

For their bedroom Sophia selected a chamber on the upper floor. Upon it she lavished her most tender skill. They had bought, in Boston, a suite of furniture; solid, substantial, of good New England maple. But Sophia was not altogether content with it; other couples could duplicate it; she wished for something unique and exquisite, appropriate to their love. So she drew, upon the head and footboard of their wide nuptial bed, copies of the Flaxman designs she admired, painted them and varnished the wood to an immaculate luster. Attenuated Grecian deities, not the stern God of the Puritans, presided over their dreams and pronounced silent epithalamia.

In the northwest corner of the Manse was a little room that had served always as the pastor's study. When Nathaniel first entered it, its walls were blackened by the smoke of eighty years, and from them portraits of the line of Concord ministers stared at him inhospitably. They looked, he thought, extraordinarily

THE OLD MANSE

like bad angels; as if their stern wrestling with the devil had communicated to them some of the qualities of their opponent. Sophia banished them to the attic. She made the room radiant with pale yellow paint and paper. She installed the furniture of Nathaniel's bachelor lodgings in Boston, and substituted for the Puritan worthies the pictures which she had painted for him during their engagement. In this room she placed their books. One of the cases bore a vivid purple vase which she supplied with fresh flowers every day. On Nathaniel's secretary she placed Margaret Fuller's wedding gift, a handsome bronze vase which they filled with sprays of fern.

After Sophia had completed her alterations, Nathaniel approved of his study. Its dimensions pleased him, for he found it difficult to compress his thoughts sufficiently to write comfortably in a spacious room. He liked the view from its windows. Two of these, set with small old-fashioned panes, looked out over the orchard toward the river. A graceful willow, brushing against the eaves, shaded them from the afternoon sun. A third window, facing north, commanded a broader view of the river; this was the window from which Doctor Emerson had witnessed the outbreak of rebellion, where now were the ruins of the contested bridge and a new commemorative monument. Late in the afternoon the little study was drenched in pale golden light. Sophia loved to enter it then, and find her beautiful husband meditating in the radiance of sunset.

(III)

The Manse contained many mysterious closets and dark recesses where the ghosts of former inhabitants might find concealment by day. Nathaniel disbelieved in the existence of supernatural presences. Sophia did not share his skepticism. One night shortly after their arrival at the Manse, they lay abed talking until nearly midnight. Nathaniel was startled by the shattering of a pause; Sophia's agitated whisper, asking why he had touched her shoulder; he had not touched it. Before he could reply, she seemed to know; she clung to him in fright, aware of a third presence in their room, and implored him not to leave their bed. He arose, searched the chamber and adjacent entry, but found nothing. He sought to persuade her that the touch had been imaginary; his incredulity irritated her. She was convinced that a ghost had visited their bedside, and believed it to be associated with the apparition of Doctor Harris, which, in Nathaniel's Custom House days, had manifested itself to him in the Boston Athenæum. She regarded it as potentially malevolent. It did not occur to her to explain the visit as a protest against her introduction of pagan gods into a bedchamber traditionally sacred to Puritan pieties.

The incident was a prelude to many others. George Hillard and his wife came out from Boston to spend a week-end at the Manse. On the evening of their arrival, after dinner, Sophia led her guests into the parlor. Nathaniel threw himself upon a sofa at some distance from the others, silent under the cover of their talk. An ominous silence interrupted his meditation and, looking up, he saw that Hillard's face was a mask of fear and that the ladies seemed painfully agitated. To their surprise he had not heard the rustling, as of a minister's silk robe, that had passed among them; to their annoyance, he refused to believe that they had heard it. But Sophia accepted the clerical ghost with seriousness. She declared that it heaved deep sighs in one corner of the parlor, that it rustled paper, as if leafing over a sermon, in the long upper gallery, and that she had heard it pounding upon Nathaniel's study table in a frenzy of nocturnal composition. The restlessness, immaterial theologian was sometimes attended by a maidservant, whom Sophia heard in the kitchen at midnight, grinding coffee, ironing, or cooking. They never profited by her ghostly labors.

(IV)

Life flowed by, a tide of indolent contentedness. As Nathaniel confided to the journal which they were jointly writing, there was, indeed, nothing to write about. "Happiness," he said, "has no succession of events, because it is a part of eternity; and we have been living in eternity ever since we came to this old Manse." "My life, at this time," he recorded on another day, "is more like that of a boy, externally, than it has been since I was really a boy. It is usually supposed that the cares of life come with matrimony; but I seem to have cast off all care, and live with as much easy trust in Providence as Adam could possibly have felt before he had learned that there was a world beyond Paradise. My chief anxiety consists in watching the prosperity of my vegetables, in observing how they are affected by the rain or sunshine, in lamenting the blight of one squash and rejoicing at the luxurious growth of another. It is as if the original relation between man and Nature were restored in my case, and as if I were to look exclusively to her for the support of my Eve and myself,—to trust to her for food and clothing, and all things needful, with the full assurance that she would not fail me. The fight with the world,—

the struggles of a man among men,—the agony of the universal effort to wrench the means of living from a host of greedy competitors,—all this seems like a dream to me. My business is merely to live and enjoy; and whatever is essential to life and enjoyment will come as naturally as the dew from heaven. This is, practically at least, my faith. And so I awake in the morning with a boyish thoughtlessness as to how the outgoings of the day are to be provided for, and its incomings rendered certain."

Their daily routine was as languid as the current of the Concord. At dawn Nathaniel bathed in the river, and before breakfast returned to catch the day's supply of fish. After breakfast he worked in his garden, gathering such vegetables as were ready for their table. Then he rambled along the margin of the river in search of flowers, often returning with masses of pond-lilies, which in their "sweet prudishness" reminded him of Sophia, or with clusters of white arrow-head, blue pickerel-weed and scarlet cardinal-flowers. He went to his study and read, or wrote in his journal, permitting time to drift on until the dinner hour, while in a room below Sophia was engaged in painting or modeling. After dinner they went walking through the neighboring woods or along the river valley. They had an early tea, and went to the little study to watch the sunset, a bouquet of painted flowers above the river. In the delicious long evenings that were seldom interrupted by visitors, they sat in the study, Sophia sewing while Nathaniel read aloud from the old English writers; Shakespeare for thought, Spenser for music, Milton, whom they dared to dislike when he went to heaven. On warm moonlit nights they sat under the trees and talked; or in a burst of gaiety they ran races up and down their avenue; or Sophia, to the delight of the Irish servant, danced before her husband to the accompaniment of their music-box.

As for the drudgery of literature, Nathaniel found that even the contemplation of it was disagreeable. Happiness, or the contentment which he identified with it, was sufficiently absorbing as a career.

(v)

To live in Concord, as Sophia's mother reminded her, was to be where "native Apollos and Platos spring up in your everyday walk." At the other end of the village was the dwelling of Mr. Emerson, the Academy of a community which cherished Athenian ideals in a Spartan environment. Concord enjoyed the international celebrity of its philosopher with philosophic appreciation. He was always to be met in the woods or on the roads, at the Athenæum or the emporium of Wolcott and Holden. He was neighborly and agreeable to talk with. A little coterie of literary folk treated him with reverence; the outside world regarded him as a prophet; Concord had no objections, for he was a sound Yankee and a good neighbor. It accepted indulgently, and not without satisfaction, Mr. Emerson's increasing fame.

Mr. Emerson sat like a deprecatory sun in the center of a system of revolving satellites; Alcott, Thoreau,

Ellery Channing, the Curtis brothers, Edmund Hosmer, the Hoars. This local constellation was constantly being enriched by wandering stars; Margaret Fuller, Theodore Parker, George Bancroft, Hillard, Bradford, Hedge and others. Disciples arrived from England, Germany and distant Asia. There were always those whom, after several years of residence in Concord, Nathaniel described as "a variety of queer, strangely-dressed, oddly-behaved mortals, most of whom took on themselves to be important agents of the world's destiny, yet were simply bores of a very intense water." For Mr. Emerson, in his office of lay-preacher to the universe, irresistibly attracted all reformers, bewildered moralists, and inventors of new sects or esoteric cults.

The Emersons had inaugurated the custom of receiving guests on one evening of every week. On these evenings Mr. Emerson would sit for hours in a corner of the library, his narrow shoulders hunched forward, his small head rising from an uncomfortable peaked collar bandaged in a high black stock. Usually, he sat with his legs crossed, one foot tucked under the calf of the other leg, so that he appeared to have braided up an inconvenient body and resembled a domestic eagle embarrassed by its talons. He spoke little, contenting himself with an infrequent question or brief sentence. He believed himself unequal to sustained flights, preferred silence to speech, and listened with patience.

Nathaniel, who attended these gatherings very seldom, recalled the spectacle with amusement. Margaret Fuller, handsomely gowned, her coarse fair hair coiled in an elaborate chignon, making men laugh uneasily at the sharpness of her satire; Mr. Alcott, looking like a starved and crested crane, talking interminably, as if infatuated with the sound of his own voice, his eyes wandering from one to another listener in childish confidence of their enjoyment; Mr. Thoreau, whom Nathaniel thought "as ugly as sin; long-nosed, queer-mouthed, with uncouth and somewhat rustic, though courteous manners," standing apart from all groups in ironical detachment. . . .

Mr. Alcott loved language with an insatiable passion. He was distressed by naked ideas, and fussily protected his thoughts from exposure. The obscurity which veiled even his casual remarks gave him, among his admirers, a reputation for profound wisdom. He decorated the infinite with polysyllabic garlands, despised facts, and believed all practical problems to be beneath the attention of a philosopher. Mr. Emerson regarded him as the "prince of conversers," but also remarked that he was an air plant, having no roots. Nathaniel considered this a generous estimate. He agreed with Mr. Emerson that Mr. Alcott "lives tomorrow, as today, for further discourse, not to begin a new celestial life," and avoided him whenever possible.

Nathaniel had come to heartily dislike Margaret Fuller, but believing her to be a dangerous woman, he did not betray his feelings. He resented her self-confidence, her rudeness, her undisguised scorn of intellectual deficiency; his vanity protested against her assumption of superiority. He thought that he perceived, beneath the surface of admirable qualities with which she had adorned it, the essential coarseness and stolidity of her nature. He ridiculed, to Sophia alone, her avowed efforts to become the wisest and greatest woman of the time. He conceded her scholarship, enjoyed her talent for malicious satire, and disagreed with Mr. Emerson, who thought her too much interested in personal gossip and who admitted that she made him laugh more than he liked. But Nathaniel's dislike of her did not prevent him from enjoying an occasional talk with Margaret, as upon one occasion when, meeting her of a Sunday afternoon reclining in the shade of Sleepy Hollow, he sat down beside her and talked with her for two hours about "autumn, and about the pleasures of being lost in the woods, and about the crows, whose voices Margaret had heard, and about the experiences of early childhood, whose influence remains upon the character after the recollection of them has passed away, and about the sight of mountains from a distance, and the view from their summits, and about other matters of high and low philosophy." One could talk with Margaret, even though distrusting her. And when their conversation was interrupted by the arrival of Mr. Emerson who, "in spite of his clerical consecration, had found no better way to spend the Sabbath than to ramble among the woods," and who told them that there were Muses in the woods and whispers to be heard in the breezes, Nathaniel was surprised to find that it was already tea time. . . .

Nathaniel had been attracted by the silence of Mr. Thoreau; the agitated fluency prevailing at Mr. Emerson's evening parties made Mr. Thoreau's taciturnity impressive. He was an inmate of the Emerson household in the dual office of acknowledged disciple and general help. He labored in Mr. Emerson's garden in return for his keep, and did odd jobs of surveying or carpentry when he required money. For the most part, he spent his days prowling about in the woods or idling on the river in his canoe. This eccentric conduct had given scandal in Concord, for Mr. Thoreau had taught school during several years, and his sudden rejection of all recognized modes of gaining a livelihood was inexplicable. Mr. Emerson believed him to be a true poet, and delighted in his gift for metaphysical speculation. As he came to know Mr. Thoreau more intimately, Nathaniel prized him for quite different reasons.

Ellery Channing, who had married Margaret Fuller's sister, Ellen, did not impress Nathaniel very favorably upon first acquaintance. "He is one of those queer and clever young men," Nathaniel reported in his journal, "whom Mr. Emerson (that everlasting rejecter of all that is and seeker for he knows not what) is continually picking up by way of a genius." Ellery agreed with Mr. Emerson's estimate of him. He considered his verses too sacred to be sold for money; Nathaniel, having read the verses at Mr. Emerson's request, was certain that Ellery would never be harassed by offers of gold. He liked Ellery well enough, thought that there was "some originality and self-inspiration in his character, but none, or very little, in his intellect," and found his efforts to be original somewhat tedious.

Nathaniel formed no very high opinion of the merits of Mr. Edmund Hosmer, a farmer of Concord to whom Mr. Emerson's admiration had contributed the reputation of being a philosopher. One Sunday morning Nathaniel and George Hillard had called at Mr. Emerson's on their way to Walden Pond. Mr. Emerson, as Nathaniel recorded, "from a scruple of his external conscience detained us till after people had got into church, and then accompanied us in his own illustrious person." He took them to call upon Mr. Hosmer, a short, sturdy, middle-aged man, who proceeded immediately to utter "thoughts that had come to him at the plough, and that had a sort of flavor of the fresh earth about them." Nathaniel disliked Mr. Hosmer's oracular manner; he spoke "as if the truth and wisdom were uttering themselves by his voice"; as if, having acquired the rôle of prophet, he was attempting to fill it to the satisfaction of his listeners. "It would be amusing," Nathaniel reflected, "to draw a parallel between him and his admirer, —Mr. Emerson, the mystic, stretching his hand out of cloudland in vain search for something real; and the man of sturdy sense, all whose ideas seem to be dug out of his mind, hard and substantial, as he digs potatoes, carrots, beets and turnips out of the earth. Mr. Emerson is a great searcher for facts, but they seem to melt away and become unsubstantial in his grasp."

(VI)

With tender concern Sophia watched the effect upon Nathaniel of this preliminary immersion in Concord life. Mr. Emerson, having assumed the office of sponsor, fell into the habit of calling almost daily at the Manse, upon one or another pretext, with the purpose

RALPH WALDO EMERSON

of enticing them into more active participation. Sophia herself would have been delighted had he succeeded, but, as she expected, his kindly tentatives were destitute of efficacy. With a gentleness equal to Mr. Emerson's, Nathaniel managed to evade unwelcome invitations; all invitations seemed to be equally unwelcome, but his consistent rejection of them seemed never to embarrass Mr. Emerson. "His panoply of reserve," Sophia confided to her mother, "is a providential shield and a breast-plate." His shyness and disinclination to society were, Sophia knew, attributable to his peculiar sensibility and long isolation. She realized that she must indulge them, for he could no longer change the habit of his life. She learned that he disliked visiting and that, although graciously hospitable to visitors, his courtesy in this instance was ceremonious and not instinctive. Sometimes she regretted that Nathaniel did not possess the gift of speech, like Mr. Emerson; this would have made the situation less difficult. But Nathaniel, she finally concluded, was not born to mix in general society; his vocation was to observe, not to be observed; his genius enforced its special asceticism; her function was to serve that genius.

She studied, with equal attention, the effect produced by Nathaniel upon Mr. Emerson and his circle. "Mr. Emerson delights in him; he talks to him all the time, and Mr. Hawthorne looks answers," she told a friend. "He seems to fascinate Mr. Emerson. Whenever he comes to see him, he takes him away, so that no one may interrupt him in his close and dead-set attack upon his ear. Miss Hoar says that persons about Mr. Emerson so generally echo him, that it is refreshing to him to find this perfect individual, all himself and nobody else." To her mother, Sophia reported that "Mr. Emerson says his way is regal, like a prince or general, even when at the table he hands the bread."

Mr. Thoreau, in his diffident, awkward fashion, began to cultivate Nathaniel's society. Sophia realized that his efforts were unusual, and appreciated the tribute to her husband. Mr. Thoreau was reported to be cold and intolerant; Sophia, suspecting that he was excessively sensitive and therefore incapable of any but extravagant demonstrations of feeling, understood that he shunned the expression though not the experience of emotion. She thought him a pathetic figure; she guessed that the eccentric independence of his life masked a profound loneliness. She had heard that his brother John, an inseparable companion, had lately died, and wondered whether, with his brother's death, something in Mr. Thoreau had not ceased to live. After their meeting at Mr. Emerson's, Mr. Thoreau had come with him to the Manse. Mr. Emerson talked, Nathaniel listened, and Mr. Thoreau maintained an inattentive silence. Finally Sophia, thinking to amuse him, played the wedding-gift music-box. Mr. Thoreau, for the first time evincing interest, had pleaded with her to play it again and again. So naïve and so thorough had been his delight in the instrument that Mr. Emerson had found it necessary to tear him away. Nathaniel had immediately invited Mr. Thoreau to dine with them the following week.

Sophia was amused by Ellery Channing's determination to secure Nathaniel's friendship. She had known Ellery as a young lad; he had been an indulged and petted child, and had carried into maturity his childish inability to endure denial or disappointment. He admired Nathaniel, made no secret of his admiration, and desired that Nathaniel admire him. He refused to be intimidated by Nathaniel's unconcealed indifference, but persisted in his efforts to ingratiate himself. Sophia melted before his gay good humor, his invariable willingness to fall in with any of Nathaniel's moods, his facile assumption of intimacy where none existed. And she was not surprised when, after months of assiduous casual visiting and unobtrusive attentions, Ellery's efforts were rewarded by the amused tolerance of her husband.

(VII)

"My wife is, in the strictest sense, my sole companion, and I need no other; there is no vacancy in my mind any more than in my heart," Nathaniel confessed in his journal. He was aware of the depth of his immersion in happiness. Every fiber of his being responded to the ineffable experience of union. By its very intensity that experience was isolated from the stream of common life; but, because he thought of it as perpetual, it seemed a tumult with a core of peace. He was incapable of responding to other experiences, and their importunity, since it did not move him, was tedious. He was without desire, except for that intimacy which is desire and the fulfillment of desire. Other relationships were superfluous, and the unaccustomed abundance in which they were being offered to him was a source of embarrassment.

There was Mr. Emerson. . . . Nathaniel realized that at an earlier period of his life companionship with Mr. Emerson might have been fruitful. There had been times when any philosophy might have solved the questions which vexed him. He had achieved the solutions without a philosophy, and now, being happy, he felt that there were no questions to be put. Philosophy is an education for contentedness; a philosopher is the least remunerative of companions for a man already supremely contented. Notwithstanding Mr. Emerson's obvious fondness for him, Nathaniel realized that an unreserved friendship between them was impossible. He was secretly embarrassed by the indefiniteness and the inequality of their relation; to him it appeared more significant in its exclusions than in its content. He was surprised to find that Mr. Emerson, whom he assumed to be equally aware of the incompatibility of their temperaments, did not consider this obstacle insuperable. He understood that Mr. Emerson's desire greatly exceeded his own, but could discover no basis for it. A superficial contact with Mr. Emerson was more than adequate to his own needs. He was always content to see Mr. Emerson striding up the avenue to the Manse; he watched Mr. Emerson's departing figure without regret.

Their conversations, he often reflected, were a disappointment to both, but for different reasons. Ordinarily, he was silent, for he was familiar with Mr.

Emerson's opinions upon the subjects which were preoccupying him, and these opinions he did not consider especially valuable. His silence, as he knew, forced Mr. Emerson to talk, and Nathaniel was seldom interested in Mr. Emerson's speculations. Mr. Emerson's mind was fertile in abstractions. He thought that he respected facts, but often failed to recognize them, and, when they were inconsistent with his doctrines, preferred to ignore them. Nathaniel's reverence for reality prevented him from sharing Mr. Emerson's temperamental optimism, or finding substance in the mystical indefiniteness of Mr. Emerson's ideas. To him the facts upon which theories are erected were more interesting than the theories. Disembodied truth irritated Nathaniel; he trusted only what was incarnate in life, and therefore a story seemed to him more significant than any system of philosophy. So generally he listened to Mr. Emerson in silence and without special enthusiasm. He read Mr. Emerson with care; he knew, without disappointment, that Mr. Emerson found it impossible to read him. "Nathaniel Hawthorne's reputation as a writer is a very pleasing fact," Mr. Emerson had said, "for his writing is not good for anything and this is a tribute to the man." Nathaniel often wondered why Mr. Emerson admired him; still more, why Mr. Emerson was so eager for his society.

In the autumn Mr. Emerson persuaded Nathaniel to join him in a walking trip to the Shaker community near Harvard village. They were gone two days and one night; "it being the first and only night," Nathaniel recorded in his journal, "that I have spent away from my belovedest wife." Warm sunshine hung in the still air, and along the roadside were clusters of fringed gentians, thorn-bushes with red fruit, and wild apples with fruit like berries. Their walk was devoid of incident, perhaps, as Nathaniel reminded Mr. Emerson, because it requires humor or extravagance in the traveler to produce incidents in his journey. They were sober men and easily pleased, he continued, and were keeping to the outside of the land; they had not entered a single farmhouse, even by the simple method of asking for a cup of milk. He told Mr. Emerson of his experiences when, as a younger man, he had traveled on foot and by stage through New England. In those days the taverns were filled with teamsters and farmers; by striking up an acquaintance with them, the traveler was able to share in the life of the countryside. But now the taverns were cold places; the Temperance Society had emptied the bar-rooms. They entered a tavern, and Nathaniel went into the bar-room to smoke a cigar, but soon rejoined Mr. Emerson on the piazza; the old atmosphere of rural wit and passionate politics had gone forever, the bar-room was dreary and cold.

They spent the night at Harvard village, and on the following morning walked out to the Shaker community for breakfast. Mr. Emerson engaged two of the brethren in a conversation about their faith and practices. Nathaniel, having been familiar with these matters since his visit to the community at Canterbury years before, paid such scant attention to the conversation that Mr. Emerson later reproved him for having been "inclined to play Jove more than Mercurius." After a tour of the farm, they began the journey home. They talked of poetry; of the inadequacy of most of the poetry of love; of the fact that many of the best poems about love had been written by unhappy lovers. Nathaniel suggested that their disappointment had taught the poets to feel and write. Mr. Emerson cited Landor, who had been unfortunate in love, but who had written one sentence about love which was worth a divorce: "Those to whom love is a secondary thing love more than those to whom it is primary."

"After an arduous journey," Nathaniel recorded in his journal after this excursion with Mr. Emerson, "we arrived safe home in the afternoon of the second day,—the first time that I ever came home in my life; for I never had a home before."

There was Mr. Thoreau. . . . Association with Mr. Thoreau was productive of many satisfactions in which Nathaniel's relation to Mr. Emerson was deficient. Between Mr. Thoreau and himself there seemed to exist a common fund of tastes and habits which made communication easy. Both were solitary by temperament; both loved to ramble about the countryside for the sheer delight of being outdoors. Mr. Emerson revered nature as the symbol of a metaphysical principle; if he could contemplate the principle, he was satisfied to ignore the landscape. But Mr. Thoreau, like Nathaniel, adored nature for its own beauty. Mr. Thoreau was on intimate terms with all animals and with every growing thing. Nature, in return for his love, seemed to have adopted him as her special child, and to have shown him secrets unrevealed to other men. "I find him,"

Nathaniel noted early in their acquaintance, "a healthy and wholesome man to know." Talk with him, Nathaniel felt, was like listening to the murmuring of the wind in the boughs of a forest.

As their acquaintance ripened into friendship, Nathaniel came to know other aspects of Mr. Thoreau's character. He wanted, above all things, leisure to be free; by which he meant, to study, to observe nature and to write. To gain this freedom he was willing to deny himself most of the possessions which other people saved to acquire. A man, he said, is rich in proportion to the number of things he can do without. He intended permanently to escape the modern routine of incessant labor for the accumulation of unremunerative possessions. He intended to make himself absolutely independent of society. The true individualist, he said, must be a non-conformist; the non-conformist must be thoroughly self-reliant. Nathaniel recognized the doctrines of Mr. Emerson; he knew that Mr. Thoreau's admiration of Mr. Emerson verged upon awe. But Mr. Thoreau's vagabond and eccentric life made a practical application of Mr. Emerson's doctrines which, in Nathaniel's opinion, Mr. Emerson himself would ultimately find embarrassing. He remembered the inconsistency of Mr. Emerson's orthodox life with his radical doctrines. He recalled that the prophet of non-conformity had refused to go walking of a Sunday morning until after people were safely in church, and wondered what attitude he would take toward Mr. Thoreau's more radical projects. For Mr. Thoreau was prepared to carry his doctrine of non-conformity to the extreme of refusing allegiance to the state. He had, in fact, refused to pay his church tithes upon one occasion, and had been saved from jail only by the intervention of a relative who had paid them without his knowledge or consent. For Mr. Thoreau, like Nathaniel himself, was impatient of ideas that had no connection with life. He believed that one's life should illustrate one's belief. . . . Nathaniel wondered when the inevitable break with Mr. Emerson would occur.

The first time that Mr. Thoreau dined at the Manse, he took Nathaniel for a trip on the river in his boat, the Musketaquid. The boat, painted green with a border of blue, had been built by Mr. Thoreau and his brother John for the purpose of making a week's trip on the Concord and Merrimac Rivers. Skillfully paddling up the swollen Concord, between high, wooded banks, Mr. Thoreau told Nathaniel about that trip and others which he made with his brother. Now, his brother having died, Mr. Thoreau no longer had any pleasure in the boat, and wished to sell it. Nathaniel promptly offered to purchase it, and on the following day the Musketaquid became his property. He decided to change its name to the Pond-Lily, which, he said, "will be very beautiful and appropriate, as, during the summer season, she will bring home many a cargo of pond-lilies from the river's weedy shore." Not for him were the Indian exploits of Mr. Thoreau; the canoe was transformed to a lady's gondola.

There was Ellery Channing. . . . Ellery's gaiety made him an excellent companion for a day's expedition in the Pond-Lily. They would start in the morning and row upstream to the North Branch, then turn into its quiet waters, landing at a clearing in the woods where they cooked their meal over a campfire. Ellery had a pretty wit, and Nathaniel was glad to stretch out upon the ground and listen to him and be idle. These were splendid indolent days, filled with warm sunshine and the odor of pines; they refreshed Nathaniel with a feeling of freedom and peace.

(VIII)

Autumn advanced; bright days vexed by keen northwest winds that filled the orchard with fallen apples and the avenue with russet leaves. Nathaniel and Sophia paid a visit to Salem and Boston. Their journal fell into neglect; after their return Nathaniel reported that "all my scribbling propensities will be far more than gratified in writing nonsense for the press; so that any gratuitous labor of the pen becomes peculiarly distasteful."

After Thanksgiving winter came on. Sullen rains shifting to snow and sleet, covering the river meadows with ice; dreary skies; the near-by houses blotted from view by snow; the river frozen from bank to bank. In the mornings Nathaniel wrote in the study; he was working at a series of tales for *The Democratic Review* and other publications. In the afternoons Sophia joined him; they read aloud to one another and began the study of German. Before sundown they went out upon the frozen river, Nathaniel to skate, Sophia to run and slide in the waning light that transformed the black ice to a floor of burnished gold. Occasionally Mr.

Emerson and Mr. Thoreau joined them in this sport. Mr. Thoreau, who was an experienced skater, "figured dithyrambic dances and Bacchic leaps upon the ice"; Sophia considered them very remarkable but very ugly. Mr. Emerson skated as if he were too weary to hold himself erect, pitching head foremost, half lying upon the air. Nathaniel, wrapped in his great cloak, moved with the stately gravity of a statue in long, sweeping curves. "Hawthorne is a lion, a bear, a tiger," Mr. Emerson said to Sophia when he came into the Manse to rest. "The man's a satyr; there's no tiring him out." Then, with his memorable smile, Mr. Emerson added, "Hawthorne is such an Ajax that no one can cope with him." In January Mr. Emerson set out upon a lecture tour in the south, and Mr. Thoreau became their solitary visitor. The drifting snow confined them to the Manse. Woodpaths and shady groves and pleasant houses that in summer they knew well, now all but passed from their recollection.

"As to the daily course of our life," Nathaniel recorded in his journal in March, "I have written with pretty commendable diligence, averaging from two to four hours a day; and the result is seen in various magazines. I might have written more, if it had seemed worth while, but I was content to earn only so much gold as might suffice for our immediate wants, having prospect of official station and emoluments which would do away with the necessity of writing for bread. Those prospects have not yet had their fulfillment; and we are well content to wait, because an office would inevitably remove us from our happy home,—at least, from an outward home; for there is an inner one that will accompany us wherever we go. Meantime, the magazine people do not pay their debts; so that we taste some of the inconveniences of poverty. It is an annoyance, not a trouble."

The money difficulties, if not acute, were at least discouraging. O'Sullivan's *Democratic Review,* which had begun by paying five dollars a page, was now paying only twenty dollars for any contribution, and was delinquent in its payments as well. Nathaniel, who regarded his investment in Brook Farm as subject to withdrawal, had attempted to secure repayment from Mr. Ripley without success, and had asked George Hillard to undertake legal measures of collection. Meanwhile, O'Sullivan was exerting his political influence at Washington to secure for Nathaniel the office of Postmaster at Salem, an office for which Nathaniel himself had no desire except as a means of solving his financial problems.

Writing to Bridge, then stationed at the Portsmouth Navy Yard, Nathaniel candidly revealed the extent of his pecuniary difficulties. "I did not come to see you, because I was very short of cash, having been disappointed in money that I expected from three or four sources. My difficulties of this sort sometimes make me sigh for the regular monthly payments at the Custom House. The system of slack payments in this country is most abominable, and ought, of itself, to bring upon us the destruction foretold by Father Miller. It is impossible for any individual to be just and honest and true to his engagements when it is a settled principle of the community to be always behindhand. I find no difference in anybody in this respect. All do wrong alike."

Early in March Nathaniel and Sophia left the Manse for a fortnight's visit to their families in Salem and Boston. "I alone went to Salem," Nathaniel recorded in his journal, "where I resumed all my bachelor habits for nearly a fortnight, leading the same life in which ten years of my youth flitted away like a dream. But how much changed was I! At last I had caught hold of a reality which never could be taken from me. It was good thus to get apart from my happiness for the sake of contemplating it."

From Salem, Nathaniel wrote to Sophia in Boston:

"Own wife, how dost thou do? I have been in some anxiety about thy little head, and indeed, about the whole of thy little person. Art thou ill at ease in any mode whatever? I trust that thy dearest soul will not be quite worn out of thee, with the activity and bustle of thy present whereabout, so different from the intense quiet of our home. That poor home! How desolate it is now! Last night, being awake, my thoughts traveled back to the lonely old house, and it seemed as if I was wandering upstairs and downstairs all by myself. My fancy was almost afraid to be there alone. I could see every object in a sort of dim, gray light—our bed-chamber—the study, all in confusion—the parlor, with the fragments of that abortive breakfast upon the table, and the precious silver forks, and the old bronze image keeping its solitary stand upon the mantel-piece. Then, methought, the wretched Pigwigger came and jumped upon the window-sill, and clung there with her forepaws, mewing dismally for admittance, which I could not grant her, being there myself only in the spirit. Then came the ghost of the old Doctor stalking through the gallery, and down the the staircase, and peeping into the parlor; and though I was wide awake, and conscious of being so many miles from the spot, still it was quite awful to think of the ghost having sole possession of our home; for I could not quite separate myself from it, after all.

"Somehow, the Doctor and I seemed to be there tête-à-tête, and I wanted thee to protect me. Why wast not thou there in thought, at the same moment; and then we should have been conscious of one another, and have had no fear, and no desolate feeling. I believe I did not have any fantasies about the ghostly kitchen-maid; but I trust Mary left the flat-irons within her reach, so that she may do all the ironing while we were away, and never disturb us more at midnight. I suppose she comes thither to iron her shroud and perhaps, likewise, to smooth the doctor's band. Probably, during her lifetime, she allowed the poor old gentleman to go to some ordination or other grand clerical celebration with rumpled linen, and ever since, and throughout all earthly futurity (at least, as long as the house shall stand) she is doomed to exercise a nightly toil with spiritual flat-irons. Poor sinner—and doubtless Satan heats the irons for her. What nonsense is all this!—but really, it does make me shiver to think of that poor house of ours. Glad I am that thou art not there without thy husband. . . ."

(IX)

Shortly after their return to Concord came the news of Mary Peabody's engagement to Mr. Horace Mann. Mary's plans included an early marriage and a six months' wedding tour of Europe. Sophia rejoiced in her sister's happiness. "No words can ever express what a spear in my side it has been to see her year after year toiling for all but herself, and growing thin and pale with too much effort," she wrote. "I was hardly aware, until it was removed, how weighty had been the burden of her unfulfilled life upon my heart. At her engagement, all my wings were unfolded, and my body was light as air." In this mood of pleasure, Sophia went to visit her sister in Boston, leaving Nathaniel alone at the Manse for the first time since their marriage.

Her departure produced a peculiar restlessness in Nathaniel. He had resolved to spend the period of her absence in hard work at his writing; he had even vowed to himself that he would not speak a word to any human being while Sophia was gone. But he found it difficult to carry out this program. He spent a morning in splitting and sawing wood, working more briskly than ever before in his life. Physically, he had never been in better condition; he attributed it to a satisfied heart, aided by exercise and about a fair proportion of intellectual labor. When he reëntered the house after his morning's work, "it was with somewhat of a desolate feeling; yet not without an intermingled pleasure, as being the more conscious that all separation was temporary and scarcely real, even for the little time that it may last."

As the week of Sophia's absence dragged itself wearily to a conclusion, Nathaniel became more and more acutely aware of the changes worked upon his life by marriage. Without being absolutely sad, he was incessantly depressed. Sleep came to him only reluctantly as he lay alone in the wide bed; his solitary meals were a gruesome punishment; the long evenings spent under the astral lamp of the little study with Tieck and a German phrase book, or with the *Dial,* a kitten purring at his feet, were intolerable. Several days passed without his exchanging a word with another human being, and whereas this solitude had once been his normal habit, it was now displeasing to him. He was glad when friendly solicitude or casual circumstance brought Mr. Emerson or Mr. Thoreau to his door, but their visits scarcely distracted him, and he did not regret their departure. He worked sedulously every morning, but to his surprise found himself incapable of sustained concentration; his mind seemed dry and barren of ideas; he increased his efforts, but accomplished no progress. The Manse was strangely desolate. As he wandered about the house, he seemed to be revisiting the scene of a past happiness now inhabited by strangers, in which familiar objects, long forgotten, revenged his desertion of them by the wistfulness of their survival. He wound and re-wound Sophia's little music-box, but its peculiar sweetness had evaporated, and he felt that he would surely throw it out the window were he doomed to hear it long and often.

MRS. NATHANIEL HAWTHORNE

From an Unpublished Photograph Taken in 1855

Sophia returned from Boston to a troubled delight in the agitation of his welcome.

(x)

Spring advanced, sometimes with sunny days, sometimes with chill, moist, sullen ones. "There is an influence in the season," Nathaniel wrote, "that makes it almost impossible for me to bring my mind down to literary employment; perhaps because several months' pretty constant work has exhausted that species of energy,—perhaps because in spring it is more natural to labor actively than to think. But my impulse now is to be idle altogether,—to lie in the sun, or wander about and look at the revival of Nature from her death-like slumber, or to be borne down the current of the river in my boat. . . . Oh, how blest should I be were there nothing to do! Then I would watch every inch and hair's-breadth of the progress of the season; and not a leaf should put itself forth, in the vicinity of our old mansion, without my noting it. But now, with the burden of a continual task upon me, I have not freedom of mind to make such observations."

Summer came, late in June; long days, with blazing sunshine and fervid heat, glowing like molten brass; moist and sultry nights when nothing slept. "I have a sort of enjoyment in these seven-times heated furnaces of midsummer, even though they make me droop like a thirsty plant," Nathaniel wrote. "The sunshine can scarcely be too burning for my taste; but I am no enemy to summer showers. Could I only have the freedom to be perfectly idle now,—no duty to fulfill, no mental or physical labor to perform,—I should be as happy as a squash, and much in the same mode; but the necessity of keeping my brain at work eats into my comfort, as the squash-bugs do into the hearts of the vines. I keep myself uneasy and produce little, and almost nothing that is worth producing."

Economic difficulties had persisted; the hopes of government office had neither materialized nor receded; Nathaniel's small savings were dwindling, and even the immediate future seemed most insecure. The summer was a poignant ecstasy sharpened by portents of imminent disaster. Nathaniel exploited every resource; worrying at his writing, cultivating the kitchen-garden that once had been a pastime and was now a source of sustenance. Bridge, off for a long cruise to Africa on the naval vessel *Saratoga,* had proposed to write a series of articles descriptive of his adventures, and Nathaniel had undertaken to edit them for publication, accepting a share in the royalties for his labor and the use of his name.

Summer brought visitors to the Manse. First came Sophia's father, who remained a week, exercising his love of order by mowing the grass on the lawns, helping with the garden, and making minor neglected repairs to the house. He also prepared a vast quantity of modeling clay, and Sophia began to model a portrait bust of Nathaniel. When he had departed, Anna Shaw arrived looking, as Sophia reported, like Diana or Aurora in the full glory of her golden hair. During her visit Mr. Emerson came frequently to the house, and the four went walking in the woods and spent hours in talk, lying on the lawn under the stars. The Hillards came over from Boston, and Louisa Hawthorne from Salem. Ellery Channing and his wife Ellen were living in a little red cottage by the roadside; Ellery worked very hard upon the single acre of land attached to the house, and kept a small school for young children. Elizabeth Hoar, who, according to Sophia, resembled "the Rose of Sharon, though thinner than ever," occasionally dropped in at the Manse. "Mr. Hawthorne has written a little and cultivated his garden a great deal,"; Sophia wrote to a friend, "and as you may suppose, such vegetables never before were tasted. . . . When Apollos tend herds and till the earth, it is but reasonable to expect unusual effects." Sophia had planted flowers. They voyaged on the river constantly, harvesting water-lilies and cardinal flowers. They were happy.

"There has been no rain, except one moderate shower, for many weeks; and the earth appears to be wasting away in a slow fever," Nathaniel recorded in his journal at the waning of summer. "This weather, I think, affects the spirits very unfavorably. There is an irksomeness, a pervading dissatisfaction, together with an absolute incapacity to bend the mind to any serious effort. With me, as regards literary production, the summer has been unprofitable; and I only hope that my forces are recruiting themselves for the autumn and winter. For the future, I shall endeavor to be so diligent nine months of the year that I may allow myself a full and free vacation of the other three."

Autumn overtook them almost unaware; first in heart-broken brilliance, later in rags and shreds of faded color. "We are rich in blessings, though poor in money," Nathaniel remarked in his journal, concluding a rhapsody upon the loveliness of the season. A necessitous existence had become irksome. He was accustomed to economy but parsimony irritated him, less for himself than for Sophia. Besides, their restricted circumstances, he felt, were a standing indictment of his own capacity as a breadwinner, a symbol of his failure to meet the American obligation of success. On one of his visits to Salem he learned that rumors of their poverty had been circulated by the Reverend Charles W. Upham, who had recently been in Concord. "When he returned from Concord," Nathaniel told Sophia with some bitterness, "he told the most pitiable stories about our poverty and misery, so as almost to make it appear that we were suffering for food. Everybody that speaks to me seems tacitly to take it for granted that we are in a very desperate condition, and that a government office is the only alternative of the almshouse. I care not for the reputation of being wealthier than I am; but we never have been quite paupers, and need not have been represented as such." His vanity was wounded, and he himself knew; the vanity of Puritan New England which abhorred dependence and found in the very smallness of its debts the source of its misery; he could not rid himself of the inherited luxury of that pain. Besides, money and a steady supply of money was now of instant importance; for Sophia was to become a mother.

Winter descended upon them ominously; their second winter in the Manse, which they faced with an anxiety that they forbore to acknowledge to one another. But their tenderness and their affection deepened, and to the overwhelming instability of life their love opposed its own endurance. "That downy bloom of happiness, which unfaithful and ignoble poets have persisted in declaring always vanished at the touch and wear of life," Sophia told her mother, "is delicate and fresh as ever, and must remain so if we remain unprofane." Sophia had resolved to increase the family exchequer herself, and had begun a painting of Endymion which she planned to sell, through Elizabeth's bookshop, for one hundred dollars. But as work upon it progressed, Nathaniel protested that he would not permit her to sell it.

The Christmas season arrived; days that were hard and bright and cold as diamonds. Mary Bryan, the maid-of-all-work, went off to Boston for a holiday. Sophia and Nathaniel were enchanted by the complete solitude which her absence afforded them. Nathaniel undertook the office of keeping house. "He rose betimes in the mornings," Sophia informed her mother, "and kindled fires in the kitchen and breakfast-room, and by the time I came down, the teakettle boiled, and potatoes were baked and rice cooked, and my lord sat with a book, superintending. Just imagine that superb head peeping at the rice or examining the potatoes with the air and port of a monarch!" He shoveled paths through the snow, sawed and split wood, and drew buckets of water from the well. "To such uses do seraphs come when they get astray on earth," Sophia commented, adding also that "Apollo helped me by making the fires." Christmas came with a magnificent sunrise. "My husband," Sophia wrote, "was entirely satisfied with the beauty of it. He is so seldom fully satisfied with weather, things, or people, that I am always glad to find him pleased. Nothing short of perfection can content him. How can seraphs be contented with less?" Nathaniel proposed to celebrate the day by having no cooking at all. At midday they went into the village, Nathaniel going to spend his customary hour in reading at the Athenæum, and Sophia paying a call at Mrs. Emerson's, where Mr. Thoreau was dining. They returned to a "truly Paradisiacal dinner of preserved quince and apple, dates, and bread and cheese, and milk."

Nathaniel had recovered from a period of comparative sterility and was now working at his writing with an intense concentration. "I do not know what the present production is about, even"; Sophia told her mother, "for I have made it a law to myself never to ask him a word concerning what he is writing, because I always disliked to speak of what I was painting. He often tells me; but sometimes the story remains hidden till he reads it aloud to me, before sending it away. I can comprehend the delicacy and tricksiness of his mood when he is evolving a work of art. He waits upon the light in such a purely simple way that I do not wonder at the perfection of each of his stories. Of several sketches, first one and then another come up to be clothed upon with language, after their own will and pleasure. It is real inspiration, and few are reverent and patient enough to wait for it as he does."

On the third day of March Sophia gave birth to a girl, whom they named Una.

(XI)

Sophia accepted motherhood as an ineffable mystery, and to Nathaniel her radiance seemed that of a Madonna. He was utterly unable to consider the little daughter as a vital part of his being, but he was proud of having become "the regular head of a family." "If you want a new feeling in this weary life," he wrote to Bridge, "get married. It renews the world from the surface to the center." And he added of Una, "For my own part, I perceive her beauty at present rather through the medium of faith than with my actual eyesight." But he was gratified by paternity and his love for Sophia acquired overtones of adoration.

In June, Sophia and her baby visited her mother in Boston. Nathaniel, unwilling to risk again the terrors of solitude in the Manse, invited Frank Farley to stop with him during Sophia's absence. "Mr. Farley is in perfect health," he wrote to Sophia, "and absolutely in the seventh Heaven; and he talks and talks and talks, and I listen and listen and listen, with a patience for which (in spite of all my sins) I firmly expect to be admitted to the mansions of the blessed. And there is really a contentment in being able to make the poor, world-worn, hopeless, half-crazy man so entirely comfortable as he seems to be here. He is an admirable cook. We had some roast veal and a baked rice pudding on Sunday; really a fine dinner, and cooked in better style than Mary can equal, and George Curtis came to dine with us. Like all male cooks, he is rather expensive, and has a tendency to the consumption of eggs in his various concoctions, which thou wouldst be apt to oppose. However, we consume so much fish of our own catching, that there is no great violation of economy upon the whole. I have had my dreams of splendor, but never expected to arrive at the dignity of keeping a man cook. At first we had three meals a day, but now only two."

The continuing insufficiency of money could no longer be faced with childish gaiety. Sophia had been in delicate health since her confinement; the baby made its presence felt as an economic unit. "I continue to scribble tales," Nathaniel wrote to Bridge, off in Africa, "with good success as regards empty praise, some notes of which, pleasant enough to my ears, have come from across the Atlantic. But the pamphlet and piratical system has so broken up all regular literature that I am forced to write hard for small gains. If we have a Democratic President next year I shall probably get an office. Otherwise, it is to be hoped, God will provide for me and mine in some other way." The simplicity of life at the Manse had degenerated into hardship and deprivation. Nathaniel, who at thirty had thought himself well off on three hundred dollars a year, was now confronted by undisguised poverty. His income was inadequate to their small household expenses; he was in debt to the local tradesmen, and that his debts were insignificant did not alter the fact that they were unpaid.

Drastic measures were necessary, and he applied them without hesitation. Molly Bryan was discharged; meat and other food-stuffs obtainable only by purchase were eliminated from the family diet; the table was strictly limited to such vegetables as were supplied by Nathaniel's garden and the fish which he caught in the Concord. Because of Sophia's condition, Nathaniel refused to allow her any share in the household work, and undertook to do all of it himself. "I cannot well ask dear Mary to visit me while my Hyperion is cook and maid," Sophia explained to her mother. "He will not let me go into his kitchen, hardly; but it is no poetry to cook and wash dishes; and I cannot let him do it for anybody but myself alone. The only way we can make money now seems to be to save it; and as he declares he can manage until September, we will remain alone until then. It is beyond words enchanting to be so. But, I assure you, his office is no sinecure. He actually *does* everything."

At Thanksgiving Nathaniel took Sophia and the baby to Salem for a visit. "For the first time since my husband can remember," Sophia informed Mrs. Peabody, "he dined with his mother! This is only one of the miracles which the baby is to perform. Her grandmother held her on her lap till one of us should finish dining, and then ate her own meal. She thinks Una is a beauty, and, I believe, is not at all disappointed in her." After the holiday, Sophia and Una went on to Boston for a visit in West Street, leaving Nathaniel behind at "Castle Dismal" in Salem. His disinclination to composition during the summer had been aggravated by his experience of the petty, menial offices of housekeeping; he now felt the urge to creative activity, and had decided to remain for a short time in Salem and work.

He wrote to Sophia: "I am very well, dearest, and it seems to me that I am recovering some of the flesh that I lost, during our long Lent. I do not eat quite enough to satisfy mother and Louisa, but thou wouldst be perfectly satisfied, and so am I. My spirits are pretty equable, though there is a great vacuity caused by thy absence out of my daily life—a bottomless abyss, into which all minor contentments might be flung without filling it up. . . . The good that I get by remaining here is a temporary freedom from that vile burthen which had irked and chafed me so long—that consciousness of debt and pecuniary botheration, and the difficulty of providing even for the day's wants. This trouble does not pursue me here, and even when we go back, I hope not to feel it nearly so much as before. Polk's election has certainly brightened our prospects, and we have a right to expect that our difficulties will vanish in the course of a few months."

The election of President Polk had, in fact, increased the determination of Nathaniel's political friends to procure him a government office, preferably the postmastership at Salem. John O'Sullivan, in Washington, was using his influence to secure this position, but was also suggesting that Nathaniel be appointed consul at Marseilles, Genoa or Gibraltar. "What would you say to go out as a consul to China with A. H. Everett?" he inquired of Nathaniel. "It seems to me that in your place I should like it; and the trade opening there would give, I should suppose, excellent opportunity for doing a business which would soon result in fortune." To increase Nathaniel's prestige, O'Sullivan persuaded Evert A. Duyckinck to write, for *The Democratic Review,* a eulogy of Nathaniel's work, which he proposed to illustrate by a daguerreotype or a portrait drawing by Sophia. "By manufacturing you thus into a Personage," he wrote to Nathaniel, "I want to raise your mark higher in Polk's appreciation." But O'Sullivan's enthusiasm was apt to exceed his power, and the prospects of office flagged without waning. George Bancroft, Nathaniel's old superior in the Boston Custom House, offered him a minor post in the Charlestown Navy Yard at an annual salary of nine hundred dollars, as a temporary stop-gap; this Nathaniel flatly rejected.

"Had my husband been dealt justly by in the matter of his emoluments, there would not have been even this shadow upon the blessedness of our condition," Sophia wrote to her mother in referring to their pressing money difficulties. "But Horatio Bridge and Franklin Pierce came yesterday, and gave us solid hope. . . . Mr. Hawthorne was in the shed, sawing wood. Mr. Bridge caught a glimpse of him, and began a sort of waltz towards him. Mr. Pierce followed; and when they reappeared, Mr. Pierce's arm was encircling my husband's old blue frock. How his friends do love him! Mr. Bridge was perfectly wild with spirits. He danced and gesticulated and opened his round eyes like an owl. . . . My husband says Mr. Pierce's affection for and reliance upon him are perhaps greater than any other person's. He called him 'Nathaniel,' and spoke to him and looked at him with peculiar tenderness."

Having determined that Nathaniel's political interests would be served by bringing him into contact with party leaders of influence with the new administration, Bridge invited Sophia and Nathaniel to visit him during the summer at his quarters in the Portsmouth Navy Yard. Upon their arrival, they discovered that Bridge had likewise invited Senators Pierce and Atherton of New Hampshire, with their wives, Senator Fairfield of Maine, several congressmen and two of his sisters. The several weeks of holiday passed delightfully; Nathaniel was invariably charming, and the practical object of the visit was accomplished successfully.

After their return to Concord, Nathaniel and Sophia learned that their tenancy of the Manse must come to a conclusion, Mr. and Mrs. Ripley having determined to resume possession of the house. For a brief period the implications of removal filled them with dismay. There was no money, and Nathaniel's prospects of government office were as indefinite as ever they had been. An obvious solution to their difficulties presented itself in temporary separation; Nathaniel to return to the family home in Salem, Sophia and the baby to go to the Peabodys in West Street. But both found the contemplation of this solution intolerable; they avoided all reference to it, were secretly miserable, and their love became a painful ecstasy of utter despair. Writing to her mother, Sophia revealed their extremity: "Unceiled rafters and walls, and a pine table, chair and bed would be far preferable with him to an Alhambra without him even for a few months. He and Una are my perpetual Paradise; and I besieged Heaven with prayers that we might not find it our duty to separate, whatever privations we must outwardly suffer in consequence of remaining together." Heaven answered her prayers; Nathaniel arranged to share with his mother the old home in Salem.

"The three years we have spent here will always be to me a blessed memory, because here all my dreams became realities," Sophia told her mother when informing her of their decision. "I have got gradually weaned from it, however, by the perplexities that have vexed my husband the last year, and made the place painful to him. If such an involved state of things had come upon him through any fault or oversight of his own part, there would have been a solid though grim satisfaction in meeting it. But it was only through too great a trust in the honor and truth of others. There is owing to him, from Mr. Ripley and others, more than thrice money enough to pay all his debts; and he was confident that when he came to a pinch like this, it would not be withheld from him. It is wholly new to him to be in debt, and he cannot 'whistle for it,' as Mr. Emerson advised him to do, telling him that everybody was in debt, and that they were all worse than he was. His soul is too fresh with Heaven to take the world's point of view about anything."

Nathaniel now learned that his friends had abandoned their attempt to secure the Postmaster's office at Salem, this having proved impracticable, and were concentrating their efforts upon the Surveyorship or Naval Office with success practically assured for one or the other post. Accordingly, he and Sophia quietly made arrangements for their removal to Salem. To Nathaniel, the assurance of political office came as a competent relief. He was momentarily weary of literature. He had endured too much deprivation, suffered too much uncertainty. He longed, above all, for peace, for the security of a regular income, for freedom from the necessity of writing for money. The creative life once more had become unreal to him; he associated its fantastic instability, not with his own disappointments, but with the character of his Concord friendships; he was relieved to quit Concord, though not greatly pleased to return to Salem. In retrospect, the years at the Manse seemed good, but they were enough. He had talked too often with Emerson; he had had too many colloquies with Ellery Channing over campfires on the shores of the Assabeth; he had heard too much about pine trees and Indian relics from Thoreau in his cabin at Walden Pond. "Even the old Inspector," he wrote years afterward in the introduction to *The Scarlet Letter,* "was desirable, as a change of diet, to a man who had known Alcott." He felt the necessity of exercising other phases of his temperament than those which had been elicited by his Concord environment. He regarded it as an evidence of a balanced nature that, his memories of Concord being what they were, he could look forward without regret to the Custom House at Salem.

Literature, its exertion and its objects, was now of

little importance to him. Books were entirely alien. The imaginative delight which he had had in the beauty of earth and sky had disappeared. It was as if the essential nucleus of his character had become inanimate, and had withdrawn into its inertia the most precious of his gifts. He was oppressed by his awareness of this amputation, but consoled by his intuition that the new life would be only temporary, and that when another change should be essential, that change would somehow be brought about. His distaste for his art, as he sometimes realized, had its roots in a dissatisfaction with his own accomplishment, rather than in that discontent with the difficulties of his life to which he preferred to attribute it. His three years in Concord had not been productive: he had not fulfilled his own anticipations. He had written less than two score of sketches and tales; he had not intended to continue employing these forms, but had hoped to write a novel. Actually, he had conquered no new territory; he had merely exploited and deepened the vein of *Twice-Told Tales.* And his decision to suspend his creative activity was, in part at least, a revenge upon what he regarded as its inadequacy to his intention.

He had arranged with Wiley and Putnam of New York, the publishers of Bridge's *Journal of an African Cruiser,* to issue the tales and sketches composed during his residence at Concord, together with some previously uncollected papers, in a book to be entitled *Mosses from an Old Manse.* He now busied himself with writing an autobiographical introduction to the book, descriptive of his Concord days. He had determined that the

Mosses should be his last collection; unless he could do better, he had already done enough in that kind. But for this book, notwithstanding the fact that it was the record of a disappointment, he had a very real affection. "For myself," he wrote, "the book will always retain one charm—as reminding me of the river, with its delightful solitudes, and of the avenue, the garden and the orchard, and especially the dear old Manse, with the little study on its western side, and the sunshine glimmering through the willow branches while I wrote."

THE SCARLET LETTER

(1)

RETURNING to Salem, Nathaniel and Sophia took up quarters in "Castle Dismal," as Nathaniel called the old home in Herbert Street. The passing of nearly forty years had left few traces upon that citadel of oblivion. Madam Hawthorne, now a feeble old lady, remained invisible in her sunless chamber. Nathaniel and Sophia saw her only when, for a scant hour, she came to visit them. On these occasions, occurring at long intervals, she spoke little but, wraith-like in her ancient gown, stared at her son with melancholy, weary eyes. Into her room only Una was permitted to enter; the prattle of this lively infant never wearied her solitary grandmother.

Elizabeth and Louisa were now middle-aged women. They maintained the rigorous seclusion which now they would have been incapable of renouncing. Elizabeth's intrepid mind retained its vigor. She commented with sardonic amusement upon the vagaries of a world that she contemplated without elation and repudiated without regret. She had become almost an hypothetical entity; after two years of residence in the same house, Nathaniel and Sophia had seen her but once. Louisa had watched life recede with a regret that contained no bitterness. Unlike her sister, she had never possessed beauty; her existence had neither aroused desires nor demanded renunciations; life had passed in a tranquil childhood which no maturity would ever crown. Louisa was amiable and ineffectual. She adored her mother and slaved for her incessantly. She was devoted to her cats and her tiny garden. She loved her brother and his wife. But her affections played chiefly about Una, upon whose golden head she poured a love that had found no other recipient. She made exquisite dresses for the child, and bestowed them with wistful apologies. She took care of Una during Sophia's absence from the house. Una became the center of her existence.

Shortly after their arrival in Salem, Nathaniel was notified of his appointment as Surveyor of the Port. The local Democratic organization had already certified to Washington candidates for the Surveyorship and Naval Office, but pressure had been brought by Nathaniel's powerful friends, the certified candidates had been persuaded to withdraw their nominations and, following the announcement of Nathaniel's appointment, they were rewarded with subordinate positions in the Custom House. Early in spring Nathaniel was commissioned and undertook the duties of his office. These required his presence at the Custom House during four hours of every day, and secured him an annual salary of twelve hundred dollars. The assurance of a regular income was particularly welcome because Sophia was now awaiting the birth of their second child.

(II)

Nathaniel, after having corrected the proofs of the *Mosses*, had abandoned all literary activity with positive relief. He divided his time between the Custom House and Herbert Street. He had few friends in Salem other than Pike, Conolly and David Roberts. He was in a condition of comparative inertia, requiring no contact with people or ideas, but only leisure in which to be indolent and tranquil. A prescience of the renewal of his creative life occasionally beat in the silence of his existence with the dull obstinacy of a muted drum. But he was determined to wait until the impulse should assert itself more exigently, although he was content to know that it had not disappeared. His life, in its suspended vitality, was like that of a moth hardening and drying in the sunshine.

In the pillared Custom House, relic of more prosperous days, Nathaniel might have fancied himself back in Boston before his migration to Brook Farm. A little murmur of commercial activity still echoed through its pretentious walls; vessels still came, though with increasing infrequency, from Africa or South America; rusty little schooners from the British provinces discharged cargoes of firewood at the dilapidated wharf where clippers once had berthed; but maritime trade had long since deserted Salem for Boston and New York. The Custom House, however, was wrapped in ignorance of its own uselessness. Its staff of decrepit sea-dogs resembled the population of an asylum for the aged. The Custom House was, in fact, precisely such an institution, in which a benevolent government maintained comfortable berths where old hulks were permitted to decay without disturbance. The building seemed to house a lost outpost which, having failed to rejoin its regiment, had maintained a century of existence in ignorance of the conclusion of hostilities.

THE CUSTOM HOUSE AT SALEM

The Collector of the Port, General James Miller, was a veteran of Ticonderoga who held office in lieu of a pension. The infirmities of advanced age had long since incapacitated him for the performance of his duties. These had devolved upon his son, but the old General, perhaps inspired by memories of military decorum, paid periodical visits to his office where, drowsing in a comfortable arm-chair, he dreamed of the martial exploits of his youth. The actual business of the Custom House was carried on, under the direction of the General's son, by a chief clerk named Zachary Burchmore whose performance of his duties gave Nathaniel a new conception of talent. Burchmore had been employed in the Custom House from boyhood; he took pride in his incontrovertible knowledge of its routine; he was, as Nathaniel later testified, thoroughly adapted to the situation which he held. As his own subordinates Nathaniel had a group of superannuated seamen whose function it was to inspect vessels discharging in the port. As the business of the port had all but vanished, their somnolent vigils were rarely disturbed by the importunity of duty. They drowsed through the morning in the back entry, their chairs tilted against the wall, and exchanged reminiscences of adventures at sea with which all had become familiar through infinite repetition. Life for them was secure; they had no fears other than the apprehension of possible removal following a change in the political complexion of the government. When Nathaniel assumed office, the Whigs among them anticipated dismissal; but Nathaniel regarded his appointment as the reward of literary endeavor, not political service, and permitted them to continue in their sinecures.

Almost from the beginning Nathaniel found his associates dull and the routine of his office tedious. His regular stipend was gratifying, and the vacancy of his existence seemed to satisfy an inner necessity of peace. But as time wore on the dreary monotony of the Custom House, the tiresome chatter of its employees, the drabness of their occupations and their lives evoked in him the familiar depression that had been aroused by the coal-ships in Boston harbor and the stubborn fields of Brook Farm. His aversion to the new environment found expression in a semi-humorous contempt for the figures who peopled it. This contempt was made bitter by his increasing impatience with himself. He had abandoned his writing, although leisure and a measure of economic security were not lacking to him; his mind was absurdly, humiliatingly inactive; he had ceased to be a man of letters without having become a man of affairs. Nature no longer provoked his interest. The rocky coast did not tempt him to solitary walks; the wintry moon was destitute of magic. At home in Herbert Street, the two families were inconveniently housed. Every member of the household, except himself, possessed privacy, and their comfort deprived him of a room in which to be alone. Sophia was preoccupied by her household tasks, her approaching confinement and the care of Una; she could no longer spend her afternoons strolling about with him as at Concord. So Nathaniel renewed his association with Pike, Conolly and David Roberts, and struck up an acquaintance with Burchmore. These companionships gave him little actual pleasure, but served to distract him from the dissatisfaction with himself that he could neither ignore nor master. His friends were stout men with the bottle, but Nathaniel was not intimidated by their capacity for drinking. He knew himself to be incapable of becoming intoxicated, and that his companions occasionally did so failed to distress him. Nor was he especially concerned that the more conservative citizens of Salem attached some opprobrium to the term "hard drinkers," which had been fastened upon these men. He seems to have been equally unconcerned by the fact that Conolly, who had deserted the ministry for the study of law, had acquired a none too savory reputation in Salem. He was much more seriously disturbed by an hostility that had sprung up between Pike and Burchmore, the origin of which he finally traced to their mutually jealous attachment to him.

In the summer of 1846 Sophia moved to Boston for her confinement, and remained there for some months after the birth of her son, whom they named Julian. In the autumn, upon her return to Salem with the two children, they moved into a house on Chestnut Street, leaving Madam Hawthorne and her daughters in possession of "Castle Dismal." But the new quarters, chosen hastily from among immediately available houses, were inconveniently small, and contained no room which Nathaniel could appropriate as a study. "We are residing in the most stately street in Salem," Sophia informed Bridge, "but our house is much too small for our necessities. My husband has no study, and his life is actually wasted this winter for want of one. He has not touched his desk since we came to Salem, nor will not, until we can remove to a more convenient dwelling, I fear." In the autumn of the following year they moved again, this time to a house on Mall Street sufficiently large for their comfort and for the accommodation, as a separate household, of Madam Hawthorne and her daughters. "My husband's study will be high from all noise," Sophia told her mother, "and it will be to me a Paradise of Peace to think of him alone and still, yet within my reach. He has now lived in the nursery a year without a chance for one hour's uninterrupted musing, and without his desk being once opened! He—the heaven-gifted Seer—to spend his life between the Custom House and the nursery!"

(III)

The domestic life of Nathaniel and Sophia was tranquilly happy. They maintained the retired existence which they had adopted in Concord, receiving few friends and never paying visits. In November, 1846, Sophia informed her mother that they had spent an evening at the home of a neighbor with whom Mr. Emerson was stopping, and that it had been their first evening away from home since Una's birth, almost three years before. And when they had rented the Mall Street house she remarked that "it is barely possible that I may take a walk with my husband again while in the body, and leave both children at home with an easy mind." But social deprivation and petty economies did not mar her happiness. "No art or beauty," she wrote, "can excel my daily life, with such a husband and such children, the exponents of all art and beauty. I really have not even the temptation to go out of my house to find anything better."

And Nathaniel shared this intimate felicity. "Oh Phoebe," he wrote to his wife upon one of her visits to Boston, "I want thee much. My bosom needs thy head upon it—thou alone art essential. Thou art the only person in the world that ever was necessary to me.

Other people have occasionally been more or less agreeable; but I think I was always more at ease alone than in anybody's company, till I knew thee. And now I am only myself when thou art within my reach. Thou art an unspeakably beloved woman." And on the occasion of this absence, he told her of a strange dream that he had had. "My love," he wrote, "has increased infinitely since the last time we were separated. I can hardly bear to think of thy staying away yet weeks longer. I think of thee all the time. The other night, I dreamed that I was at Newton, in a room with thee, and with several other people, and thou tookst occasion to announce that thou hadst now ceased to be my wife and hadst taken another husband. Thou madest this intelligence known with such perfect composure and *sang-froid,* not particularly addressing me, but the company generally—that it benumbed my thoughts and feelings so that I had nothing to say. Thou wast perfectly decided, and I had only to submit without a word.

"But thereupon thy sister Elizabeth, who was likewise present, informed the company that, in this state of affairs, having ceased to be thy husband, I of course became hers; and turning to me, very coolly inquired whether she or I should write to inform my mother of the new arrangement! How the children were to be divided, I know not. I only know that my heart suddenly broke loose, and I began to expostulate with thee in an infinite agony, in the midst of which I awoke; but the sense of unspeakable injury and outrage hung about me for a long time—and even yet it has not quite departed. Thou shouldst not behave so, when thou comest to me in dreams!"

After the epoch-making evening when they had called upon Mr. Emerson at a neighbor's home, Nathaniel and Sophia began to relax their habits of seclusion. Nathaniel was appointed an officer of the Salem Lyceum, and they attended the lectures together. Sophia enjoyed hearing Daniel Webster's oration upon the Constitution; "a very useful lecture, and in some parts quite grand"; and admired the orator, who stood "like an Egyptian column, solid and without any Corinthian grace, but with dignity and composed majesty." Mr. Alcott spent an evening in their home when he came to Salem to lecture, and told them of his early experience as a peddler. His lecture at the Lyceum drew an audience of twelve people. "Mr. Alcott said he would commence with the Nativity, and first read Milton's Hymn," Sophia recorded in a letter. "Then he retreated to his corner and for about an hour and three quarters kept up an even flow of thought, without a word being uttered by any other person present. Then Mr. Stone questioned him upon his use of the word 'artistic,' which provoked a fine analysis from him of the word 'artist' as distinguished from 'artisan.' I thought the whole monologue very beautiful and clear." Mr. Thoreau likewise lectured in Salem, and Sophia considered his lecture "a revelation of nature in all its exquisite details." "Mr. Thoreau," she remarked, "has risen above all his arrogance of manner, and is as gentle, simple, ruddy and meek as all geniuses should be; and now his great blue eyes fairly outshine and put into shade a nose which I once thought must make him uncomely forever." Upon one occasion they attended a ball given by Mrs. George Peabody, but Sophia was more preoccupied by Mr. Peabody's Murillo Madonna than by the festivities; of the latter she recorded no description, but the painting moved her to eloquence, for it was the greatest picture she had ever seen.

The tranquillity of his domestic life and the possession of a study in which to work had impelled Nathaniel to a tentative encounter with composition. In 1847 Sophia wrote: " . . . My husband began retiring to his study on the first of November, and writes every afternoon. Have you seen the most exquisite of reviews upon 'Evangeline'—very short, but containing all?"

Nathaniel felt exceedingly virtuous in praising Longfellow's new poem. For nine years before the story of the Arcadian lovers had been told him by Horace Conolly, who had heard it from Mrs. Haliburton, one of his parishioners in South Boston. Nathaniel had jotted down the plot in his notebook for later use, but had never employed it. Conolly, after waiting for some time, told the story to Longfellow, who had been captivated by it. Longfellow acknowledged that he owed the poem to Nathaniel, for in November, 1847, after the appearance of the review, he wrote: "I was delighted to receive your note after so long a silence, and also to find that 'Evangeline' is not without favor in your eyes. Still more do I thank you for resigning to me that 'Legend of Arcady.' This success I owe entirely to you, for being willing to forgo the pleasure of writing a prose tale which might have been taken for poetry, that I might write a poem which many people take for prose."

The fruits of Nathaniel's laborious afternoons were not abundant. He produced *The Snow Image*, *The Great Stone Face*, *Main Street* and *Ethan Brand*, but made no effort to publish them. His dislike of the short tale and sketch—the only literary form in which he had practised—persisted and increased; he wrote only with the greatest difficulty and entirely without pleasure. It seemed to him that he had exhausted his invention and his facility. "At last," he wrote in December, 1848, to a New York editor who had asked him for manuscript, "at last, by main strength, I have wrenched and torn an idea out of my miserable brain; or rather, the fragments of an idea, like a tooth ill-drawn, and leaving the roots to torture me."

An unfamiliar development was taking place, the implications of which Nathaniel himself scarcely understood. He now desired, above all things, to get on with his writing, yet his accustomed medium resisted him and aroused only an irritated distaste. He was preoccupied by subjects to which that medium was obviously inadequate, yet so unsophisticated was he in the general principles of his art, and so distrustful was he of his own capacities for sustained narrative that, instead of perceiving the inadequacy of his medium, he was overwhelmed by doubt of his subjects. Actually, although he did not then realize it, he was ceasing to be a writer of short stories and was about to emerge as a novelist. This esthetic re-birth was accompanied by extraordinary psychological labor-pains; he was a prey to an humiliating awareness of temporary impotence and probable future infertility; he was afflicted, simultaneously, by doubt and desire. Never before had he been driven toward conception with greater passion; never, too, had the process of conception appeared so hazardous and uncertain.

He was infatuated by an idea, which, as it seemed to him, would neither reveal itself completely nor relinquish its possession of his mind. The germ, for it was scarcely more than that, was not new; he had fixed it, casually, in his story *Endicott and the Red Cross*, published in *The Token* for 1838. He had found, in the early records of Boston, mention of a punishment enacted by Plymouth Colony in 1658 for the crime of adultery; it had been ordered that women found guilty of this crime wear, on their uppermost garments, the initial letter A, as a public indication of their sin. When writing *Endicott* he had included in the story a description of such a woman: "Sporting with her infamy, the lost and desperate creature had embroidered the fatal token in scarlet cloth with golden thread and the nicest art of needlework." The image caught in that brief phrase had never completely vanished from Nathaniel's memory: he had often reflected upon it, idly fancying that other interpretations might be put upon the woman's defiant elaboration of the symbol of her shame. But an appropriate interpretation had never suggested itself to him. During long afternoons in the Mall Street study his imagination, engaged no more by one subject than another but casting about for material which would make the creative act inevitable, played upon the image of the scarlet letter. He realized that this symbol concentrated a theme more powerful and a story more poignant than any that he had attempted heretofore. The more he pondered its possibilities, the more certain became his conviction of the talismanic potency of the symbol; here, if it did not elude him altogether, was the germ of a great romantic tale.

(IV)

In November, 1848, the Whig candidate for the Presidency, General Zachary Taylor, was elected to office. There had been considerable ill-feeling among political leaders in Salem over developments occurring in the Custom House subsequent to the election. Just after the election of General Taylor, but during the term of President Polk, the term of General Miller, nominally Collector of the Port, came to an end. He declined reappointment, and President Polk, in the last months of his term, appointed General Miller's son in his stead. This appointment enraged the local Whigs who, under the spoils system, felt that the office was rightfully within the bestowal of the incoming administration. After the inauguration of General Taylor as President, the Whigs applied to Mr. Miller for the removal of such Democratic employees of the Custom House as were subject to his appointment, and their replacement by Whigs. Mr. Miller declined to accede to this request of his opponents, taking the ground that he would use his power of removal only after the Federal Government had given the example by making similar removals from office; namely, the removal of the Surveyor and Naval Officer. The Whigs therefore began to besiege Washington with requests for the removal of Nathaniel from the Surveyorship and that of John D. Howard from the Naval Office, and their replacement by Whig appointees.

Nathaniel learned of the attack upon his retention in office at an early date. On the day after President Taylor's inauguration he wrote to George Hillard: "I am informed that there is to be a strong effort among the politicians here to remove me from office, and that my successor is already marked out. I do not think this ought to be done; for I was not appointed to office as a reward for political services, nor have I acted as a politician since. A large portion of the local Democratic Party look coldly on me for not having used the influence of my position to obtain the removal of Whigs—which I might have done, but which I in no case did. . . . But it seems to me that an inoffensive man of letters, having obtained a pitiful little office, on no other plea than his pitiful little literature, ought not to be left to the mercy of these thick-skulled and no-hearted ruffians. It is for this that I now write you. There are men in Boston—Mr. Rufus Choate, for instance—whose favorable influence with the administration would make it impossible to remove me, and whose support and sympathy might fairly be obtained in my behalf—not on the ground that I am a very good writer, but because I gained my position, such as it is, by my literary character and have done nothing to forfeit that tenure. . . ."

On June 8th Nathaniel received a telegram from Washington announcing his removal from office. Immediately he wrote to inform George Hillard of the news; the impact of the event was little less than catastrophic, for it foreboded a return to poverty and hardship, even to acute distress:

"I am turned out of office!

"There is no use in lamentation. It now remains to consider what I shall do next. The emoluments of the office have been so moderate that I have not been able to do anything more than support my family, and pay some few debts that I had contracted. If you could do anything in the way of procuring me some stated literary employment, in connection with a newspaper, or as a corrector of the press in some printing establishment, etc., it could not come at a better time. . . . I shall not stand upon my dignity; that must take care of itself. Perhaps there may be some subordinate office connected with the Boston Athenæum. Do not think anything too humble to be mentioned to me. . . .

"The intelligence has just reached me, and Sophia has not yet heard it. She will bear it like a woman—that is to say, better than a man."

Nathaniel returned to Mall Street that day earlier than was his custom. When Sophia expressed her pleasure at his unexpected arrival, he told her that he had left his head behind him. She replied, "Then you can write your book." He smiled at this, and gently inquired whence their income was to be derived during the period of composition. But Sophia was prepared for the emergency. Unlocking a drawer of her desk, she produced the sum of one hundred and fifty dollars which she had saved from the amounts furnished by Nathaniel for household expenses. His immediate fear having been allayed, Nathaniel went to his study and began to work on the story of the scarlet letter. That evening Sophia wrote to her mother:—"I have not seen my husband happier than since this turning out. He has felt in chains for a long time, and being a *man*, he is not alarmed at being set upon his own feet again—or on his head, I might say—for that contains the available gold of a mine scarcely yet worked at all."

Some days later Nathaniel learned that Charles W. Upham, the retired clergyman whose gossip about their poverty while at the Manse had irritated him some years before, had been active in the attempt to secure his dismissal from office. This news, as Sophia remarked, roused the lion in him. He felt it to be a cowardly and secret attack on his character, and determined to vindicate himself of whatever charges had been made against him. These charges, as he learned, were that he had been appointed to office because of his partisan activities in politics; that he had conducted his office for the benefit of the Democratic Party and its workers; that he had contributed political articles to Democratic publications. In addition he was personally charged with "loafing around with hard drinkers." To this latter charge Nathaniel paid no attention whatever. But the first three charges he disproved in letters which he wrote to Hillard, to his brother-in-law Horace Mann, and other powerful friends. Hillard and Congressman Mann brought their influence, and that of such friends as they could involve in the issue, to bear upon the Administration. For a time it seemed as if a reaction in Nathaniel's favor might result; a month went by, and as Nathaniel's successor had not been appointed, he continued in office. But in July, the issue having assumed the proportions of a political scuffle in Salem circles, the Whig organization addressed a memorial to the Administration calling upon it to sustain Nathaniel's removal. Mr. Upham made several trips to Washington in behalf of a change in the Surveyorship; innumerable petitions were addressed to Washington by merchants of Salem and Whig leaders; Nathaniel's friends, now out of office, were all but powerless. Finally Captain Allen Putnam was appointed to the Surveyorship, and the incident was closed.

It was closed, but not without leaving acrimony on both sides. Nathaniel was especially bitter; he had been turned out of office, as he thought, unjustly, and although he considered that he had vindicated his character he felt abused by the charges that had been brought against him. Very early in the affair he had written to Hillard: "I repeat, that it makes me sick to think of attempting to recover this office. Neither have I any idea that it can be recovered. There is no disposition to do me justice. The Whigs knew that the charges are false. But, without intending it, they are doing me a higher justice than my best friends. I have come to feel that it is not good for me to be here. I am in a lower moral state than I have been—a duller intellectual one. So let me go; and, under God's providence, I shall arrive at something better." And writing later to

Horace Mann, Nathaniel said:—"My surveyorship is lost and I have no expectation, nor any desire, of regaining it. My purpose is simply to make such a defence to the Senate, as will insure the rejection of my successor, and thus satisfy the public that I was removed on false or insufficient grounds. Then, if Mr. Upham should give me occasion—or perhaps if he should not—I shall do my best to kill and scalp him in the public prints; and I think I shall succeed." His resentment against Upham was inexorable, and he quarreled, as well, with Horace Conolly, who had taken part in a meeting of the Whigs at which measures for Nathaniel's removal had been discussed. During the political scuffle which revolved about Nathaniel's removal, Burchmore was likewise dismissed from the Custom House. And Nathaniel, perceiving that Burchmore's position was more difficult than his own, sought to divert such influence as his friends commanded to the task of securing Burchmore's reinstatement. But the poor clerk, whose conduct of his office had given Nathaniel a new conception of talent, never regained his post, and soon afterward opened a bar-room in Salem.

(v)

Early in July, at about the time that Nathaniel's opponents were petitioning Washington to sustain his dismissal, Madam Hawthorne's health began to fail. Within a few days it became apparent that her long immolation was drawing to its inevitable end. The removal of her son from office and the subsequent gossip had been a shock to her delicate sensibility. She said little, for her indomitable pride sustained her during this cruel attack upon her peace by a world which had long forgotten her. But, unnoticed by her family, decrepitude overcame her; her fragile spirit, wearied by too great a burden of sorrow, could offer no resistance to this fresh misfortune; she was unable to believe what she was incapable of denying. Gently and silently, resembling more than ever some impalpable presence, she continued her rites and her pieties. But of these there were now too many. The past had suddenly become dim in the pitiless light of the present; and in that inhospitable brightness she could not find her way. At the end of June she took to her bed.

The hot days of July brought her no respite. The sun blazed into her room strongly, filling it with shafts of light that, like unwelcome memories, seared the eyes they would not blind. Her two daughters, paralyzed by an intuition of approaching death, were incapable of nursing her. Day after day Sophia sat by her side, fanning away the flies that tormented her with their droning, so like the whispers of evil rumor to which she could not close her ears. Her sister, Mrs. Dike, moved about the room like an unyielding shadow, cold and imperturbable and unsorrowing; often, when Elizabeth or Louisa entered her chamber, they found their mother painfully gasping for breath in Sophia's arms.

Day after day dragged on; the scorching, intolerable fury of July. Nathaniel sat in the nursery or at a window overlooking the blazing yard, writing bitter, useless letters to his friends, and watching over the children at their play. Within, the house was hushed by the expectancy of death. But in the little yard, where the grass was bleached and lifeless, Una and Julian played carelessly, their shrill voices making bright, gay patterns upon the silence. As he watched them, Nathaniel knew the mood of irony at last, for day after day, while his mother lingered on the verge of death, the children reënacted her illness in their play. And this grave, unwitting parody of the end of life in its beginning seemed to him the more poignant because of its innocence.

"At about five o'clock," he recorded in his notebook, "I went to my mother's chamber, and was shocked to see such an alteration since my last visit. I love my mother; but there has been, ever since boyhood, a sort of coldness of intercourse between us, such as is apt to come between persons of strong feelings if they are not managed rightly. I did not expect to be much moved at the time—that is to say, not to feel any overpowering emotion struggling just then—though I knew that I should deeply remember and regret her. Mrs. Dike was in the chamber; Louisa pointed to a chair near the bed, but I was moved to kneel down close to my mother and take her hand. She knew me, but could only murmur a few indistinct words; among which I understood an injunction to take care of my sisters. Mrs. Dike left the chamber, and then I found the tears slowly gathering in my eyes. I tried to keep them down, but it would not be; I kept filling up, till, for a few moments, I shook with sobs. For a long time I knelt there, holding her hand; and surely it is the darkest hour I ever lived. Afterwards I stood by the open window and looked through the crevice of the curtain. The shouts, laughter and cries of the two children had come up into the chamber from the open air, making a strange contrast with the death-bed scene. And now, through the crevice of the curtain, I saw my little Una of the golden locks, looking very beautiful, and so full of spirit and life that she was life itself. And then I looked at my poor dying mother, and seemed to see the whole of human existence at once, standing in the dusty midst of it. Oh, what a mockery, if what I saw were all,—let the interval between extreme youth and dying age be filled up with what happiness it might! But God would not have made the close of life so dark and wretched, if there were nothing beyond; for then it would have been a fiend that created us and measured our existence, and not God. It would be something beyond wrong, it would be insult to be thrust out of life and annihilated in this miserable way. So, out of the very bitterness of death, I gather the sweet assurance of a better state of being."

On the last day of July Madam Hawthorne faded into death, silently and graciously in the dying twilight. "My husband came near a brain fever, after seeing her for an hour," Sophia wrote her mother on the following day. "I thought I could not stay through the final hour, but found myself courageous for Louisa's and Elizabeth's sakes; and her disinterested, devoted life exhaled in a sigh, exquisitely painful to hear when we knew it was the last sigh—but to her not painful. I am too tired to rest yet."

In the days immediately following Madam Hawthorne's death, exhaustion overtook the whole family. Illness succeeded it, aggravated, in the case of Nathaniel, by undeniable pecuniary embarrassment. Elizabeth Peabody, hearing from Sophia of the emergency, came on from Boston and assumed charge of the household until the crisis had passed. Nathaniel wished only to quit Salem forever. "I mean," he wrote to Horace Mann, "as soon as possible—that is to say, as soon as I can find a cheap, pleasant, healthy residence—to remove into the country and bid farewell forever to this abominable city; for, now that my mother is gone, I have no longer anything to keep me here."

Actually, however, Nathaniel was on the brink of despair. His mother's illness and death and the subsequent illness of the family had absorbed all the little money that Sophia had saved. He was now without funds and without immediate prospect of securing any; he was without a position and did not know where to turn for one; he had an unfinished story in work, but no hope of finding a publisher for it. In the emergency, Sophia had turned to the making for sale of little decorative articles, such as lampshades; but the income from this source was insufficient even for their most elementary needs.

But when the outlook appeared most hopeless a check for one hundred dollars arrived; an evidence that kind-hearted John O'Sullivan had not forgotten the debt which the defunct *Democratic Review* had so long neglected to cancel. Another substantial check arrived from Francis Shaw, accompanied by a touching letter to Sophia from his wife, pleading that Nathaniel accept the money either as a gift or a loan. Finally, in January, Nathaniel received this letter from George Hillard:

"It occurred to me and some other of your friends that, in consideration of the events of the last year, you might at this time be in need of a little pecuniary aid. I have therefore collected, from some of those who admire your genius and respect your character, the enclosed sum of money, which I send you with my warmest wishes for your health and happiness. I know the sensitive edge of your temperament; but do not speak or think of obligation. It is only paying, in a very imperfect measure, the debt we owe you for what you have done for American Literature. Could you know the readiness with which every one to whom I applied contributed to this little offering, and could you have heard the warm expressions with which some accompanied their gift, you would have felt that the bread you had cast upon the waters had indeed come back to you.

"Let no shadow of despondency, my dear friend, steal over you. Your friends do not and will not forget you. You shall be protected against 'eating cares' which, I take it, means cares lest we should not have enough to eat."

To which Nathaniel replied: "I read your letter in the vestibule of the Post Office; and it drew—what my troubles never have—the water to my eyes; so that I was glad of the sharply cold west wind that blew into them as I came homeward, and gave them an excuse for being red and bleared.

"There was much that was very sweet—and something too that was very bitter—mingled with that same moisture. It is sweet to be remembered and cared for by one's friends—some of whom know me for what I am, while others, perhaps, know me only through a generous faith—sweet to think that they deem me worth upholding in my poor work through life. And it is bitter, nevertheless, to need their support. It is something else besides pride that teaches me that ill-success in life is really and justly a matter of shame. I am ashamed of it, and I ought to be. The fault of a failure is attributable—in a great degree at least—to the man who fails. I should apply this truth in judging of other men; and it behooves me not to shun its point or edge in taking it home to my *own* heart. Nobody has a right to live in the world unless he be strong and able, and applies his ability to good purpose.

"The money, dear Hillard, will smooth my path for a long time to come. The only way in which a man can retain his self-respect, while availing himself of the generosity of his friends, is by making it an incitement to his utmost exertions, that he may not need their help again. I shall look upon it so—nor will shun any drudgery that my hand shall find to do, if thereby I may win bread."

(VI)

Sophia had informed her mother early in the autumn that "Mr. Hawthorne writes *immensely*. I am almost frightened about it. But he is well now, and looks very shining." For three months Nathaniel worked unremittingly at his story, quitting his study only for brief intervals at Sophia's urgent persuasion. His mood was surprising even to himself. He was driven to his task by an inexorable compulsion that made him totally oblivious to the practical issues of life. He forgot the affair of the Surveyorship, the attack upon his character, the prospect of economic destitution only temporarily postponed. But despite his concentration upon his story, he was doubtful of its merit, and almost convinced of its probable failure to find a publisher. The story of the woman branded with a scarlet letter was taking shape as a longer tale than any that he had previously written, but aside from its greater length, he perceived in it no dissimilarity to his earlier work. He considered it too depressing in subject and mood to appear alone, and intended it to form one of a new collection of stories such as his previous books had been.

One wintry afternoon he was surprised to receive a visit from James T. Fields, of the Boston publishing house of Ticknor, Reed and Fields. Fields was scarcely more than an acquaintance, but Nathaniel knew him as a capable man of business, and liked his cordiality.

When Fields entered the little study over the sitting room, he found Nathaniel hovering about the stove. They fell into a talk about Nathaniel's future prospects, and, as Fields had expected, Nathaniel was in a very despondent mood.

"Now," said Fields, "is the time for you to publish, for I know that during these years in Salem you must have got something ready for the press."

THE HAWTHORNE HOUSE

Here *The Scarlet Letter* was written. (14 Mall St., Salem)

"Nonsense," Nathaniel replied bitterly. "What heart had I to write anything when my publishers have been so many years trying to sell a small edition of *Twice-Told Tales?*"

"But," Fields said, "you would have good chances now with something new."

"Who would risk publishing anything for *me,* the most unpopular writer in America?"

"I would," Fields responded. "And I would start with an edition of two thousand copies of anything you write."

"What madness! Your friendship for me gets the better of your judgment. No, no! I have no money to indemnify a publisher's losses on my account."

Fields looked at his watch; it would soon be time for him to take the train for Boston. He had no time to lose in trying to discover what Nathaniel's literary work had been during these last few years in Salem. He asked Nathaniel what he had been writing. Nathaniel shook his head and gave Fields to understand that he had produced nothing.

At that moment Fields noticed a bureau in a corner of the room. And suddenly it occurred to him that somewhere in it was a story on which Nathaniel had been working. He asked Nathaniel; Nathaniel, with an expression of surprise, shook his head in denial.

Fields rose to take his leave, and urging Nathaniel not to follow him into the cold entry, promised to return within the course of the next few days. He was hurrying down the stairs when he heard Nathaniel calling after him from the study, asking him to wait a moment. Then Nathaniel stepped into the entry with a roll of manuscript in his hands.

"How in Heaven's name," he asked, "did you know this thing was there? As you found me out, take what I have written, and tell me, after you get home and have time to read it, whether it is good for anything. It is either very good or very bad,—I don't know which."

On his way up to Boston, Fields read the germ of *The Scarlet Letter*. Before he slept that night Fields wrote Nathaniel a note of enthusiastic praise, promising to return to Salem on the following day to arrange for publication of the story. When he arrived he found Nathaniel reluctant to believe in his enthusiasm. Nathaniel said frankly that he considered Fields mad, and laughed sadly at Fields' repeated expression of admiration.

With a remarkable intuition of the literary problem that had been perplexing Nathaniel, Fields urged that the story be expanded into a novel, and published independently. Upon this suggestion he stood firmly and dismissed Nathaniel's objections that the somber mood of the story would arouse the hostility and diminish the number of its readers.

Convinced at last by Fields' praise, Nathaniel took up the story, invigorated now by the compulsion of a new ambition.

On February 4, 1850, Nathaniel wrote to Horatio Bridge: "I finished my book only yesterday, one end being in press in Boston, while the other was in my head here in Salem; so that, as you see, the story is at least fourteen miles long.

"My book, the publisher tells me, will not be out before April. He speaks of it in tremendous terms of approbation. So does Mrs. Hawthorne, to whom I read the conclusion last night. It broke her heart, and sent her to bed with a grievous headache, which I look upon as a triumphant success.

"Judging from its effect on her and the publisher, I may calculate on what bowlers call a ten-strike. Yet I do not make any such calculation. Some portions of my book are powerfully written; but my writings do not, nor ever will, appeal to the broadest class of sympathies, and therefore will not obtain a very wide popularity. Some like them very much; others care nothing for them and see nothing in them. There is an introduction to this book giving a sketch of my Custom House life, with an imaginative touch here and there, which may, perhaps, be more widely attractive than the main narrative. The latter lacks sunshine, etc. To tell you the truth, it is—(I hope Mrs. Bridge is not present)—it is positively a hell-fired story, into which I found it almost impossible to throw any cheerful light."

Nathaniel had read the last scene of *The Scarlet Letter* to Sophia just after writing it or, as he recorded years later, he had "tried to read it rather, for my voice swelled and heaved as if I were tossed up and down on an ocean as it subsides after a storm. But I was in a very nervous state then, having gone through a great diversity of emotion, while writing it, for many months. I think I have never overcome my own adamant in any other instance."

Now, with the book completed and in press, Nathaniel began to suffer from the reaction of all the crowded, tragic days of the preceding six months. "I should like to give up the house which I now occupy at the beginning of April, and must soon make a decision as to where I shall go. I long to get into the country, for my health lately is not quite what it has been for many years past. I should not long stand such a life of bodily inactivity and mental exertion as I have lived for the last few months. An hour or two of daily labor in a garden, and a daily ramble in country air, or on the sea shore, would keep me all right. Do not allude to this matter in your letters to me, as my wife sermonizes me quite sufficiently on my habits; and I never own up to not feeling perfectly well. Neither do I feel anywise ill; but only a lack of physical vigor and energy, which reacts upon the mind."

(VII)

The Scarlet Letter was published, at the beginning of April, 1850, in an edition of four thousand copies. Up to the very last moment Nathaniel had been doubtful of its success. Less than a month before publication he had written to Fields: "I pray Heaven the book may be a quarter part as successful as your prophecy. Nevertheless, I don't expect even this small modicum of luck. It is not in my cards." In less than ten days, however, the original edition was exhausted, and another was hastily put in press. To his extreme surprise, Nathaniel realized that he was no longer "the most unpopular writer in America," but probably the most famous, and certainly the most widely discussed. There could be no doubt, now, that the book had won artistic recognition as well as material success. It achieved, likewise, a certain sensational notoriety; *The Church Review,* for example, after severely reprobating the theme of the book, asked, "Is the French era begun in our literature?"

There was, as Nathaniel realized, ample cause for the orthodox to be disconcerted by *The Scarlet Letter.* The theme itself, as he had developed it, was scarcely apt to comfort conventional readers. His romance portrayed, as he believed impartially and objectively, the consequences of what society calls sin. He had not condemned either Hester Prynne or Arthur Dimmesdale for their sin; their love, having had a consecration of its own, never caused them repentance. Hester's elaboration of the badge of her shame into a beautiful emblem was paralleled, in her life, by the elaboration of the sin into nothing but beauty. Because of her sin she achieved a moral career, and having entered upon it she became more loving, more comprehending, and intellectually more emancipated than if she had not sinned. In the story as he had written it, punishment was meted out to the wronged husband and the lover; to the husband, for having determined upon a hideous revenge; to the lover, because he had been too cowardly to make public acknowledgment of his passion. The novel therefore challenged society's right to restrict the freedom of individual passion. But its import was even more radical. It raised the question whether sin itself, rather than the repentance of sin, is not a source of the highest good. Into this novel he had put the yield of his observation of life and of his study of the doctrines of Emerson. Like Hester Prynne, he had been companioned by thoughts which, had they been known, would have been held more dangerous than the sin of the scarlet letter.

The Scarlet Letter enunciated Nathaniel's intellectual radicalism with a directness and detachment which he was never again to equal. Although superficially an historical romance of Puritan times, actually it was an inexorably realistic study of the world as it is, in which Nathaniel had justified the self-reliant individual, and expressed his contempt for the society which hedges that individual about with conventions devoid of spiritual validity. Probably his own recent conflict with society in the matter of his post at the Custom House, and certainly his inherited, injured sense of superiority, had contributed to the directness and the objectivity of his presentation.

He had added to the novel an autobiographical introduction dealing with his experience in the Custom House, in which he expressed under a veil of satire all the ill-feeling which he bore his fellow-townsmen.

"As to the Salem people," he wrote to Bridge a few days before leaving Salem, "I really thought that I had been exceedingly good-natured in my treatment of them. They certainly do not deserve good usage at my hands after permitting me to be deliberately lied down—not merely once, but at two several attacks—on two false indictments—without hardly a voice being raised on my behalf; and then sending one of the false witnesses to Congress, another to the Legislature, and choosing another as the mayor.

"I feel an infinite contempt for them—and probably have expressed more of it than I intended—for my preliminary chapter has caused the greatest uproar that has happened here since witch-times. If I escape from town without being tarred and feathered, I shall consider it good luck. I wish they would tar and feather me; it would be such an entirely novel kind of distinction for a literary man. And, from such judges as my fellow-citizens, I should look upon it as a higher honor than a laurel crown."

The introduction to *The Scarlet Letter* was, in fact, Nathaniel's valedictory to Salem:

"Soon my old native town will loom upon me through the haze of memory, a mist brooding over and around it; as if it were no portion of the real earth, but an overgrown village in cloudland, with only imaginary inhabitants to people its wooden houses, and walk its homely lanes, and the unpicturesque prolixity of its main street. Henceforth it ceases to be a reality of my life. I am a citizen of somewhere else. My good townspeople will not much regret me; for though it has been as dear an object as any, in my literary efforts, to be of some importance in their eyes, and to win myself a pleasant memory in this abode and burial-place of so many of my forefathers—*there* has never been, for me, the genial atmosphere which a literary man requires, in order to ripen the best harvest of his mind. I shall do better amongst other faces; and these familiar ones, it need hardly be said, will do just as well without me."

THE STORY TELLER

(1)

WITH his wife and children and household goods Nathaniel set out for Lenox in the Berkshires late in April, 1850. He had rented a little red farm house on the great hillside overlooking Stockbridge Bowl, with comfortable grounds and a wide view over the rugged Berkshire landscape. "We seem to have such a large house *inside,* though outside the little reddest thing looks like the smallest of ten-feet houses," Sophia reported upon arrival. "Mr. Hawthorne says it looks like the Scarlet Letter." Within, the house soon bore much the same aspect as their former dwellings. They had brought with them from Salem many of the Hawthorne heirlooms; bits of ancient furniture and Oriental objects remaining from the voyages of Nathaniel's father and grandfather. They had likewise brought the casts, the paintings and engravings with which Sophia had always surrounded herself. There was a pretty garden in front of the house, an orchard behind it, and at one side a barnyard with a two-story chicken-coop that sheltered a brood of pet chickens.

Nathaniel intended to settle once more into the happy seclusion of family life. "It is about a mile and a half from the village," he wrote to Burchmore in June, "whither I have not been since my arrival. Neither have I seen a single newspaper (except an anti-slavery paper) since the day I left Boston, and I know no more of what is going on in the world than if I had emigrated to the moon. I find it very agreeable to get rid of politics and the rest of the damnable turmoil that has disturbed me for three or four years past; but I must plead guilty to some few hankerings after brandy and water, rum and molasses, and occasional sugar, and other civilized indulgences of the like nature."

Nathaniel was making one of his periodic retreats from reality, always necessary when the pressure of circumstance became too insistent. Such a retreat had again become inevitable; the tediousness of his office, his dismissal and the aspersions of his character that accompanied it, his mother's illness and death, the subsequent foretaste of destitution while engaged upon *The Scarlet Letter*—the hard hostility of reality had been too much for him. The previous year had exacted a heavy toll in strength and energy. On his arrival at Lenox he was, according to Sophia, "so perfectly weary and worn with waiting for a place to be, to think and to write in" that "at last he gave up utterly" and "took cold because so harassed in spirit; and this cold, together with brain work and disquiet, made a tolerable nervous fever. His eyes looked like two immense spheres of troubled light; his face was wan and shadowy, and he was wholly uncomfortable." He had, in fact, begun to age; he was less vigorous than at any previous period of his life, less adventurous in his projects, more easily fatigued and more thoroughly weary. He was forty-six years old. The taste of fame had been sweet, though awaited overlong. But it had brought with it the ominous suggestion of unremitting effort; the popularity of his work might diminish at any time, and his future work was the only barrier to penury upon which he could rely.

Apart from the beauty of its landscape, Lenox offered numerous advantages as a place of residence. To any writer less deliberately solitary than Nathaniel, its cultivated and tolerably amusing society might have seemed an attraction; to him that attraction was purely incidental. Lenox and its environs had not yet become a center of fashion, but they had already drawn as summer residents a group of people engaged in the arts. At Stockbridge Mrs. Sedgwick had opened her academy for young ladies; close by resided the novelist G. P. R. James and L. W. Mansfield, author of *The Pundison Letters;* at Pittsfield Herman Melville was writing and farming; the actress Fanny Kemble was to be met furiously riding up and down the lanes on her great black mare. During the summer many friends and acquaintances came to the region for brief visits; Bridge arrived as soon as they had begun to establish themselves, and remained to assist with their installation; the Celtically improbable John O'Sullivan reappeared for a day; Fields, Holmes, Lowell, Duyckink, and Whipple were among the professional colleagues who made the little red house on the hill a stopping-place on Berkshire holidays. Nathaniel abandoned the hope of solitude for the summer. Sophia soon remarked that they seemed to see more society than ever before, and Nathaniel painstakingly filled his notebook with lists of visitors and chronicles of amiable distractions—dinners in Stockbridge and Pittsfield, and long mountain drives with agreeable companions. Lenox was more frivolous in its amusements than Concord had been, and the atmosphere of easy informality which enveloped its social life was gratifying after the monotonous solemnities of Salem. The fame of *The Scarlet Letter*, as Nathaniel soon became aware, made him easily the most distinguished member of this society, and his consciousness of that prestige contributed to his relations with it an assurance that had been totally lacking in Concord, where his insubstantial reputation had been eclipsed by those of nearly every other resident. Most of the summer passed in the indolent acceptance or bestowal of hospitality. Nathaniel found his new friends congenial. "I met Melville the other day," he wrote to Bridge, "and liked him so much that I have asked him to spend a few days with me before leaving these parts." Nathaniel knew the circumstances of professional success at last; unknown visitors besieged his door for interviews or autographs; strangers lingered at the gate for a glimpse of him; every mail brought him letters from admirers whose praise might have been more heartening had it revealed any discrimination.

(II)

With the beginning of autumn Nathaniel found himself in the familiar existence of the past, modified now only in one important respect. He was once again living in retirement with his family, and was remote from the world. But, as the immediate past receded from his thoughts, the world began to seem no longer cold and hostile, but warm and kindly. In his winter solitude at Lenox Nathaniel found no cause to complain of neglect, but was refreshed and encouraged by the tangible evidence of approval and esteem.

He had begun, in September, a new novel—or, as he preferred to call it, romance—*The House of the Seven Gables.* He wrote diligently and regularly, but the story moved more slowly than he had anticipated. Occasionally he had to wait for an access of energy, and his progress was further impeded by his inexperience; he had never before attempted a book of equivalent scope or equal variety of tone. But notwithstanding his own feeling that the book was proceeding slowly, as compared with previous work of another kind, its composition was notably rapid. On January 13, 1851, Sophia noted in her diary: "In the evening my husband said he should begin to read his book. Oh, joy unspeakable!" On successive days thereafter she recorded her enthusiastic delight in the new book, and on January 27 she wrote to her mother: "*The House of the Seven Gables* was finished yesterday. Mr. Hawthorne read me the close, last evening. There is unspeakable grace and beauty in the conclusion, throwing back upon the sterner tragedy of the commencement an ethereal light, and a dear home-loveliness and satisfaction. How you will enjoy the book. . . ."

The book was sent to press immediately; proofs began arriving in February, and Nathaniel corrected them in the post-office, that there might be no delay in publication. Advance orders had poured in upon Ticknor, Reed and Fields, and after the book had been issued, in March, a chorus of praise arose in the press. Nathaniel himself was pleased by his book. He preferred it to his earlier volumes and, as he wrote to Pike, felt that "it is more characteristic of the author, and a more natural book for me to write, than *The Scarlet Letter* was." To Bridge he expressed himself with greater candor:

"*The House of the Seven Gables*, in my opinion, is better than *The Scarlet Letter;* but I should not wonder if I had refined upon the principal characters a little too much for popular appreciation; nor if the romance of the book should be found somewhat at odds with the humble and familiar scenery in which I invest it. But I feel that portions of it are as good as anything I can hope to write, and the publisher speaks encouragingly of its success.

"How slowly I have made my way in life! How much is still to be done! How little worth—outwardly speaking—is all that I have achieved! The bubble reputation is as much a bubble in literature as in war, and I should not be one whit the happier if mine were world-wide and time-long than I was when nobody but yourself had faith in me.

"The only sensible ends of literature are, first, the pleasurable toil of writing; second, the gratification of one's family and friends; and, lastly, the solid cash."

The House of the Seven Gables was Nathaniel's valedictory to his past. Into this book he put his memories of childhood and youth; he drew upon his family legend of ancestral curse and vanished deeds for its plot; in its theme he studied the perpetuation of the past in the present as environment and inheritance, a problem which his own early experience had fully illustrated. The excellence of the novel derives from his memories and his brooding upon them. The insignificant and sterile life of the house on Pyncheon Street, with its air of shabby gentility, its isolation from the world, its odor of decay, its concentration upon the past; this was the life of Herbert Street as he remembered it. In Pyncheon Street, as in Herbert Street, life was made up of monotonous trivialities; little talks and walks, the passing of neighbors in the street, the purchase of some delicacy for the table. In Pyncheon Street, as in Herbert Street, life was sustained by family pride, and was embittered by it. From his memory of his own environment Nathaniel drew the mass of realistic detail which makes the novel seem almost a genre painting of New England, an expansion of one of his own earlier realistic sketches of rural life.

On its moral side, the book gives a pessimistic account of Emerson's doctrine of compensation. Judge Pyncheon, who permits his innocent cousin to languish in prison, dies of apoplexy; of an illness, not a retribution. Clifford, the innocent victim, and Hepzibah, the devoted sister, are not rewarded for the injuries they have suffered. Emerson might have said that the innocence of the one and the loyalty of the other would constitute, of themselves, a reward. Nathaniel portrayed the one as a broken man, and the other as a grim and unlovely old woman; in life the consequences of being even an innocent victim are disastrous, and there are no amends. In the character of Holgrave he studied the application to life of the Transcendental doctrine of self-reliance; he shared Holgrave's impeachment of the past in so far as the past restricts the life of the present, and in leaving Salem it was the past that he embodied in his book from which he hoped to liberate himself.

To his sister Louisa, Nathaniel wrote after the publication of the novel: "I receive many complimentary letters from poets and prosers, and adoring ones from young ladies; and I have almost a challenge from a gentleman who complains of me for introducing his grandfather, Judge Pyncheon. It seems there really was a Pyncheon family formerly resident in Salem, and one of them bore the title of Judge and was a Tory at the time of the Revolution—with which facts I was entirely unacquainted. I pacified the gentleman with a letter."

This letter no doubt amused Nathaniel, for he had modelled the character of Judge Pyncheon upon the Reverend Charles W. Upham of Salem, and intended the portrait as his revenge for Upham's connection with his removal from the Surveyorship. Upham had been the prime mover in that affair, but had assured Doctor Peabody that his efforts were engaged in securing Nathaniel's retention in office. The portrait was recognizable in Salem; even Elizabeth Hawthorne, in her seclusion, recognized "some points of resemblance, such as the warm smiles, and the incident of the daguerreotype bringing out the evil traits of his character, and his boasts of the great influence he had exerted for Clifford's release."

After completing *The House of the Seven Gables* Nathaniel rested for several months, enjoying the end of winter and the spring with Una and Julian, tramping, fishing and flower-gathering with them, and recording the chronicle of their activities in his notebooks. In May a second daughter was born, whom they named Rose. "I think," Nathaniel wrote to Pike, "I feel more interest in her than I did in the other children at the same age, from the consideration that she is to be the daughter of my age—the comfort (at least, so it is to be hoped) of my declining years—the last child whom I expect or intend to have."

He began on the fifth of June, and completed by mid-July, *A Wonder Book for Boys and Girls,* a pleasurable task which grew out of his story-telling to his own children, and which was accomplished with ease. During the spring Fields had asked him for a volume of his previously uncollected stories and sketches. He had been so doubtful of the value of his later stories and sketches that he had not retained copies of any; he therefore borrowed the collection made by his sisters, and from it compiled *The Snow Image and Other Twice-Told Tales,* which he dedicated to Bridge. "I don't know what I shall do next," he told Bridge. "Should it be a romance, I mean to put an extra touch of the devil into it, for I doubt whether the public will stand two quiet books in succession without my losing ground. As long as people will buy, I shall keep at work, and I find that my facility for labor increases with the demand for it." It was the sharpest spur of future necessity that now urged him to more rapid production. Just after the birth of Rose, Elizabeth Peabody, whose appetite for ameliorative measures only increased with the years, had written to him suggesting the advantages of life insurance. In replying to her suggestion Nathaniel revealed his perplexity concerning the economic aspect of the future:

"The subject of life insurance is not new to me. . . . I know that it is an excellent thing in some circumstances—that is, for persons with a regular income, who have a surplus, and can calculate precisely what it will be. But I have never yet seen the year, since I was married, when I could have spared even a hundred dollars from the necessary expense of living. If I can spare it this year, it is more than I yet know; and if this year, then probably it would be wanted the ensuing year. Then our expenditure must positively increase with the growth of our children and the cost of their education. I say nothing of myself—nothing of Sophia—since it is probably our duty to sacrifice all the green margin of our lives to these children, whom we have seen fit to bring into the world. In short, there is no use in attempting to put the volume of my convictions on paper. I should have insured my life, years since, if I had not seen that it is not the thing for a man, situated like myself, to do, unless I could have a reasonable certainty of dying within a year or two. We must take our chance, or our dispensation of Providence. If I die soon, my copyrights will be worth something, and might—by the efforts of friends who undoubtedly *would* exert themselves—be made more available than they have yet been. If I live some years I shall be as industrious as I may, consistently with keeping my faculties in good order; and not impossibly I may thus provide for Sophia and the children."

In August Sophia, with Una and the baby, went off to visit her mother, now residing with the Manns at West Newton. Nathaniel remained at home with Julian, and amused himself by writing, day by day, an exhaustive record of his adventures with Julian and the pet rabbit which the boy had adopted.

(III)

Ever since their first meeting Nathaniel had been singularly attracted by Herman Melville. He had been prepared to be interested by Melville, whose life of romantic wandering seemed to him the fulfillment of all his own boyhood dreams of adventure. Melville, as he knew, had roamed the world in whaling ships and had been a captive in Polynesia, and the thoroughly picturesque account of his experiences given in *Typee* and *Omoo* had aroused Nathaniel's curiosity. As it turned out, Melville's stories of his life in the South Seas were more fantastic and extraordinary than Nathaniel had anticipated. Almost immediately after their first meeting, Nathaniel had invited Melville to pass a few days at the little red house. Melville had come, and they had spent two memorable days in incessant talk. In the evening, before the fire, Melville had spoken of his adventures. As he talked, he seemed to be again living through the events that he described; he acted them in vivid pantomime, and lost himself in the drama of his past. So eloquent was his story-telling, and so convincing, that when he had finished he found it difficult to break the spell that he had woven, and summon his hearers back to the reality of a Berkshire fireside. At the end of his visit the children adored him, and Sophia could not decide whether she did not think him a very great man.

From that first visit his acquaintance with Melville had progressed with what seemed to Nathaniel incredible rapidity. Suddenly, almost imperceptibly, this hitherto unknown young man who was fifteen years his junior had established himself as an intimate friend. Scarcely a week passed that did not find Melville riding over the six long miles from Pittsfield with his great Newfoundland dog for an evening of talk with Nathaniel. If Melville had been prevented from coming in person, Nathaniel usually received as a substitute a fat, discursive letter. To Nathaniel it seemed that their talks ranged through all manner of subjects with bewildering inclusiveness. "Melville and I had a talk," he recorded after one of their customary evenings, "about time and eternity, things of this world and the next, and books, and publishers, and all possible and impossible matters, that lasted pretty deep into the night. At last he rose, and saddled his horse, and rode off to his own domicile, and I went to bed. . . ."

They had come a long way from Melville's adventures in the South Seas. Nathaniel's original curiosity had expanded into interest and admiration; he had begun to feel a very real affection for Melville. In mind and in temperament they were absolutely unlike. Melville was highly emotional, impulsive, and capricious. He gave himself absolutely, without reservation or reticence. He took understanding for granted, and wished always to accelerate experience to its maximum velocity. In friendship he knew no middle ground; the slow growth of years must be anticipated, and a possessive intimacy established at once, or the attempt be abandoned. He oscillated between moods of extravagant gaiety, and others of equally extravagant despair. In his moments of melancholy, depression descended upon Melville like a cloud, through which his bitter laughter boomed destructively. At such times an indrawn, dim look came into his eyes; a strange glance that, as Sophia once remarked, "does not seem to penetrate through you, but to take you into himself."

"Time and eternity" claimed many of their conversations. "Have ready a bottle of brandy," Melville commanded by letter, "for I always feel like drinking that heroic drink when we talk ontological heroics together." Notwithstanding the vein of Yankee shrewdness in Melville's character, his temperament drove him toward unsolvable problems; he was impatient of human ignorance of the nature of life, and his mysticism was an assertion of his discontent. Unlike Nathaniel, who studied reality in terms of moral experience, Melville cared about neither reality nor morals. He was concerned only about ultimate destiny, and he was tortured by metaphysical doubts. To him the universe seemed a meaningless chaos; and as he looked at the world, he saw it only as the scene of an immitigable conflict between the careless forces of nature and the savagery of man. He professed complete skepticism, but found no comfort even in the profession; doubt was fundamentally repugnant to him, and belief an absolute necessity. He would have loved Deity could he have believed in it; since he could not believe even in his own disbelief, he cursed it superbly. Nathaniel listened quietly on many a long evening, while Melville poured out his tumultuous philosophy, talking in the little parlor that overlooked the black Berkshire hills until the last distant lights had winked out, the moon had set, the gin or brandy had been consumed, and their mouths refused more cigars.

Melville was putting his perplexities, his agitated interrogation of God and man and nature into *Moby Dick*. He was doubtful of his ability to write the book that he had conceived, and uncertain of his prospects of winning an audience for it. He compared Nathaniel's ascending literary destiny with his own, and found his own contemptible. "What 'reputation' H. M. has is horrible," he remarked to Nathaniel. "Think of it! To go down to posterity is bad enough, any way; but to go down as a 'man who lived among the cannibals'! When I speak of posterity, in reference to myself, I only mean the babies who will probably be born in the moment immediately ensuing upon my giving up the ghost. I shall go down to some of them, in all likelihood. *Typee* will be given to some of them with their gingerbread." Private difficulties—the infelicity of his married life and the unprosperous condition of his finances—were adding to the burden of his depression. In his lonely unhappiness he turned with greater eagerness to his friendship with Nathaniel, hoping to find in it the solace and the certainty that life had denied him.

"In a week or so, I go to New York to bury myself in a third-story room and slave on my 'Whale' while it is driving through the press," he told Nathaniel in one of his frequent letters. "*That* is the only way I can finish it now,—I am so pulled hither and thither by circumstances. The calm, the coolness, the silent grass-growing mood in which a man *ought* always to compose,—that, I fear, can seldom be mine. Dollars damn me; and the malicious Devil is forever grinning in upon me, holding the door ajar. My dear Sir, a presentiment is on me,—I shall at last be worn out and perish, like an old nutmeg grater, grated to pieces by the constant attrition of the wood, that is, the nutmeg. What I feel most moved to write, that is banned—it will not pay. Yet, altogether, write the *other* way I cannot. So the product is a final hash, and all my books are botches."

"Shall I send you," he asked Nathaniel another time, "a fin of the 'Whale' by way of a specimen mouthful? The tail is not yet cooked, though the hell-fire in which the whole book is broiled might not unreasonably have cooked it ere this. This is the book's motto (the secret one): *Ego non te baptismo in nomine*—but make out the rest for yourself."

Nathaniel undoubtedly was puzzled by the mysterious malady of Melville's spirit, evident in the moods of intense despondency which possessed him with increasing frequency. Both in conversation and by letter Melville was prolific in confidences. Nathaniel must have been frequently embarrassed by Melville's impulsive abandonment of reticence; the tone of Melville's remarks must have been more disturbing than their meaning, for the meaning was usually all but incomprehensibly vague. Melville's agonized skepticism was, in all likelihood, not the cause but the symptom of his malady. That malady was undoubtedly an intolerable loneliness; a hopeless awareness of the necessity for a companionship so intimate and so understanding that it could have been satisfied only by love. Melville's marriage was scarcely happy; it is probable that he was unsuited to marriage and it is likely that he was incapable of being physically attracted to women. In his work the almost complete absence of women is notable, as is the almost total absence of sex.

Melville's admiration for Nathaniel as a man of letters was extravagant. He had written anonymously, for Duyckink's *Literary World,* an essay on Nathaniel's work, in which eulogy had far exceeded the limits of even laudatory criticism. When *The House of the Seven Gables* was published, he wrote a letter of enthusiastic praise to Nathaniel. No doubt Melville's praise delighted Nathaniel, but the extremity of Melville's admiration must have embarrassed him. His pleasure in Melville's companionship was great but it began to become uneasy. In strange and disturbing ways, Melville revealed a passionate dependence upon their friendship. In his letters there was an obscure note of urgency, a lack of serenity, as if their intercourse had in some important way failed to satisfy Melville completely. Intimations of the obstinate necessity of Melville's loneliness crept into their relationship. He must have suffered because these indefinite avowals provoked no response. He must have been aware that Nathaniel would always remain inaccessible to his emotion, and this awareness must have caused him pain. Above all, the serenity with which Nathaniel confronted an emotion which perhaps he did not understand, but which certainly he could neither wish to satisfy nor hope to extinguish, must have been the most painful of wounds. Nathaniel had offered Melville his companionship and his friendship. He had nothing more to give. He was no longer young, and the time for romantic friendship had long since passed. He was incapable of sharing the ecstasies and the pangs which their relations yielded to Melville. No doubt he desired neither ecstasies nor pangs. No doubt he desired only peace.

When *Moby Dick,* which was dedicated to Nathaniel, issued from the press, Melville sent him an early copy, and Nathaniel wrote to Melville immediately upon reading it.

"Your letter," Melville said in his reply, "was handed to me last night on the road going to Mr. Morewood's, and I read it there. Had I been at home, I would have sat down at once and answered it. In me divine magnanimities are spontaneous and instantaneous—catch them while you can. The world goes round, and the other side comes up. So now I can't write what I felt. But I felt pantheistic then—your heart beat in my ribs and mine in yours, and both in God's. A sense of unspeakable security is in me at this moment, on account of your having understood the book. I have written a wicked book, and I feel spotless as the lamb. Ineffable socialities are in me. I would sit down and dine with you and all the gods in old Rome's Pantheon. It is a strange feeling—no hopefulness is in it, no despair. Content—that is it; and irresponsibility; but without licentious inclination. I speak now of my profoundest sense of being, not of an incidental feeling.

"Whence come you, Hawthorne? By what right do you drink from my flagon of life? And when I put it to my lips—lo, they are yours and not mine. I feel that the Godhead is broken up like the bread at the Supper, and that we are the pieces. Hence this infinite fraternity of feeling. Now, sympathizing with my paper, my angel turns over another page. You did not care a penny for the book. But, now and then as you read, you understood the pervading thought that impelled the book—and that you praised. Was it not so? You were archangel enough to despise the imperfect body, and embrace the soul. Once you hugged the ugly Socrates because you saw the flame in the mouth, and heard the rushing of the demon,—the familiar,—and recognized the sound; for you have heard it in your own solitudes.

"My dear Hawthorne, the atmospheric skepticisms steal into me now, and make me doubtful of my sanity in writing to you thus. But, believe me, I am not mad, most noble Festus! But truth is ever incoherent, and when the big hearts strike together, the concussion is a little stunning. Farewell. Don't write a word about the book. That would be robbing me of my miserly delight. I am heartily sorry I ever wrote anything about you—it was paltry. . . .

"This is a long letter, but you are not at all bound to answer it. Possibly if you do answer it, and direct it to Herman Melville, you will missend it—for the very fingers that now guide this pen are not precisely the same that just took it up and put it on this paper. Lord, when shall we be done changing? Ah, it's a long stage, and no inn in sight, and night coming, and the body cold. But with you for a passenger, I am content and can be happy. I shall leave the world, I feel, with more satisfaction for having come to know you. Knowing you persuades me more than the Bible of our immortality.

"What a pity, that, for your plain, bluff letter, you should get such gibberish! Mention me to Mrs. Hawthorne and to the children, and so, good-by to you, with my blessing!"

Whether Nathaniel replied or failed to reply to this letter is unknown. One fancies that he did not. To these tragic avowals of necessity and desire he could have made but one reply. Silence would have been the most considerate of rejections; the least embarrassing to himself, and the least painful to Melville. But whatever Nathaniel's method of communication, Melville became aware that this, too, had failed him. And with this realization began the last phase of his despondency; six more years of effort to write for publication, and afterward the thirty-four years of silence. . . .

(IV)

When Sophia returned from her holiday at West Newton, it was with a new plan for the immediate future. Her brother-in-law Horace Mann and his family were to spend the winter in Washington, leaving the house at West Newton vacant. Sophia proposed renting it for the winter. For some time past Nathaniel had been considering the purchase of a home for himself and his family, and had requested Pike and Bridge to look out for suitable properties. "I find that I do not feel at home among these hills, and should not like to consider myself permanently settled here," he had written to Pike. "I do not get acclimated to the peculiar state of the atmosphere and, except at midwinter, I am continually catching cold, and am none so vigorous as I used to be on the sea coast." No home had yet been found, and Nathaniel, anxious only not to spend another winter at Lenox, readily assented to a temporary stay at West Newton.

December, 1851, found the family established in the Mann home, a comfortable cottage in a dreary suburb on the Charles River near Boston. It found Nathaniel already engaged in the composition of his third novel. "When I write another romance," he had told Pike in the previous July, "I shall take the community for a subject, and give some of my experiences and observations at Brook Farm." It was this novel, *The Blithedale Romance,* upon which he was now working. West Newton was but a few miles from Roxbury, and although Ripley's Utopia had long since disappeared, the scene of its brief life remained practically unaltered. For Nathaniel this proximity to the scene of his story was convenient but not essential; his notebooks covering the period of his sojourn at Brook Farm yielded a mass of precise, minute observations; his memory, reviving these impressions with greater enjoyment than he had anticipated, served him admirably. His subject continued to support his interest throughout the process of composition. It was his first attempt to write a novel of contemporary life, and he enjoyed the opportunities for realism and for humor which his material provided. He was certain that his book would arouse interest, for the passing years had conferred upon the experiment at Brook Farm a romantic respectability. Now that it had disappeared, the New England mind had begun to regard the experiment with the indulgence of maturity toward the gallant follies of youth. Moreover, public interest in the community and its members had been revived by the recent death of Margaret Fuller who, returning from a long residence in Italy with her young Italian husband and her child, had been drowned in the wrecking of their vessel within sight of the shores of her native land.

Nathaniel worked at his novel throughout the winter, and finished it on the first of May, 1852, almost exactly ten years after his arrival at the Farm in the midst of a blizzard. In it he embodied his reflections upon the perils of reform, in the character of Hollingsworth, and upon self-reliance as regards women, in the character of Zenobia. The thesis of the novel was that a good ideal brings a man to a worthy end only if it does not alienate him from the natural order of life. Hollingsworth, through the selfish and exclusive cultivation of the philanthropic ideal, is shown as bringing misery into the lives of two people, and becoming himself a failure. Zenobia's natural emancipation is shown not to be capable of saving her from disaster through disappointed love. Nathaniel explicitly denied that he had included in his novel any portraits of actual residents of the community at Brook Farm, but the public identified Zenobia with Margaret Fuller, and accepted the book as a picture of life at the Farm.

During the winter Nathaniel had continued his search for a permanent home. His thoughts had drifted back to Concord, and he had addressed an inquiry to Ellery Channing. Channing's reply had been an invitation to pay a visit: "Nobody at home but myself," he wrote, "and a prospect of strong waters. . . . Emerson is gone, and nobody here to bore you. The skating is damned good." Nathaniel declined the invitation, having *Blithedale* on his desk. But word got about Concord that he was looking for a suitable residence, and ultimately the house which Mr. Alcott then inhabited was offered to him. Mr. Alcott's conscientious efforts to ameliorate a recalcitrant universe had never been financially remunerative. His residence was largely the property of Mr. Emerson, and he was content that it remain so, for it seemed to him fitting that a sage be maintained by those to whose lives his presence added luster. Mr. Alcott therefore moved into a neighboring cottage, thereby permitting Nathaniel to purchase, for the sum of fifteen hundred dollars, a house and some forty-two acres of land. Nathaniel, seeing his purchase for the first time in mid-winter, reported to Sophia that "it seemed fit only for a menagerie of cattle"; Sophia thought it "a horrible old house." They moved to Concord early in June.

The Wayside, as they named their new home, had been a small square house standing almost flush with the Lexington Road. Across the highway there were broad meadows and a brook; behind the house the ground rose steeply to a ridge elevated about one hundred feet above the highway and meadows. When Mr. Alcott had taken possession of the place, he had begun to wreak upon it his unique architectural taste. He admired the Gothic, and sought to imitate cathedrals he had never seen in rustic structures of perilous frailty. He had set up a gable in front of the house, appended a double bow-window, added a small wing and constructed porches along the front. He had placed summer houses in the meadow and on the crest of the ridge, and had set up rustic fences along the highway. He had likewise terraced the hillside. Nathaniel and Sophia made no changes to the exterior of the dwelling, and limited their alterations of the interior. "It is really astonishing," Sophia wrote to her mother, "what magical changes have been wrought inside the horrible old house by painters, paperers and carpenters, and a little upholstery." Shortly thereafter she remarked, "We find The Wayside prettier and prettier." And again, "The Study is the pet room, the temple of the Muses and the Delphic shrine."

"The hillside," Nathaniel wrote to George William

Curtis, "is covered chiefly with locust trees which come into luxuriant blossom in the month of June, and look and smell very sweetly, intermixed with a few young elms and white pines and infant oaks—the whole forming a thicket rather than a wood. Nevertheless there is some very good shade to be found there. I spend delectable hours there in the hottest part of the day, stretched out my lazy length, with a book in my hand or some unwritten book in my thoughts. . . . In front of the house, on the opposite side of the road, I have eight acres of land. On the hither side my territory extends some little distance over the brow of the hill, and is absolutely good for nothing, in a productive point of view, though very good for many other purposes. I know nothing of the history of the house except Thoreau's telling me that it was inhabited, a generation or two ago, by a man who believed he should never die."

Concord, as Nathaniel soon became aware, was very much what it had been ten years before. The changes which he perceived were not in the place but in himself. Time had touched his old friends very lightly. Thoreau and Ellery Channing wandered over the countryside and paddled on the river as they had always done, and stopped at The Wayside for long talks with Nathaniel as they had formerly been wont to stop at the Manse. Mr. Emerson's deliberate, slow smile was still as serene as ever; one found him now, seated on his doorstep, a young daughter on his knee, supervising the efforts of his son to ride a pony on the front lawn. Only Mr. Hosmer had changed. He was now an old man, and when he called at The Wayside it was not easy for him to climb the terraced hill behind the house. But, having reached the summit, he still discoursed indefatigably, thereby proving his right to a place in Concord society, where neither obstacles nor infirmities were permitted to interfere with conversation. For these old friends, however, Nathaniel soon discovered that he had less time than formerly. For The Wayside had become as magnetic in its attraction as the home of Mr. Emerson; visitors streamed into it, and Nathaniel became accustomed to receiving delegations of callers in his study. Presently there were to be found among these visitors a sprinkling of Democratic politicians. The Presidential convention was about to take place, and Franklin Pierce was prominently mentioned as the party's candidate. The convention took place. Pierce was nominated. And shortly thereafter, Nathaniel received from Pierce a request that he prepare Pierce's campaign biography.

(v)

Pierce's request embarrassed Nathaniel, for the task which it proposed was peculiarly distasteful to him. He held Pierce in affection as one of the oldest and most valued of his friends; but Pierce was a politician, and for politicians as a class he felt only a hearty contempt. He knew that his refusal would deeply hurt Pierce. He knew, likewise, that whether or not he complied with the request, he would be offered a lucrative post in the government service if Pierce were elected, and in the event of his compliance, this post would seem to be his payment. This was his principal objection to an enterprise which he considered alien to the profession of letters. Yet he was aware of his very real indebtedness to Pierce; during their long friendship Pierce had never failed to exercise his political influence to Nathaniel's advantage. This Nathaniel could not forget; it constituted a valid claim upon his services. In the circumstances he could scarcely reproach Pierce for having indicated an acceptable repayment, and one which to Pierce seemed entirely correct. Yet his realization that Pierce regarded the request as entirely natural did not make it any less objectionable.

In the dilemma which Pierce's request provoked, Nathaniel found his conscience divided by the claims of obligation reënforced by friendship, and adherence to an ideal of personal dignity. After reflecting for several days he sought to persuade Pierce that the task of writing the biography might be performed more advantageously by some one else. This evasion Pierce met with a flat denial. One or two more attempts of the same kind having met with a similar response, Nathaniel reluctantly signified his consent. In accepting, Nathaniel privately resolved to refuse any office that Pierce might offer him if elected. "I have consented," he notified Fields, "somewhat reluctantly however, for Pierce had now reached that altitude where a man careful of his personal dignity will begin to think of cutting his acquaintance. But I seek nothing from him, and therefore need not be ashamed to tell the truth of an old friend."

To tell the truth about Pierce as he knew him was

Nathaniel's intention; he did not purpose writing a eulogy of his friend. He recognized in Pierce the representative of certain political principles which, in so far as he himself possessed any, were also his. He admired Pierce's administrative ability, and although he had no illusions about Pierce's character and intelligence, he believed him capable of serving his country efficiently as its chief executive. As a loyal Democrat, Pierce stood for the preservation of the Union at any cost. He accepted unquestioningly the party doctrine regarding slavery; he was committed to a policy of non-interference and protection, and had voted for both the Compromise and the Fugitive Slave Law. His attitude toward the issue of slavery was attended with considerable unpopularity in the northern states; nowhere more than in Massachusetts, which was the center of the movement for negro emancipation. At about the time when Nathaniel was writing his defense of Pierce's pro-slavery platform, his fellow-citizens of Concord were holding a meeting in the Town Hall to commemorate the abolition of slavery in the British West Indies.

Nathaniel was personally without any conviction in respect to the problem of slavery. Although his Concord friends were prominent in the movement for Abolition, he not only failed to share their views, but regarded the movement, as he regarded other reforms, with skepticism, as being probably more fertile in evil than the condition which it sought to remedy. On this issue he had adopted, automatically and without any display of interest, the accepted views of his party.

Only a year before he had written to Burchmore on the subject of the Free Soil controversy:—"As for myself, being entirely out of political life, I act upon other considerations. I have not, as you suggest, the slightest sympathy for the slaves; or, at least, not half so much as for the laboring whites, who, I believe, as a general thing, are ten times worse off than the Southern negroes. Still, whenever I am absolutely cornered, I shall go for New England rather than the South; and this Fugitive law cornered me. Of course, I knew what I was doing when I signed that Free Soil document, and bade farewell to all ideas of foreign consulships or other official stations, so that I doubt whether you and I ever go to Rio together. Perhaps you may go alone if you wish it. I don't care a copper for office." He disapproved the Fugitive Slave Law, not because it strengthened the powers of the slave-holders, but because it seemed to him an abdication of New England's autonomy.

In his *Life of Franklin Pierce* he wrote of the issue: "There is still another view, and probably as wise a one. It looks upon slavery as one of those evils which Divine Providence does not leave to be remedied by human contrivance, but which, in its own good time, by some means impossible to be anticipated, but of the simplest and easiest operation, when all its uses shall have been fulfilled, it causes to vanish like a dream. There is no instance, in all history, of the human will and intellect having perfected any great moral reform by methods which it adapted to that end." Here spoke, surely, the creator of Holgrave and Hollingsworth, and the

realistic critic of Transcendentalism. Ten years later he knew that he had been a failure as a prophet; the "means impossible to be anticipated, but of the simplest and easiest operation" wherewith Providence caused slavery "to vanish like a dream" proved to be the Civil War.

Nathaniel completed the *Life of Pierce* late in August, with great relief, for the task had been almost intolerably repugnant to him. His feelings toward the book after its completion he revealed in a letter to Bridge:—

"I did not send you the *Life of Pierce*, not considering it fairly one of my literary productions.

"I was terribly reluctant to undertake this work, and tried to persuade Pierce—both by letter and *viva voce*—that I could not perform it so well as many others; but he thought differently, and, of course, after a friendship of thirty years, it was impossible to refuse my best efforts in his behalf at this—the great pinch of his life.

"Other writers might have made larger claims for him, and have eulogized him more highly; but I doubt whether any other could have bestowed a better aspect of sincerity and reality upon the narrative, and have secured all the credit possible for him without spoiling all by asserting too much.

"Before undertaking it, I made an inward resolution that I would accept no office from him; but, to say the truth, I doubt whether it would not be rather folly than heroism to adhere to this purpose in case he should offer me anything particularly good. We shall see. A foreign mission I could not afford to take. The consulship at Liverpool I might. I have several invitations from English celebrities to come over there, and this office would make all straight."

(VI)

While Nathaniel had been writing the *Life of Pierce* catastrophe had paused near The Wayside. Louisa Hawthorne, on her way from a holiday at Saratoga Springs to a visit with her brother, had died in the burning of a Hudson River steamer. The shock of this news, which reached him just when he was expecting his sister's arrival, was severe. Nathaniel took it in silence, and continued his irksome work on the biography, but when the book had been completed he cast about for a change of scene which might restore his spirits and invigorate him. He had been invited by the President of Bowdoin to visit the college at the celebration of its semi-centennial; Pierce had asked him to come on an expedition to the Isles of Shoals. He decided to combine these invitations, and set out from Concord alone. Pierce and several other politicians joined him on the Isles for a few days, but he lingered on after their departure, looking at the sea, copying out the records of the quaint old church at Gosport, and listening to the legends of the sea-bound community told him by Celia Thaxter and her husband. He then proceeded to Brunswick, arriving too late for most of the ceremonies, and fortunately too late for the eulogies of himself pronounced by orator and poet. "It was rather a dreary affair," he informed Bridge, who had not attended. "Only eight of our classmates were present, and they were a set of dismal old fellows whose heads looked as if they had been out in a pretty copious shower of snow. The whole intermediate quarter of a century vanished, and it seemed to me as if they had undergone a miserable transformation in the course of a single night, especially as I myself felt just about as young as when I graduated. They flattered me with the assurance that time had touched me tenderly, but alas! they were each a mirror in which I beheld the reflection of my own age."

Nathaniel was absent from The Wayside for nearly three weeks. The children, Sophia told her mother, missed him miserably; she herself could not eat while facing his empty chair at table, and lost several pounds of flesh during his absence. "On that bright Friday afternoon," she wrote in describing his return, "I put the vase of delicious rosebuds, and a beautiful China plate of peaches and grapes, and a basket of splendid golden Porter apples on his table; and we opened the western door and let in a flood of sunsetting. Apollo's 'beautiful disdain' seemed kindled anew. Endymion smiled richly in his dream of Diana. Lake Como was wrapped in golden mist. The divine form in the Transfiguration floated in light. I thought it would be a pity if Mr. Hawthorne did not come that moment. As I thought this, I heard the railroad-coach—and he was here. He looked, to be sure, as he wrote in one of his letters, 'twice the man he was.' " And a few days later, she wrote again: ". . . On the first of October we all (except Rosebud) took a walk. We mounted our hill, and 'thorough brush, thorough briar,' till we came out in Peter's Path, beyond the Old Manse. All that ground is consecrated to me by unspeakable happiness; yet not nearly so great happiness as I now have, for I am ten years happier in time, and an uncounted degree happier in kind. I know my husband ten years better, and I have not arrived at the end; for he is still an enchanting mystery, beyond the region I have discovered and made my own. Also I know partly how happy I am, which I did not well comprehend ten years ago. We went up the bare hill opposite the Old Manse, and I descended on the other side, so I could look up the avenue and see our first home for the first time in seven years."

Nathaniel hoped, so he had told Bridge, to commence a new novel which, he remarked, "if possible I mean to make more genial than the last." Melville came to visit him in Concord, and suggested a story which he had heard on a recent visit to Nantucket. For a while Nathaniel's imagination toyed with the plot, which he thought might be set in the lonely Isles of Shoals, but finally he abandoned the project because of the tragic nature of the story, and suggested that Melville employ it himself. In the absence of any compelling subject, he turned once again to the always profitable field of stories for children, and during the winter composed *Tanglewood Tales*, completing the book in March.

In March Franklin Pierce was inaugurated President, and shortly thereafter informed Nathaniel, through his publisher W. H. Ticknor, that the Consulate at Liverpool—the most remunerative office in the President's gift—would be offered to him should he choose to accept it. At first Nathaniel was partly disposed to reject the appointment; the prospect of the dreary routine of official life was anything but alluring to him. But James T. Fields reminded him that the years spent in Liverpool would be the means of securing to his family financial independence and to himself freedom of the necessity of writing for money. The appointment to Liverpool was tendered and accepted, and, on March 26, 1853, was confirmed by the Senate. Felicitations were general. Even Charles Sumner, leader of the anti-slavery party in the Senate, wrote a note that, as Sophia said, "fairly shouted as with a silver trumpet, it was so cordial and strong in joy. So from all sides Mr. Hawthorne seems chosen by acclamation, as General Pierce was."

Nathaniel began to make preparations for departure from The Wayside. His close friendship with the President was a matter of public knowledge, and The Wayside was soon overrun by office-seekers who considered Nathaniel a possible dispenser of patronage. In writing to O'Sullivan, Nathaniel took up the case of one applicant, the poet R. H. Stoddard: "He tells me he is a Democrat; but as to hard-shell or soft-shell, or Barnburner or Hunker, he don't know the difference one from another. His habits and character are unexceptionable; he has shown a good deal of poetic talent, and a small appointment in his favor would reflect credit on the source whence it should come. His claim on me is, that he wrote a biography of my distinguished self in a magazine; and biographies of great men ought to be rewarded—and sometimes are." Nearest Nathaniel's heart, however, was the project of securing from the President a consular appointment for Herman Melville, who was now in a state of extreme depression following the failure of his new book, *Pierre: or The Ambiguities.*

After his appointment had been confirmed, Nathaniel was summoned to Washington by the President. He persuaded Ticknor to join him on his first trip to the capital, and spent two weeks in the journey. During his stay at Washington he was entertained at the White House on several occasions, and was amused to observe the reserved and dignified address assumed by Pierce when on public view, and the easy familiarity of his comradeship in private. Nathaniel had two requests to lay before Pierce; his own appointment to the Consulate at Manchester, and the appointment of Melville. With respect to an appointment for Melville, Nathaniel found himself unable to accomplish anything. With his own affair he achieved greater success; the President could not appoint him to Manchester as well as to Liverpool but, realizing that the additional income would be welcome to Nathaniel, he promised to withhold making any appointment to Manchester during Nathaniel's tenure, thus diverting the fees to the Liverpool consulate. His business concluded, Nathaniel remained for a few days in Washington to enjoy the invitations which had poured in upon him. He soon found the existence of a literary lion to be somewhat tedious, and did not regret returning to The Wayside.

At The Wayside preparations for their departure were rapidly going forward. Sadness visited them once more; this time with the death of Sophia's mother.

There was a certain melancholy, also, in their awareness that they were about to give up their home for an indefinite period of foreign residence, among strangers and unfamiliar scenes. "I burned great heaps of old letters, and other papers, a little while ago, preparatory to going to England," Nathaniel recorded in his notebook just before their departure. "Among them were hundreds of Sophia's maiden letters. The world has no more such, and now they are all dust and ashes. What a trustful guardian of secret matters is fire! What should we do without fire and death?"

(VII)

One hot July morning in 1853 a little knot of people clustered at the deck-rail of the Cunard steamship *Niagara,* and waved farewell to their friends ashore. As the paddle-wheels began churning the water of the slip, a long cannonade rang out; an official salute to the departing American Consul at Liverpool. On the deck of the ship, as it got out into the waters of Boston harbor, a bustle of activity began. The little knot of travelers separated. But on the after-deck, gazing back toward the sun-drenched buildings of Boston, stood the new consul, pensively watching New England fall away behind him. . . .

OUR OLD HOME

(I)

LIVERPOOL rose out of the Mersey fog; a stony labyrinth under sodden skies, chill and forbidding. The gloomy English comforts of their hotel intimated no hospitality, but seemed inexorably hostile. Outdoors a brown, soupy rain fell incessantly. Hovering over the coal-grate in their dismal apartment, Nathaniel and Sophia succumbed to melancholy. They were aliens here, and they were unwelcome. Their hearts sank when they recalled that they were to remain for four years. This was July in England! The children wept for The Wayside. . . .

(II)

Not long after their arrival in Liverpool, Nathaniel and Sophia met Grace Greenwood, who was about to sail for America after a year spent in London. It seemed to Nathaniel that Grace's usually ebullient spirits were unduly depressed. "This," he reflected, "undoubtedly is partly due to her regret in leaving England, where she has met with great kindness, and the manners and invitations of which, I suspect, she likes better than an American ought. She speaks rapturously of the English hospitality and warmth of heart. I likewise have already experienced something of this, and apparently have a good deal more of it at my option. I wonder how far it is genuine, and in what degree it is better than the superficial good feeling with which the Yankee receives foreigners—a feeling not calculated for endurance, but a good deal like a brushwood fire. We shall see."

A month later they rented a villa at Rock Park, a genteel suburb across the Mersey from Liverpool and, after they had moved into it, Nathaniel confided to his notebook a melancholy premonition that he would always remain a stranger in England: "It was a dismal, rainy day yesterday, and we had a coal fire in the sitting room, beside which I sat last evening as twilight came on, and thought, rather sadly, how many times we have changed our home since we were married. In the first place, our three years at the Old Manse; then a brief residence at Salem, then at Boston, then two or three years at Salem again; then at Lenox, then at West Newton, and then again at Concord, where we imagined that we were fixed for life, but spent only a year. Then this farther flight to England, where we expect to spend four years, and afterwards another year or two in Italy, during all which time we shall have no real home. For as I sat in this English house, with the chill, rainy English twilight brooding over the lawn, and a coal fire to keep me comfortable on the first evening of September, and the picture of a stranger . . . gazing down at me from above the mantelpiece,—I felt that I should never be quite at home here."

(III)

The Consulate comprised two dreary rooms in a building near the docks; a "small patch of America, with English life encompassing it on all sides." Here, in September, Nathaniel began to spend six hours of every day in the performance of duties not unlike those which had been his at the Salem Custom House. On busy days, when steamers cleared for America, he signed innumerable documents for a fee of two dollars each. "The autograph of a living author has seldom been so much in request at so respectable a price," he reflected. The entry of the Consulate was always thronged by "the most rascally set of sailors that ever were seen; dirty, desperate, and altogether pirate-like in aspect," who sought assistance from the Consul. Americans of every type in distress haunted Nathaniel, claiming his charity; for these cases no provision was made by the government, and such relief as he chose to bestow was a private expenditure. "It is impossible (or at any rate very disagreeable)" he told Bridge, "to leave a countryman to starve in the streets, or to hand him over to the charities of an English workhouse; so I do my best for the poor devils." He soon learned that his official station required his occasional presence at public ceremonies. Within a week of taking office he had been invited to a banquet given at the Town Hall by the Lord Mayor of Liverpool. "Heaven knows I had rather dine at the humblest eating-cellar in the city," he remarked, "inasmuch as a speech will doubtless be required of me." To his astonishment he found himself capable of oratory, and his fear of it disappeared though his reluctance remained. "Anybody may make an after-dinner speech who will be content to talk onward without saying anything . . ." he observed. "I hardly thought it was in me, but, being once started, I felt no embarrassment, and went through it as coolly as if I were going to be hanged."

Politics contributed heavily to making Nathaniel's official post less agreeable than he had anticipated. The sympathy of the English government and press for the Abolitionist cause had exasperated the Democratic Party, and had revived among its ranks the ancient Anglophobia. This partisan attitude toward England as a political entity Nathaniel had adopted with his other political doctrines, and residence in Liverpool served only to emphasize it. It appears repeatedly in his notebooks and correspondence; characteristically, for example, in October, 1854, after the false reports of the fall of Sebastopol. "The people, for several days, have been in the utmost anxiety, and, latterly, in the highest exultation, about Sebastopol—and all England, and Europe to boot, have been fooled by the belief that it had fallen. This, however, now turns out to be incorrect; and the public visage is somewhat grim in consequence. I am glad of it. In spite of his actual sympathies, it is impossible for a true American to be otherwise than glad. Success makes an Englishman intolerable; and already, on the mistaken idea that the way was open to the prosperous conclusion of the war, the *Times* had begun to throw out menaces against America. I shall never love England till she sues to us for help, and, in the meantime, the fewer triumphs she obtains, the better for all parties."

Nathaniel's attitude toward the issue of slavery suffered no change during his term of office, although the issue was perceptibly drawing toward a great national crisis. His views of the matter were unpopular in England, and, for the most part, they were absolutely incomprehensible to the few Englishmen whose good opinion he came to value. It was characteristic of him, however, that, having taken a stand, its unpopularity increased the obstinacy of his adherence to it. "I do assure you," he wrote to his sister-in-law Elizabeth Peabody, who was taking an active part in the agitation for Abolition; "I do assure you that, like every other Abolitionist, you look at matters with an awful squint, which distorts everything within your line of vision; and it is queer, though natural, that you should think that everybody squints, except yourselves. Perhaps they do; but certainly *you* do." And he reaffirmed this attitude in a letter to Bridge written just before his resignation of the consulate: "I regret that you think so doubtfully (or, rather, despairingly) of the prospects of the Union; for I should like well enough to hold on to the old thing. And yet I must confess that I sympathize to a large extent with the Northern feeling, and think it about time for us to make a stand. If compelled to choose, I go for the North. At present we have no country—at least none in the sense an Englishman has a country. I never conceived, in reality, what a true and warm love of country is till I witnessed it in the breasts of Englishmen. The States are too various and too extended to form really one country. New England is quite as large a lump of earth as my heart can really take in.

"Don't let Frank Pierce see the above, or he would turn me out of office, late in the day as it is. However, I have no kindred with, or leaning toward, the Abolitionists."

(IV)

Nathaniel's awareness of being a stranger in England persisted, notwithstanding the solicitude of his friends and the inroads upon his leisure made by English hospitality. "Englishmen are not made of polishable substance—" he remarked in his notebook; "not of marble, but rather of red free-stone. There is a kind of roughness and uncouthness in the most cultivated of them. After some conversance with them as a people, you learn to distinguish true gentlemen among them, but at first it seems as if there were none." And, at another time, he observed: "There are some English whom I like—one or two for whom, I might almost say, I have an affection; but still there is not the same union between us as if they were Americans. A cold, thin medium intervenes between our most articulate approaches. It puts me in mind of Aladdin, when he went to bed with the Princess, but placed the cold steel blade of his scimitar between. Perhaps, if I were at home, I might feel differently; but in this foreign land I can never forget the distinction between English and American."

His first impressions of Englishwomen were decidedly unfavorable, and he found no occasion to modify them materially during his residence in England. After two months of Liverpool, he recorded in his notebook this savage description of the British matron: "The women of England are capable of being more atrociously ugly than other human beings; and I have not yet seen one whom we should distinguish as beautiful in America. They are very apt to be dowdy. Ladies often look like cooks and housemaids, both in figure and complexion:—at least to a superficial observer, although a closer inspection shows a kind of dignity, resulting from their quiet good opinion of themselves and consciousness of their position in society. . . . As a general rule, they are not very desirable objects in youth, and, in many instances, become perfectly grotesque after middle age:—so massive, not seemingly with pure fat, but with solid beef, making an awful ponderosity of frame. You think of them as sirloins, and with broad and thick steaks on their immense rears. They sit down on a great round space of God's footstool, and look as if nothing would ever move them; and indeed they must have a vast amount of physical strength to be able to move themselves. Nothing of the gossamer about them; they are elephantine, and create awe and respect by the muchness of their personalities. Then, as to their faces, they are stern, not always positively forbidding, yet calmly terrible, not only by their breadth and weight of feature, but because they show so much self-reliance, such an acquaintance with the world, its trials, troubles, changes, and such internal means of defense:—

such *aplomb*:—I can't get at my exact idea, but without anything salient and offensive, or unjustly terrible to their neighbors, they seem like seventy-four gun ships in time of peace:—you know that you are in no danger from them, but cannot help thinking how perilous would be their attack if pugnaciously inclined, and how hopeless the attempt to injure them."

Nathaniel had acquired two friends, Henry Bright and Francis Bennoch, of whose sincerity he entertained no doubts, and for them he had as much affection as he was capable of entertaining for any Englishman. Bright was an Oxford graduate of literary inclination, slender talent and large means. His father was a prosperous merchant and ship-owner; his mother had aristocratic connections; they resided at a charming country place, Sandheys, not far from the city. Bright had visited America and had been introduced to Nathaniel by Mr. Emerson while at Concord; he had likewise become friendly with Thoreau and Ellery Channing, and their common acquaintance established a bond between Nathaniel and Bright. Bright was about thirty years old, homely in that British fashion which passes for distinction of appearance, good-humored and voluble. He cherished the image of an ideal England, a land of spacious parks and ancient houses where life flowed evenly into patterns of beauty. He had an esthetic appreciation of all ceremony, and a delight in all tradition which preserved an unbroken continuity with the splendid past. He was humorously determined to overcome what he considered Nathaniel's natural, but absurd, democratic prejudices against the social results of an aristocratic system. Nathaniel's other friend, Bennoch, was a wealthy silk-merchant of London, and a close friend to Fields and Ticknor. Bennoch was a patron of the arts, generous in his benefactions to writers, and enjoyed in consequence a wide acquaintance in literary circles. His wit, his tenderness and his simplicity recommended him to Nathaniel, who found him a delightful companion. Under the guidance of these two oddly contrasted friends, Nathaniel began his investigation of English life.

Nathaniel was attracted and Sophia excited by the novelty of the society which began to claim their time. Sophia acknowledged that she had never been capable of imagining such luxury and splendor as enveloped the lives of their English acquaintances. She filled her letters to her father and Elizabeth with expressions of amazement. The footmen in livery at Sandheys; the lustrous velvet lawn at Norris Green, into which her feet sank as into a "downy enchantment"; the mosaic-paved corridors of Green Bank; the gold and crystal drawing room at Poulton Hall; the magnificent dinner service at Liscard Vale—all these evoked a rapturous astonishment. Nathaniel endured the interminable hospitality of formal dinner parties with philosophy but without enjoyment. He was consoled by the delicate taste in wines frequently displayed by his hosts, but the functions which he attended seemed to him only agreeable, not heart-warming, and after the novelty had worn off he ceased to find them even agreeable. "He left me," Sophia wrote home in allusion to a function which Nathaniel had attended alone, "with a powerful

NATHANIEL HAWTHORNE

From a Photograph Taken in Boston, 1862

anathema against all dinner parties, declaring he did not believe anybody liked them, and therefore they were a malicious invention for destroying human comfort."

Writing to Ticknor of his social activities, Nathaniel remarked: "I do need somebody to drink with, now and then. Englishmen are not to be trusted, to that extent. I dined with two of the sons of Burns, last Saturday, and got into great favor with them—partly by the affection which I showed for the whisky bottle." Mr. Bramley Moore, a wealthy merchant and former Lord Mayor of Liverpool, invited Nathaniel to dine at his country place and meet Samuel Warren, the author of *Ten Thousand a Year*. The dinner proved to be not very agreeable to Nathaniel. "The eatables and drinkables were very praiseworthy; and Mr. Bramley Moore circulated his wines more briskly than is customary at gentlemen's tables. . . . But he alludes to the cost of wines and other things that he possesses—a frailty which I have not observed in any other Englishman of good station. . . . I hope, on the whole, that he will not ask me to dinner any more, though his dinners are certainly very good." After the dinner Warren made an informal address extolling Nathaniel, who was compelled to reply in kind. "If either of us said too much," he observed in his notebook, "let Mr. Bramley Moore's first rate champagne, and very agreeable hock, and excellent sherry, and forty-five year old Madeira, and port genuine from the vineyard, and his magnum of admirable claret bear as much of the blame as can anywise be attributed to them."

Nathaniel pondered incessantly his own attitude toward the society with which he had become acquainted in England. He was not aware that his capacity to understand and judge it was limited by prejudice, by his own pride of caste, by a lifelong habit of solitude, and by the unfailing Yankee disposition to disparage whatever is unfamiliar. The people whom he met were, with few exceptions, representative not of the old aristocracy but of the new Victorian middle class, the possessors of the wealth created by the industrial revolution. Had he chosen to compare them with the merchant families of Salem, he might have perceived that their only superiority was in a greater facility in assuming the privileges of wealth, and he might have realized that this facility was due to the existence, in England, of an aristocratic tradition which provided the necessary example for imitation. But Nathaniel did not make this observation. The society which had been his lifelong environment had made a virtue of its necessary frugality; in New England the ability to do without was esteemed a social grace, and an inclination to luxurious ways of living was considered vulgar. Nathaniel's personal tastes were baroque rather than simple, although his circumstances had always condemned him to ways of simplicity, or even meagerness. In England he came in contact with a society that satisfied his instincts for luxury but contradicted his traditions of frugality. He was attracted and repelled by it; he deplored its attraction for him, and sought to justify on rational grounds the repugnance toward it which two centuries of New England asserted through him.

He resented what Sophia termed "the unmistakable

English sense of superiority to the rest of mankind." "It is very queer," he observed after visiting a country house where the hostess had repeated some gossip reflecting discredit upon the breeding of a former American Minister—"It is very queer, the resolute guzzling of our manners, when we are really and truly much better figures and with much better capacity of polish, for drawing room or dining room, than they themselves are. . . . John Bull cannot make himself fine, whatever he may put on. He is a rough animal, and his female is well adapted to him." It did not occur to him, presumably, that in making this criticism he was indulging a sense of superiority as obtrusive as that which he attributed to the British. He resented not only their assumption of superiority, but what his New England traditions asserted to be the grossness of their material comfort. "The best thing a man born in this island can do," he reflected, "is to eat his beef and mutton and drink his porter, and take things as they are, and think thoughts that shall be so beefish, muttonish, portish, and porterish that they shall be matters material rather than intellectual. In this way an Englishman is natural, wholesome and good; a being fit for the present time and circumstances, and entitled to let the future alone."

Nathaniel explored British society as he found it represented in Liverpool from the point of view of a superior alien who was proud to be out of harmony with his environment, who anticipated its hostility and had prepared against it provocative defenses of prejudice. He cherished the democratic convictions appropriate to an American traveling abroad, forgetting that at home he had complained of the leveling social effects of democracy. Only reluctantly did he come to feel the appeal of English life, and to perceive, though not to acknowledge, the advantages of a society hereditarily fixed by a system of caste and disciplined by ancestral example to the assumption of its traditional responsibilities and privileges. England, he came to feel, as time wore on, had singularly set him free. "All past affairs, all home conclusions, all people whom I have known in America and met again here," he confessed, "are strangely compelled to undergo a new trial. It is not that they suffer by comparison with circumstances of English life and forms of English manhood or womanhood; but, being free from my old surroundings, and the inevitable prejudices of home, I decide upon them absolutely." He had not, as he thought, been emancipated from his old surroundings and the inevitable prejudices of home; he was never to be thoroughly emancipated from them; and Europe, where he always considered himself an alien, was ultimately to make his native land foreign to him. But he was already far removed from the simplicity of Salem and Concord when he wrote: "I have grown woefully aristocratic in my tastes, I fear, since coming to England. I am conscious of a certain disgust at going to dine in a house with a small entrance-hall and a narrow staircase, parlor with chintz curtains, and all other arrangements on a similar scale. This is pitiable." Thus did the great houses of England revenge his early indifference to them!

On the whole, however, he considered himself happy

in England, as he confessed in a touching entry in his journal on Christmas Day of 1854: "I think I have been happier this Christmas than ever before,—by my own fireside, and with my wife and children about me,—more content to enjoy what I have,—less anxious for anything beyond it in this life. My early life was perhaps a good preparation for the declining half of life; it having been such a blank that any thereafter would compare favorably with it. For a long, long while I have occasionally been visited with a singular dream; and I have an impression that I have dreamed it ever since I have been in England. It is, that I am still in college—or, sometimes, even at school—and there is a sense that I have been there unconscionably long, and have quite failed to make such progress as my contemporaries have done; and I seem to meet some of them with a feeling of shame and depression that broods over me, as I think of it, even when awake. This dream, recurring all through these twenty or thirty years, must be one of the effects of that heavy seclusion in which I shut myself up for twelve years after leaving college, when everybody moved onward, and left me behind. How strange that it should come now, when I may call myself famous and prosperous!—when I am happy, too!"

(V)

Although he felt out of place in England, Nathaniel soon discovered that he had no least desire to return to America. He contemplated with distinct aversion the ultimate necessity of resuming his residence at home, and was determined to postpone it for as long a term as possible. He had undertaken his consular post with the foreknowledge that he would dislike its official duties; he had been prepared to accept all the wearying and disagreeable circumstances of office in order to acquire permanent financial independence. He kept this purpose fixed in his mind, practised an economy almost as rigorous as that which he had been compelled to maintain in America, and was rewarded with the knowledge that, for the first time in his life, he was putting money aside.

Scarcely six months of his consular term had passed when he returned to George Hillard the money that had been given him during the dark days at Salem when he had been writing *The Scarlet Letter:* "I herewith send you," he wrote to Hillard, "a draft on Ticknor for the sum (with interest included) which was so kindly given me by unknown friends, through you, about four years ago.

"I have always hoped and intended to do this, from the first moment when I made up my mind to accept the money. It would not have been right to speak of this purpose before it was in my power to accomplish it; but it has never been out of my mind for a single day, nor hardly, I think, for a single working hour. I am most happy that this loan (as I may fairly call it, at this moment) can now be repaid without the risk on my part of leaving my wife and children utterly destitute. I should have done it sooner; but I felt that it would be selfish to purchase the great satisfaction for myself, at any fresh risk to them. We are not rich, nor are we ever likely to be; but the miserable pinch is over.

"The friends who were so generous to me must not suppose that I have not felt deeply grateful, nor that my delight at relieving myself from this pecuniary obligation is of any ungracious kind. I have been grateful all along, and more so now than ever. This act of kindness did me an unspeakable amount of good; for it came when I most needed to be assured that anybody thought it worth while to keep me from sinking. And it did me even greater good than this, in making me sensible of the need for sterner efforts than my former ones, in order to establish a right for myself to live and be comfortable. For it is my creed (and was so even at that wretched time) that a man has no claim on his fellow creatures, beyond bread and water and a grave, unless he can win it by his own strength or skill. But so much the kinder were those unknown friends whom I thank again with all my heart."

To Bridge, some three months later, he confessed his distaste for his office, and his disinclination to return to America: "I like my office well enough, but any official duties and obligations are irksome to me beyond expression. Nevertheless, the emoluments will be a sufficient inducement to keep me here, though they are not above a quarter part what some people suppose them.

"It sickens me to look back to America. I am sick to death of the continual fuss and tumult and excitement and bad blood which we keep up about political topics. If it were not for my children I should probably never return, but—after quitting office—should go to Italy, and live and die there. If Mrs. Bridge and you would go too, we might form a little colony amongst ourselves, and see our children grow up together. But it will never do to deprive them of their native land, which I hope will be a more comfortable and happy residence in their day than it has been in ours. In my opinion, we are the most miserable people on earth."

There was a note of increasing satisfaction in Nathaniel's frequent letters to Ticknor who, back in Boston, was attending to his investments. "I suppose Baring Brothers have already advised you of my depositing £300 to your credit," he wrote in December, 1853. "If it had been £3000, I would kick the office to the devil and come home again. I am sick of it, and long for my hillside; and what I thought I should never long for—my pen. When once a man is thoroughly imbued with ink he can never wash out the stain." Two months later he wrote, playfully:—"Redding has published a list of the monied men of Massachusetts. I consider myself one of them, since you tell me I have $3000 safely invested. Send me the pamphlet, for I ought to be acquainted with the names of my brethren." At the end of April, 1854, Nathaniel learned of the probable introduction in Congress of a bill revising the emoluments of American consuls, and wrote to Bridge, then in Washington, asking him to use his influence with President Pierce to exempt the Liverpool consulate from the proposed reductions. "It will seriously affect the emoluments of this office"; he told Ticknor, "but if nothing happens, I shall get rather more than $20,000 out of it. The truth is, it is a devilish good office if those jackasses at Washington (of course, I do not include the President under this polite phrase) will but let it alone." And again he wrote, "I could not possibly live in this infernal hole if it were not for the pleasure of occasionally sending you a thousand or two of dollars." In June he referred once more to his financial prospects: "I shall fairly bag $10,000 within the year—and my expenses here have been very heavy, too. If I can have full swing of the emoluments for one year more I shall not grumble much; though (to tell you the truth) I do not see how it will be possible for me to live, hereafter, on less than the interest of $40,000. I can't imagine how I ever did live on much less than that. It takes at least $100,000 to make a man quite comfortable—don't you think so?—and even then he would have to deny himself a great many very desirable things. To sum up the matter, I shall try to be content with a little, but would far rather have a great deal." Nathaniel was discovering the familiar fact that no income, whatever its extent, is quite satisfactory, since desires increase always a little more rapidly than income.

The prospect that his official income might be seriously reduced by act of Congress caused Nathaniel considerable apprehension. In the summer of 1854 he wrote Ticknor, noting that the objectionable bill had already been reported in Congress, and that, if passed, the injury to his interests would be irreparable: "However, I am so sick and weary of this office, that I should hardly regret it if they were to abolish it altogether. What with brutal shipmasters, drunken sailors, vagrant Yankees, mad people, sick people, and dead people (for just now I have to attend to the removal of the bones of a man who has been dead these twenty years) it is full of damnable annoyances. . . . After all there are worse lives than that of an author—at least, when he is so fortunate in his publishers as I am. I suppose some persons would console themselves with the dignity of that office, and public and private dinners, and the excellent opportunity of playing the great man on a small scale; but this is to me a greater bore than all the rest; so that you see I have nothing to comfort myself with but the emoluments."

Nathaniel was aware that he could do nothing personally to prevent the proposed law from affecting his official income. He could make no appeal directly to President Pierce because of the delicate nature of their relationship. "Write me about Pierce," he asked Bridge upon one occasion, "and how his health and spirits are. I ought to write to him, but it is a devilish sight harder to write to the President of the United States (especially when he has been an intimate friend) than to a private man. It is my instinct to turn the cold shoulder on persons in his position." "I feel somewhat desirous that you should remain in Washington," he had advised Bridge previously, "not on your own account but on Pierce's. I feel a sorrowful sympathy for the poor fellow (for God's sake don't show him this) and hate to have him left without one true friend, or one man who will speak a single word of truth to him. There is no truer man in the world than yourself, and unless you have let him see a coolness on your part, he will feel the utmost satisfaction in having you near him. You will soon find, if I mistake not, that you can exercise a pretty important influence over his mind." Bridge had remained in Washington and, having the President's confidence, had attempted to induce him to block the passage of the objectionable bill. In this he was unsuccessful; the President opposed the bill, but seemed without power to prevent its passage. Nathaniel's letters to Ticknor reflected his irritation or pleasure, as the news which he received from Washington proved unfavorable or propitious to his interests. "It now looks as if I should nearly or quite make up the $20,000. . . . before July," he wrote in April, 1855, "and if the President adheres to his purpose of keeping the old system in force, the subsequent six months can hardly fail to give me five or six thousand more. If so, I shall be well enough satisfied."

In March, 1855, Bridge notified him that Congress had passed the bill. Nathaniel had made up his mind that the reduced emoluments would make a continued term of office unprofitable, and in acknowledging Bridge's efforts in his behalf, he intimated an intention of resigning from the service, and returning to his writing. "All through my life I have had occasion to observe that what seemed to be misfortunes have proved in the end to be the best things that could possibly have happened to me; and so it will be with this—even though the mode in which it benefits me should never be made clear to my apprehension. It would seem to be a desirable thing enough that I should have had a sufficient income to live comfortably upon for the rest of my life, without the necessity of labor; but, on the other hand, I might have sunk prematurely into intellectual sluggishness—which now there will be no danger of my doing; though, with a house and land of my own, and a good little sum at interest beside, I need not be under very great anxiety for the future. When I contrast my present situation with what it was five years ago, I see a vast deal to be thankful for; and I still hope to thrive by my legitimate instrument—the pen." And a few weeks later he referred to the matter again: "We are in good spirits—my wife and I—about official emoluments. I shall have about as much money as will be good for me. Enough to educate Julian, and portion off the girls in a moderate way, that is, reckoning my pen as good for something. And, if I die, or am brain-stricken, my family will not be beggars, the dread of which has often troubled me in the past."

Nathaniel was reconciled to the prospect of giving up his office by the fact that the climate of England had proved unfavorable to Sophia's health. She had developed a serious bronchial affection, and had been advised of the necessity of removing to a semi-tropical climate. It was Nathaniel's purpose to establish his family in Italy for a year before returning home. President Pierce, informed of this, authorized Bridge to offer Nathaniel the post of chargé d'affaires at Lisbon, to which court he had lately appointed John O'Sullivan minister. Nathaniel decided to decline this post, the duties of which promised to be more irksome than those of the consulate. Meanwhile the O'Sullivans, who had visited Nathaniel in England on their way to Portugal, invited Sophia to spend the winter with them in Lisbon and Maderia. This invitation she accepted at Nathaniel's urgent solicitation, arranging to take her daughters with her and leave Julian with his father in Liverpool. It was at about this time that Nathaniel, weary to death of Liverpool and of the Consulate, returned from a holiday in the country, and expressed his acute exasperation in a note to Henry Bright: "I have come back (only for a day or two) to this black and miserable hole," adding the postscript, "I don't mean to apply the above disparaging adjective to my consulate, but to all Liverpool and its environs—except Sandheys and Norris Green."

A few weeks later he made an entry in his journal that gives the measure of his discontent. "For the last week or two I have passed my time between the hotel and the Consulate, and a weary life it is, and one that leaves little of profit behind it. I am sick to death of my office—brutal captains and brutal sailors; continual complaints of mutual wrong, which I have no power to set right, and which, indeed, seem to have no right on either side; calls of idleness or ceremony from my traveling countrymen, who seldom know what they are in search of at the commencement of their tour, and never have attained any desirable end at the close of it; beggars, cheats, simpletons, unfortunates, so mixed up that it is impossible to distinguish one from another and so, in self-defense, the consul distrusts them all. I see many specimens of mankind, but have come to the conclusion that there is but little variety among them after all."

(VI)

Sophia was to sail from Southampton in October, 1855. During their residence of two years in England, Nathaniel and Sophia had made a number of little excursions about the country. They had been to the Isle of Man, to Chester, to Conway in Wales; they had spent some weeks on the Welsh coast at Rhyl; they had visited Leamington, Stratford, Lichfield and Uttoxeter, and had spent a fortnight at the Lakes. These little tours had made Nathaniel familiar with an England which he could love without reservation, for neither landscape nor history presented vexing moral problems, but were a pure delight existing only to be enjoyed. Like most Americans of his time, Nathaniel felt sentimental obligations, as a tourist, toward culture, and the mere sight of places rich in literary or historical associations was sufficient to induce him to fill page after page of his notebooks with minute accounts of expeditions afield and his emotions of discovery. These notebook records satisfied his lifelong habit of reproducing in words the data of observation, and they served as an opiate to the desire for creative composition. He had come to England weary of literary effort. His ambition was all but satisfied by the success that he had already achieved; the urgent need for creative activity had all but disappeared, and despite his occasional complaints against an immersion in affairs which made him both too busy and too tired to write, he was not displeased by having so excellent an excuse for his literary sterility. His notebooks, therefore, in addition to satisfying a habit that by now had come to be almost instinctive, provided an adequate outlet for a fitful and diminishing compulsion to expression. They reveal that he traveled about England in the mood and with the perceptions of a cultivated tourist engaged in a vacation pilgrimage to the more obvious shrines. He enjoyed picturesque antiquity and loved the soft and misty English landscape. He sought out old places with the reverent devotion of one coming from a land where all places are new. He preferred the satisfactions of a tourist to the hospitalities accorded a distinguished visitor. "I don't think I am a good sight-seer;" he observed after one excursion, "at least I soon get satisfied with looking at set sights, and wish to go on to the next." But the statement itself indicates that, in his excursions about England, he was in fact a "good sight-seer" and but little else.

During their two years of residence in England, neither Nathaniel nor Sophia had visited London. They decided to devote the month preceding Sophia's departure for Lisbon to this visit, and accordingly the family took lodgings in George Street, Hanover Square, early in September. They devoted themselves with indefatigible energy to the task of seeing the city. Sophia organized their methodically planned expeditions to the principal points of interest, but more than these Nathaniel enjoyed the opportunities which he took for aimless wanderings on foot about London. "Yesterday forenoon I went out alone," he noted in characteristic vein, "and plunged headlong into London, and wandered about all day, without any particular object in view, but only to lose myself for the sake of finding myself unexpectedly among things that I had always read and dreamed about." Nathaniel's first visit to London was memorable, for the city fulfilled his imagination of it, and not once during his stay of a month did its enchantment or his ecstatic appreciation of it diminish. It was also somewhat remarkable, in view of his exceptional facilities for meeting the distinguished men and women of the day, for the fact that with a single exception he met nobody of importance and made no effort to do so. The single exception was made in the case of Leigh Hunt, whom Nathaniel and his family sought out in his shabby Hammersmith lodgings; and Nathaniel's visit to the old, impoverished and neglected poet was a charming interlude in the incessant sightseeing that preoccupied him. Finally the visit to London came to an end. Nathaniel took his family to Southampton, put Sophia and the two girls on their steamer, and returned with Julian to Liverpool and the boarding house of Mrs. Blodgett.

(VII)

Mrs. Blodgett's boarding house on Duke Street was the resort of Yankee sea-captains. It was as much an American island in the midst of Liverpool as was the Consulate. Nathaniel remarked that the smell of tar and bilge-water was somewhat strongly perceptible in the conversations that occurred at table or in the smoking-room, and that the boarders were alive "to an extent to which the Englishman never seems conscious of life." "The captains," he reported, "talk together about their voyages, and how they manage with their unruly mates and crews; and how freights are in America; and of equinoctial gales and the qualities of different ships and their commanders, and how crews, mates and masters have deteriorated since their remembrance. . . . In my official intercourse with them, I do not generally see their best side; as they are seldom before me except as complainants, or when summoned to answer to some complaint made by a seaman. But hearing their daily talk, and listening to what is in their minds, and their reminiscences of what they have gone through, one becomes sensible that they are men of energy, fit to be trusted, and retaining a hardy sense of honor and a loyalty to their own country, the stronger because they have compared it to many others."

This was, in fact, just such an environment as Nathaniel had become familiar with in his Custom House service; he appreciated its simplicity, its hardihood and the total absence of all social pretensions; he associated happily and familiarly with Mrs. Blodgett's boarders, and was regarded by them with respect for his official station and with much fondness as a companion. After dinner the company was wont to retire to the smoking room, and there spend the evening in a haze of blue vapor at whist or conversation. In these diversions Nathaniel always had a genial share. Christmas day was an occasion of special festivity at Mrs. Blodgett's; the maidservants hung mistletoe about the house, trapped the unwary lodgers beneath it, and exacted kisses and shillings from them. Nathaniel joined in the merry-making, but was exempted from osculatory forfeits. He had laid aside, it seemed, the man of letters and had once again become a practical man of affairs indistinguishable from those with whom his duties brought him into daily contact.

Yet he was, on the whole, unhappy. "I have suffered woefully from low spirits for some time past;" he confessed in his notebook, "and this has not often been the case since I grew to be a man, even in the least auspicious periods of my life. My desolate bachelor condition, I suppose, is the cause. Really, I have no pleasure in anything, and I feel my tread to be heavier, and my physical movement more sluggish, than in happier times. A weight is always upon me. My appetite is not good. I sleep ill, lying awake till late at night, to think sad thoughts and to imagine somber things, and awaking before light with the same thoughts and fancies still in my mind. My heart sinks always as I ascend the stairs of my office, from a dim augury of ill news from Lisbon that I may perhaps hear,—or black-sealed letters, or some such horrors. Nothing gives me any joy. . . . I am like an uprooted plant, wilted and drooping. Life seems so purposeless as not to be worth the trouble of carrying it any further."

(VIII)

Nathaniel made several visits to London before his resignation from office and departure for Italy. On these occasions he became familiar with the city itself, which never lost for him its first appealing magic; and he saw, under the guidance of Bennoch and Richard Monckton Milnes, a good deal of London literary society. He did not meet the most celebrated writers of the day; Thackeray, Dickens, George Eliot, Trollope, Arnold, Swinburne and Carlyle he never saw; Tennyson he saw and admired at the Manchester Exhibition, regretting that they had not become acquainted; the Brownings he met at one of Monckton Milnes's breakfast parties, but came to know well only in Florence. It was clearly a disappointment to him that he had no talk with those writers whom, like Thackeray and Dickens, he greatly admired as artists, and about whose characters and temperaments his curiosity expressed itself candidly in his notebooks. But London literary society—a society of minor writers and powerful journalists—began by attracting him and ultimately bored him. His early years of obscurity had, as he acknowledged, made him indifferent to praise and neglect, and they had likewise robbed him of that clear confidence in his own distinction which might have enabled him to meet the more famous English writers of the day on equal terms without embarrassment. His hereditarily wounded pride, his consciousness of inferiority, revealed themselves in London, as previously in America, through an unflinching disposition to minimize celebrated or successful people. So aggravated was Nathaniel's mingled diffidence and indifference that Monckton Milnes, who made every effort to take him about in London society, finally desisted under the impression that Nathaniel had taken a dislike to him. Nathaniel's honest but not invariably discerning admirers fared little better. He was acclaimed, publicly and privately, by innumerable people; but he was inveterately skeptical of such praise, and usually it aroused only his dislike or suspicion of the person uttering it. Having been, as he termed it, lionized at one admirable dinner party, he confessed his discomfort in characteristic terms: "It is ungracious, even hoggish, not to be gratified with the interest they expressed in me; but then it is really a bore, and one does not know what to do or say. I felt like the hippopotamus, or—to use a more modest illustration,—like some strange bug imprisoned under a tumbler, with a dozen eyes watching whatever I did."

Nathaniel's temperament, as he was almost certainly not aware, was responsible for the impression produced upon him by the men of letters with whom he came into most frequent contact, and by literary society in general. It was likewise responsible, in some degree, for the circumstance that he failed to meet the most distinguished of his contemporaries. His experience of English literary and intellectual circles was, on the whole, a bitter disappointment to him. For most of the people whom he met and came to know he retained no very high regard or esteem. He considered himself, in the end, to have been disillusioned; but there persisted a secret, naïve and strangely wistful conviction that he had somehow missed the best, an inability to understand how it had so happened, and an unacknowledged sense of injury in the frustration. It was not until his return from Italy that he came to care for what London, in this field, offered him.

He compiled in his notebooks with inexorable candor the accumulation of his individual impressions; the tone of these portraits varied from the affectionate sympathy through which he saw Leigh Hunt to the vitriolic burlesque which he poured upon the portly mediocrity of Martin Tupper; but the portrait sketches, however interesting, are less satisfactory as portraits of their subjects than as portraits of Nathaniel. Scarcely any of the subjects pleased him, and he indulged his propensity for disparagement and derogation with perverse and savage delight.

He paid a visit, in Bennoch's company, to Martin Farquhar Tupper, and found that popular philosopher a person for whom he immediately felt a kindness and instinctively knew to be a bore. Tupper, he thought, was "really a good man, most domestic, most affectionate, most fussy; for it appeared as if he could hardly sit down, and even if he were sitting he still had the effect of bustling about." "I liked him," Nathaniel observed after enduring the agony of Tupper's demonstrative hospitality for several hours, "and laughed in my sleeve at him, and was utterly weary of him; for, certainly, he is the ass of asses." But in recording his visit, Nathaniel spared Tupper no touch of caricature; he had noted everything, from the bookcases filled exclusively with Tupper's works, to the autographed portraits of all the children of Queen Victoria taken at the age when she deemed it appropriate for them to read *Proverbial Philosophy*.

Nathaniel met Charles Reade at a supper party in Park Lane, but Reade made so little impression that he evaded conversation with him. "I wish I could know exactly what the English style good conversation," he reflected after another function at which he had engaged in talk with the playwright Tom Taylor, who was reputed for his wit. "Probably it is something like plum pudding,—as heavy, but seldom as rich."

Nathaniel was invited to dine at the Reform Club and met Douglas Jerrold. Jerrold, despite his air of infirmity, his excessively bent back and very gray hair, was a commanding figure. In the tone of Jerrold's voice and expression, Nathaniel caught the racy note of the humorist. Jerrold's talk was shrewd, satirical and cynical; he reminded Nathanicl, by "a tincture of something at once wise and humorously absurd" in what he said, of Ellery Channing. During the evening Jerrold spoke appreciatively of Emerson, Longfellow and Lowell. Nathaniel mentioned Thoreau and proposed sending his works to their host, who, being connected with the press, might be disposed to draw some attention to them. Douglas Jerrold asked why he should not also receive them. "I hesitated a little," Nathaniel recorded afterward, "but as he pressed me, and would have an answer, I said that I did not feel so sure of his kindly judgment on Thoreau's books; and it so chanced that I used the word 'acrid,' for the lack of a better, in endeavoring to express my idea of Jerrold's way of looking at men and books. . . . Jerrold said no more, and I went on talking with Doctor Mackay but, in a minute or two, I became aware that something had gone wrong and, looking at Douglas Jerrold, there was an expression of pain and emotion on his face. By this time a second bottle of Burgundy had been opened . . . and that warm and potent wine may have had something to do with the depth and vivacity of Mr. Jerrold's feelings. But he was indeed greatly hurt by that little word 'acrid.' 'He knew,' he said, 'that the world considered him a sour, bitter, ill-natured man, but that such a man as I should have the same opinion was almost more than he could bear.' As he spoke, he threw out his arms, sank back in his seat, and I was really a little apprehensive of his actual dissolution into tears. Thereupon I spoke, as was good need, and though, as usual, I have forgotten everything I said, I am sure it was to the purpose, and went to this good fellow's heart, as it came warmly from my own." After Jerrold's too-susceptible feelings were mollified, they became the best of friends.

At a reception given in their honor, Nathaniel met the famous singer Jenny Lind, who sent word that she desired him to be presented to her. "There was," he commented, "a gentle peremptoriness in the summons that made it something like being commanded into the presence of a princess; a great favor, no doubt, but yet a little humbling to the recipient. . . . Jenny Lind is rather tall,—quite tall, for a woman—and not in the least plump; extremely light hair, a longish nose, tending upward at the end, pale, and a little scrawniness about the neck—certainly no beauty, but with sense and self-reliance in her aspect and manners. . . . Her conversation is quite simple and I should have great faith in her sincerity; and there is about her the manner of a person who knows the world, and has conquered it. She said something or other about *The Scarlet Letter;* and, on my part, I paid her such compliments as a man could pay who had never heard her sing, nor greatly cared to hear her. . . . On the whole I was not greatly interested in Madame Goldschmidt, nor sorry to take an early opportunity of assigning my seat to somebody else." On the same occasion Nathaniel met the novelist Samuel Lover, "a most good-natured, pleasant Irishman, with a shining, twinkling visage," who sang some Irish songs, "his own in music and words, to which the comicality of his face contributed almost as much as his voice and words."

The climax of Nathaniel's excursions into London society was a breakfast party given in his honor by Richard Monckton Milnes. Monckton Milnes's breakfasts were, at the time, the most distinguished parties given in London; only celebrities were invited to them, and the divergent worlds of politics, letters, the arts and scholarship met familiarly in the stately dining room in Upper Brook Street. To meet Nathaniel the host had invited, among others the Brownings, Macaulay, the Marquis of Lansdowne, the American historian Ticknor, and the mother and sister of Florence Nightingale. Nathaniel arrived late and found the company already assembled, and took his place next to Elizabeth Barrett Browning. They talked of spiritualism, to which she was greatly attracted despite her husband's objections to it; and of Miss Bacon's theory of Shakespeare, about which Nathaniel had lately had occasion to learn, and which horrified Mrs. Browning. "She is one of that quickly appreciative and responsive order of women with whom I can talk more freely than with any man," Nathaniel reflected afterward, "and she has, beside, her own originality wherewith to help on conversation though, I should say, not of a loquacious tendency." "I like her very much," he remarked, "a great deal better than her poetry which I could hardly suppose to have been written by such a quiet person as she." Nathaniel had been too much engaged by conversation with Mrs. Browning to pay much attention to the other guests. He had, however, been impressed by a portly, gray-haired, distinguished looking man who talked very little; suddenly he realized that the man was Macaulay. Macaulay, as Nathaniel had heard, was apt to arrogate all the talk to himself; on this occasion he was prevented from doing so, Nathaniel supposed, by the fact that conversation kept to American subjects, and the presence of his American colleague Ticknor prevented Macaulay from assuming authority. "I am glad to have seen him, —a face fit for a scholar, a man of the world, a cultivated intelligence."

As the guests left the table and adjourned to the library, a youthful, handsome, brown-haired man introduced himself to Nathaniel as Robert Browning. "He is very simple and agreeable in manner," Nathaniel remarked, "gently impulsive, talking as if his heart were uppermost. He spoke of his pleasure in meeting me, and his appreciation of my books; and—which has not often happened before—mentioned that *The Blithedale Romance* was the one he admired most. I wonder why. I hope I showed as much pleasure at his praise as he did at mine; for I was glad to see how pleasantly it moved him."

Nathaniel left the breakfast party with the feeling that he had been offered the best that English society afforded. But, thinking it over afterward, he found one point open to criticism. The criticism that he recorded in his notebook is perhaps the most complete illustration of Nathaniel's self-consciousness in the presence of social superiors. "I liked greatly the manners of almost all—yes, as far as I observed,—all the people at this breakfast, and it was doubtless owing to their being all people of high rank or remarkable intellect or both. An Englishman can hardly be a gentleman, unless he enjoy one or another of these advantages; and perhaps the surest way to give him good manners is to make a lord of him, or rather of his grandfather or great-grandfather. In the third generation, scarcely sooner, he will be polished into simplicity and elegance, and his deportment will be all the better for the homely material out of which it is wrought and refined. The Marquis of Lansdowne would have been a very commonplace man in the common ranks of life; but it has done him good to be a nobleman. Not that his tact is quite perfect. In going up to breakfast, he made me precede him; in returning to the library, he did the same, although I drew back, till he impelled me up the first stair, with gentle persistence. By insisting upon it, he showed his sense of condescension much more than if, when he saw me unwilling to take precedence, he had passed forward, as if the point were not worth either asserting or yielding. Heaven knows it was in no humility that I would have trodden behind him."

(IX)

"It is a very disagreeable office; but some amusing incidents happen occasionally," Nathaniel remarked of the consulate in a letter to Ticknor; "for instance, I send home by this steamer a Doctor of Divinity, who has been out here on a spree, and who was brought to my office, destitute, after a week's residence in a brothel! He shook in his shoes, I can tell you. Not knowing whether I should ever have another opportunity of preaching to a Doctor of Divinity (an orthodox man, too) I laid it on without mercy; and he promised never to forget it. I don't think he ever will."

An equally ironical circumstance involved Nathaniel in an adventure entirely characteristic of his nature and completely at variance with his philosophy. In early life he had imagined the situation of a reformer who makes converts to a new theory but, while addressing a meeting, is discovered to be an escaped lunatic. This represented his view of theories in any field, and his antipathy to all theorists. Yet when Miss Delia Bacon applied to him for assistance in securing publication for her *Philosophy of the Plays of Shakespeare,* Nathaniel capitulated in very short order and put himself entirely at her service.

He met her but once, in her humble London lodgings; a tall, dark-haired woman of striking appearance and refined manners. She had been living in absolute solitude, existing only for and by her theory, for she confessed to Nathaniel that she could no longer bear the society of people who did not accept it. Their conversation convinced him that she was "unquestionably a monomaniac; this great idea had thrown her off her balance but, at the same time, it has wonderfully developed her intellect and made her what she otherwise would not have been."

"Evidently too," he reflected after his talk with her, "she thinks that Providence has brought me forward at this critical juncture when she could not have done without me. For my part I would rather that Providence would have employed some other instrument; but still I have little or no scruple or doubt about what I ought to do. Her book is a most remarkable one, and well deserves publication, and towards that end she shall have every assistance that I can render. Her relatives are endeavoring to force her home by witholding from her all sources of support; but, in my opinion, if taken from England now, she would go home as a raving maniac, and I shall write to them and suggest this view of the case. Meanwhile, as she must be kept alive, it devolves on me to supply her with some small means for that purpose. As to her designs on Shakespeare's grave, I see no way but to ignore them entirely and leave Providence to manage that matter in its own way. If I had it in my power to draw her out of her delusions on that point, I should not venture to do so; it is the condition on which she lives in comfort and joy and exercises great intellectual power, and it would be no business of mine to unhabilitate her for this world by showing her a miserable fact."

Instead of showing Delia Bacon a "miserable fact," Nathaniel arranged, after considerable effort, for the publication of one thousand copies of her book, at his expense, of which, upon his own responsibility, he ordered five hundred imprinted with the name of Ticknor and Fields and sent to them for sale in America. As the English publishers refused to accept the book, even upon these conditions, without an introduction signed by himself, Nathaniel was under the embarrassing necessity of prefacing the thesis which he absolutely disbelieved. The preface which he wrote failed to satisfy the exigent author of a quite unreadable work, who demanded that it be made more favorable to her theory. Nathaniel, who felt that he had already gone to the limit of his conscience in what he had written, refused to modify the preface. For a time matters seemed at a deadlock, but Miss Bacon's "severe and passionate displeasure" was finally dispelled by Bennoch's tactful intervention, the preface was accepted and the book was published. It fell flat in both England and America, and its failure served only further to derange the mind of its unfortunate and lonely author. Miss Bacon survived the publication of her book only two years, most of which she spent in an institution for the insane. Nathaniel lost more than a thousand dollars in the venture, and did not live to see the subsequent wholesale conversions to the theory that he had launched without believing. His correspondence with Miss Bacon displayed an all but indefatigible patience, and exceptional delicacy and conscientiousness. She had engaged his sympathies much as Frank Farley had, long years before at Brook Farm. "You say nothing about the state of your funds," he wrote to her at one time. "Pardon me for alluding to the subject, but you promised to apply to me in case of need. I am ready." He endured without complaint the violence of her anger even while making himself responsible for her maintenance and the production of her book. And, so gentle was he when his sympathies were aroused, that he failed completely to perceive the inconsistency of his conduct with his philosophy.

(x)

In June, 1856, Sophia and her daughters returned from Madeira, where they had spent the winter. That summer the family spent at Bennoch's home in Blackheath, near London, removing in the autumn to Southport, a seaside town some twenty miles from Liverpool. Here they remained during the winter and spring, and, after short sojourns at Manchester for the exhibition and at Leamington, they again went up to London before leaving England for Italy.

While they were residing at Southport, in November, 1856, Herman Melville made his appearance in Liverpool on his way to Constantinople. Melville looked much as he used to, Nathaniel thought; he was perhaps a little paler and a little sadder, and his gravity and reserve of manner were noticeable. "I felt rather awkward at first," Nathaniel confessed in his account of their meeting, "because this is the first time I have met him since my ineffectual attempt to get him a consular appointment from General Pierce. However, I failed only from lack of real power to serve him; so there was no reason to be ashamed, and we soon found ourselves on pretty much our former terms of sociability and confidence. Melville has not been well of late; he has been affected with neuralgic complaints in his head and his limbs, and no doubt had suffered from too constant literary occupation, pursued without too much success, latterly, and his writings, for a long while past, have indicated a morbid state of mind. So he left his place at Pittsfield, and has established his wife and family, I believe, with his father-in-law in Boston, and is thus far on his way to Constantinople. I do not wonder that he found it necessary to take an airing through the world, after so many years of toilsome pen-labor following after so wild and adventurous a youth as his was. I invited him to come and stay with us at Southport as long as he might remain in this vicinity; and, accordingly, he did come, on the next day, taking with him, by way of baggage, the least little bit of a bundle, which, he told me, contained a nightshirt and a toothbrush. He is a person of very gentlemanly instincts in every respect, save that he is a little heterodox in the matter of clean linen.

"He stayed with us from Tuesday till Thursday; and, on the intervening day, we took a pretty long walk together, and sat down in a hollow among the sand hills (sheltering ourselves from the high, cool wind) and smoked a cigar. Melville, as he always does, began to reason of Providence and futurity, and of everything that lies beyond human ken, and informed me that he had 'pretty much made up his mind to be annihilated;' but still he does not seem to rest in that anticipation, and, I think, will never rest until he gets hold of a definite belief. It is strange how he persists—and has persisted ever since I knew him, and probably long before—in wandering to and fro over these deserts, as dismal and monotonous as the sand hills amid which we were sitting. He can neither believe, nor be comfortable in his unbelief; and he is too honest and courageous not to try to do one or the other. If he were a religious man, he would be one of the most truly religious and reverential; he has a very high and noble nature and is better worth immortality than most of us."

Nathaniel took Melville to Chester, and introduced him to Henry Bright, who guided him about Liverpool; he saw Melville once again on the day before his departure. "He said that he already felt much better than in America, but observed that he did not anticipate much pleasure in his rambles, for the spirit of adventure is gone out of him. He certainly is much overshadowed since I saw him last; but I hope he will be brighter as he goes onward." This proved to be their last meeting. If Melville had had a forlorn hope, when he came to Liverpool, of reëstablishing the former intimacy, he was thoroughly disillusioned. He never again made any effort to see Nathaniel.

(XI)

With the election of James Buchanan as President in the autumn of 1856, Nathaniel planned to bring his tedious consular duties to an end. In March, 1857, he wrote to Ticknor, "I should suppose I might count on the interest of nearly or quite $30,000. This would have seemed a fortune to me five or six years ago; but our ideas change with our circumstances, and I now perceive that it is a bare competence. But the embroidery and trimming shall come out of my inkstand." To Bridge in Washington he sent a formal resignation to be delivered to Mr. Buchanan after his inauguration, and effective in August. "It will," he said in his letter to Bridge, "be a great relief to me to find myself a private citizen again; and I think the old literary instincts and habits will begin to revive in due season. I doubt, however, whether I shall publish a book until after my return to the United States, which probably will not be in less than two years. I expect to live beyond my income while on the Continent, but hope to bring myself up again after my return with my literary labors and the economy of living on my own homestead."

After the acceptance of his resignation by the President, Nathaniel was briefly involved in an international controversy. The British press had been exercised by the cruelties practised by American shipmasters on their crews; the matter had been debated in Parliament, and a formal protest had been lodged with the United States government by Lord John Russell. To this the Secretary of State, General Lewis Cass, had replied in a manner reflecting, as Nathaniel thought, discredit upon American consular officials. Having himself protested vigorously against the cruelties sanctioned under American maritime law, Nathaniel now sent a despatch to

Secretary Cass sharply criticizing the government's attitude as expressed by the Secretary. This drew from General Cass a reply vindicating Nathaniel in his official conduct. Elizabeth Peabody wrote to congratulate him upon his humanitarian effort in this matter, and his reply embodies his final judgment upon his consular career. No doubt he meant his skepticism concerning the value of conscious philanthropy to chill, if possible, the Abolitionist ardor of his philanthropic sister-in-law.

"I do not know," he wrote, "what Sophia may have said about my conduct in the Consulate. I only know that I have done no good; none whatever. Vengeance and benficence are things that God claims for Himself. His instruments have no consciousness of His purpose; if they imagine they have, it is a pretty sure token that they are *not* His instruments. The good of others, like our own happiness, is not to be attained by direct effort, but incidentally. All history and observation confirm this. I am really too humble to think of doing good! Now, I presume you think the abolition of flogging was a vast boon to seamen. I see, on the contrary, with perfect distinctness, that many murders and an immense mass of unpunishable cruelty—a thousand blows, at least, for every one that the cat-of-nine-tails would have inflicted—have resulted from that very thing. There is a moral in this fact which I leave you to deduce. God's ways are in nothing more mysterious than in this matter of trying to do good."

THE AMBITIOUS GUEST

(I)

ROME, which they reached in mid-January by way of Paris and Marseilles, greeted Nathaniel and his family with a succession of cold, bright days that chilled them into misery. Day after day Nathaniel sat by the fireside clothed more amply than ever before in his life, shivering under his thickest great-coat. A fortnight after his arrival one finds him recording: "I shall never be able to express how I dislike the place and how wretched I have been in it; and soon, I suppose, warmer weather will come, and perhaps reconcile me to Rome against my will. Cold narrow lanes, between tall, ugly, mean-looking, whitewashed houses, sour bread, pavements most uncomfortable to the feet, enormous prices for poor living; beggars, pickpockets, ancient temples and broken monuments, and clothes hanging to dry about them; French soldiers, monks and priests of every degree; a shabby population smoking bad cigars—these would have been some of the points of my description." One pictures a disgruntled tourist savagely cursing the incomprehensible accidents of foreign travel. . . .

(II)

Lodgings were finally secured in the Palazzo Larazani, Via Porta Pinciana, and the family settled into its appointed duty of sight-seeing. Nathaniel had been looking forward to a prolonged freedom from tasks of any kind, his first carefree leisure in many years. The inescapable obligation to culture slightly irked him. But to Sophia the whole of Italy was sacred ground, and she maintained an incessant ecstasy of devotion to history, architecture, painting and sculpture, sending home to her sister Elizabeth rhapsodic accounts of her belated exposure to innumerable masterpieces. "But I am in Rome, Rome, *Rome!*" she wrote. "I have stood in the Forum and beneath the Arch of Titus, at the end of Sacra Via. I have wandered about the Coliseum, the stupendous grandeur of which equals my dream and hope. I have seen the sun kindling the open courts of the Temple of Peace. . . . (It is now called Constantine's Basilica.)" Meanwhile Nathaniel was observing that "if you tread beneath the triumphal arch of Titus or Constantine, you had better look downward than upward, whatever be the merit of the sculptures aloft," and expressing his disgust at the ordure to be found everywhere except in the most frequented streets. They had in common a passion for precision of information. . . .

(III)

Rome subjected them to the impact of Catholicism, against which every fiber of tradition quivered in prejudice. Through the narrow streets shambled ill-kempt brown-garbed monks, and Penitents with faces concealed under pointed hoods; Sophia bridled at the thought of their superstition, and warned her children against contamination by their doctrine. But

St. Peter's dome, whenever it came into view, ironically questioned her preconceptions, and the Madonnas which she adored threatened her assurance. Nathaniel submitted to the fascination of this new experience without reluctance and with characteristic curiosity.

"St. Peter's," he recorded after a fourth or fifth visit, "offers itself as a place of worship and religious comfort for the whole human race, and in one of the transepts I found a range of confessionals, where the penitent might tell his sins in the tongue of his own country, whether French, German, Polish, English, or what not. If I had a murder on my conscience, or any other great sin, I think that I should have been inclined to kneel down there and pour it into the safe secrecy of the confessional. What an institution that is! Man needs it so that it seems as if God must have ordained it. The popish religion certainly does apply itself most closely and comfortably to human occasions; and I cannot but think that a great many people find their spiritual advantage in it who would find none at all in our formless mode of worship. You cannot think that it is all a farce, when you see peasant, citizen and soldier coming into the church, each on his own hook, and kneeling for moments or for hours, directing his silent devotion to some particular shrine; too humble to approach his God directly, and therefore asking the mediation of some saint who stands beside the Infinite Presence. In the church of San Carlos, yesterday, I saw a young man standing before a shrine, writhing and wringing his hands in an agony of contrition. If he had been a Protestant, I think he would have shut all that up within his heart and let it burn there till it seared him."

The churches of the Eternal City with their superb decoration and elaborate ritual, the throngs of people preoccupied by their devotions, above all the whole range of Italian painting communicated to Nathaniel a perception of the mystery of religious emotion which nothing in his previous experience had furnished. "Occasionally today," he remarks after a visit to a gallery, "I was sensible of a certain degree of emotion in looking at an old picture; as, for example, by a large, dark, ugly picture of Christ bearing the Cross and sinking beneath it, when somehow or other, a sense of His agony and the fearful wrong that mankind did (and does) its Redeemer, and the scorn of His enemies, and the sorrow of those who loved Him, came knocking at my heart and got entrance there. Once more I deem it a pity that Protestantism should have entirely laid aside this mode of appealing to the religious sentiment." At fifty-four an entirely new field of perception opened itself to him through the medium of an art whose language he scarcely understood. It was as though, deprived in his youth of all beauty, he had unconsciously awaited this inevitable revelation. Its effect was so gradual as to be all but imperceptible to himself, but it was decisive and complete. "No place," he finally came to write, "ever took so strong a hold of my being as Rome, nor ever seemed so close to me and so strangely familiar."

(IV)

Nathaniel spent three months in Rome and, for perhaps the first time in his life, began to live among people on terms of constant and intimate association. He found a congenial, and for his purposes a profitable, society awaiting him in the colony of American and English artists who were then residing in Rome. "I suppose," he reflected after some experience of this environment, "there is a class feeling among the artists who reside here, and they create a sort of atmosphere among themselves which they do not find anywhere else, and which is comfortable for them to live in. Nevertheless they are not generous nor gracious critics of one another; and I hardly remember any full-breathed and whole-souled praise from sculptor to sculptor or from painter to painter. They dread one another's ill-word, and scrupulously exchange a little attentions, for fear of giving offense; they pine, I suspect, at the sight of one another's successes, and would willingly keep a rich stranger from the door of any studio save their own. Their public is so much more limited than that of literary men that they have the better excuse for their petty jealousies."

Almost immediately after establishing himself in Rome, Nathaniel sought out two former acquaintances, the sculptor William Wetmore Story, whom he had known casually as a clerk in the Salem law-office of David Roberts, and the painter Thompson, who had made a portrait of him in Boston eight years before. For Thompson's work Nathaniel conceived a very high admiration, avowing that his pleasure in it was greater than in that of any other painter except the greatest of the old masters. Story exercised a strong personal fascination; he was gay, witty and worldly, but he was also sensitive, and a vein of melancholy occasionally showed beneath the sparkling surface of his mind. Nathaniel deplored Story's excessive facility and believed that he would do better things were it more difficult for him to do merely good ones. But having met few artists and none intimately, Nathaniel enjoyed listening to Story's talk about art, and he found Story a congenial and diverting companion whose breakfast parties always were pleasant and whose friends were charming and cultivated people.

He met two women artists whose unfamiliarly independent lives aroused his curiosity and interest. A Miss Lander, originally from Salem, requested Nathaniel to sit for a bust; at the sittings he attempted to draw her out, being, as he confessed, "a little inclined to take a similiar freedom with her moral likeness to that which she was taking with my physical one." "There are," he noted, "very available points about her and her position; a young woman, living in almost perfect independence, thousands of miles from her New England home, going fearlessly about these mysterious streets, by night as well as by day, with no household ties, no rule or law but that within her, yet acting with quietness and simplicity and keeping, after all, within a homely line of right. In her studio she wears a sort of pea-jacket, buttoned across her breast, and a little foraging cap just covering the top of her head." Miss Harriet Hosmer, a pupil of the English sculptor John Gibson and the sharer of his studio, was a small, brisk, bird-like person whose habitual costume, approximating as closely as possible that of a man, never failed to excite

Nathaniel's interest. Her mind was direct and hard and capable, like a man's, and Nathaniel studied her eagerly, puzzled by her deliberate repudiation of the conventions and conditions of her sex.

There were acquaintances whom Nathaniel saw during the winter; Mrs. Jameson, a little old lady who had written a series of books on Italian art, with whom he discussed painting and sculpture; Miss Bremer, the Swedish novelist, whose quarters were on the brow of the Tarpeian Rock; the poet William Cullen Bryant, aged and infirm, "with a weary look in his face as if he were tired of seeing things and doing things," whose coldness seemed the most significant quality of his character.

What he gained, as he thought, from his intimate association with painters and sculptors, was some comprehension of the elements and processes of their arts, which he attempted to turn back upon the classic masterpieces in the Roman galleries. But he failed to acquire an understanding even of the intention of these arts; his contact with them were purely literary and restricted him to an appreciation of such works as embodied some moral concept or abstract idea, and it was always the concept and not its expression which moved him. Under the influence of Sophia's enthusiasm, he came to admire the more sentimental pictures of Guido Reni and Raphael, but his response to Italian painting was not even amateurish and, despite his conscientious visits to the famous collections, he remained essentially a stranger to their contents. He learned even less about sculpture than about painting; his aversion to the representation of the nude was perhaps the keenest emotion which that art aroused, and he recurred to it again and again. "Man is no longer a naked animal," he remarked; "his clothes are as natural to him as his skin, and sculptors have no more right to undress him than to flay him." The works of his American contemporaries satisfied him more thoroughly than any masterpieces; nor is it singular that they did so, being for the most part conceived in terms of an attitude toward art scarcely more sophisticated than his own.

The real benefit of his painstaking esthetic pilgrimages came with his perception of the existence of a realm of experience which he had never known. That he was now incapable of making it, in any vital sense, his own was a source of occasional regret to him. But the knowledge of its existence, the realization that it might be susceptible of mastery by persons more fortunately equipped than himself, was in some oblique way stimulating to his mind. "I wonder," he speculated after visiting the Vatican gallery of sculpture, "whether other people are more fortunate than myself, and can invariably find their way to the inner soul of a work of art. I doubt it; they look at these things for just a minute, and pass on, without any pang of remorse, such as I feel, for quitting them so soon and so willingly. I am partly sensible that some unwritten rules of taste are making their way into my mind; that all this Greek beauty has done something toward refining me, though I am still, however, a very sturdy Goth." It seemed to him that the capacity to enter freely into the experience of art extended the range of life beyond the bounds by which he had hitherto assumed it to be restricted. The possession of that capacity, which he himself lacked, seemed to him to assure an existence richer, more varied and more significant than any that he had previously conceived. Art, which he failed to understand and largely failed to appreciate, enlarged his conception of life. Again and again in his notebooks he referred to the contrast between the meagerness of life in America, with one whole domain of possible experience all but closed to it, and the illimitable richness of life in Europe. His esthetic pilgrimages made him a more savage critic of the civilization of his native land.

(v)

"Rome struck me very disagreeably at first, but rather improves upon acquaintance, and has a sort of fascination which will make me reluctant to take final leave of it," Nathaniel informed Ticknor. "I wish I were a little more patriotic; but to confess the truth I had rather be a sojourner in any other country than return to my own. The United States are fit for many excellent purposes, but they certainly are not fit to live in." The fact is that he enjoyed not Rome but his own impression of it, and more particularly, the indolent and carefree existence which he led there. The Rome that he knew was the tourist's Rome; he delighted in wandering about its narrow streets as he had previously delighted in wandering about London, and he came to know both cities in somewhat the same way, acquiring a familiarity with whatever both retained of the past, but passing over with a minimum of attention their contemporary aspects. His social contacts were restricted to American or English people, and he became acquainted with no Italians. It is scarcely surprising that, having been sensible of almost impassible barriers between himself and the English, he considered the obstacles to comprehension of the Italians as absolutely insurmountable and decided to leave the native world of Italy unexplored in its inaccessible mystery. He came to know Rome, then, only as an exciting and bewildering museum. He found beauty in its picturesque ruins, its fountains and brilliant gardens, its palaces and churches and soft blue skies. He observed with exceptional precision the more striking features of that portion of Roman life which any casual visitor might have witnessed as a spectacle, and the accumulated details which he recorded deceptively make his descriptions seem less superficial than actually they are.

Nevertheless, what to a cosmopolitan or more sophisticated mind would have seemed a peculiarly barren experience, was to him infinitely stimulating and supremely important. The three months that he spent in Rome made him aware of the existence of a world of which he had hitherto been all but ignorant; a world that, by contrast, made his previous environment seem meager, vulgar and provincial; a world whose tones of richness and splendor moved him profoundly in spite of his confessed incapacity to completely assimilate and possess them. Rome aroused his dormant creative impulse, and furnished it with its most impressively significant materials.

When, in May, 1858, he removed with his family to Florence, it was with the intention, as he described it, of coming "to close grip with a romance which I have been trying to tear out of my mind." The germ of this romance had been suggested by the Faun of Praxiteles. After seeing the statue, Nathaniel had described it in his notebook and remarked: "This race of fauns was the most delightful of all that antiquity has imagined. It seems to me that a story, with all sorts of fun and pathos in it, might be contrived on the idea of their species having become intermingled with the human race; a family with the faun blood in them having prolonged itself from the classic era till our own days. The tail might have disappeared by dint of constant intermarriage with ordinary mortals; but the pretty, hairy ears should occasionally reappear in members of the family; and the moral instincts and intellectual characteristics of the faun might be most picturesquely brought out, without detriment to the human interest of the story. Fancy this combination in the person of a young lady!" This was the physical symbol which his imagination invariably required as a basis for invention; but the moral idea which preoccupied him was one suggested by his first view of Michelangelo's "Last Judgment": "At the last day—I presume, that is, in all future days, when we see ourselves as we are—man's only inexorable judge will be himself, and the punishment of his sins will be the perception of them."

Florence was in every way attractive. June and July were spent in the Casa Bella, near the Casa Guidi, where the Brownings were residing; in August Nathaniel rented the old villa of Montaüto, on the hill of Bellosguardo, just outside the city, and the family removed there to remain until October. During the first two months of their sojourn in Florence, Nathaniel's existence seemed to him only a continuation of his life in Rome. He explored the city and its galleries tirelessly, went frequently into society, and failed to settle down into the task of writing his book. "The atmosphere, or something else," he remarked in mid-June, "causes a sort of alacrity in my mind and an affluence of ideas, such as they are; but it does not thereby make me the happier. I feel an impulse to be at work, but am kept idle by the sense of being unsettled with removals to be gone through, over and over again, before I can shut myself into a quiet room of my own and turn the key. I need monotony, too, an eventless exterior life, before I can live in the world within."

The monotony of an eventless exterior life was clearly lacking during the early months of Nathaniel's Florentine residence. Across the street from the Casa Bella was the studio of Hiram Powers, the sculptor of the "Greek Slave," who was then enjoying his greatest celebrity. Powers quickly won Nathaniel's regard. "The man and his talk are fresh, original, and full of bone and muscle, and I enjoy him much," Nathaniel recorded. Powers stimulated by a vigorous iconoclasm. His theories of sculpture, which he never wearied of discussing, impressed Nathaniel as being extravagantly unconventional when compared to the decorous notions of Story and his other Roman acquaintances. One day when they were talking of the use of color in sculpture, a practice which Gibson had revived but which Powers deprecated, Powers asserted that everything capable of expression by a painter in color is equally capable of expression in colorless marble. Nathaniel asked whether Powers could model a blush. "Yes!" Powers cried, "I once proposed to a painter to express a blush in marble if he would express it in picture."

Powers respected neither the classics nor his contemporaries. He took a cynical delight in explaining, to Nathaniel's horrified dismay, precisely why he considered the Medici Venus a deplorably defective work. In similar fashion he destroyed, by his capricious criticism, the works of his principal contemporaries. But art was only one of Powers's varied interests. His principal diversion was mechanical invention, and in his studio he had fitted up an admirably complete workshop. "You see, I am a bit of a Yankee," he remarked to Nathaniel when displaying the machines which he had invented and constructed. He was convinced that flying would be a future form of locomotion—after the moral condition of mankind had been so improved as to obviate its possible bad uses—and had made several attempts to invent a practicable flying machine. He was, besides, much interested in spiritualism and, being a Swedenborgian, plunged into metaphysics with characteristic energy. He was never more oracular than when discussing his philosophical ideas. "He sees too clearly what is within his range to be aware of any region of mystery beyond," Nathaniel reflected, feeling that Powers's ultimate thought always left you with an inclination to think a little further for yourself.

Nathaniel remembered especially one warm summer evening when they had spent hours on the terrace-roof of Powers's studio, looking out over the city toward the hills, listening to the Florentine bells. "We talked, furthermore," he recorded, "about instinct and reason, and whether the brute creation have souls, and, if they have none, how justice is to be done them for their sufferings here; and Mr. Powers came finally to the conclusion that brutes suffer only in appearance, and that God enjoys for them all that they seem to enjoy, and that man is the only intelligent and sentient being. We reasoned high about other states of being, and I suggested the possibility that there might be beings inhabiting this earth, contemporaneously with us and close beside us, but of whose existence and whereabouts we could have no perception, nor they of ours, because we are endowed with different sets of senses; for certainly it was in God's power to create beings who should communicate with nature by innumerable other senses than those few which we possess. Mr. Powers gave hospitable reception to this idea, and said that it had occurred to himself; and he has evidently thought much and earnestly about such matters; but he is apt to let his idea crystallize into a theory before he can have sufficient data for it. . . . The atmosphere of Florence, at least when we ascend a little way into it, suggests planetary speculations. Galileo found it so, and Mr. Powers and I pervaded the whole universe; but finally crept down his garret stairs, and parted, with a friendly pressure of the hand."

Nathaniel recalled also, as typical of the pleasant

intercourse that developed between the two families, an evening spent with the Brownings in their dimly-lit drawing room at Casa Guidi. Mrs. Browning, her pallor framed in masses of dark curls, seemed to him to be scarcely embodied and almost elf-like. "It is marvelous, . . ." he reflected, "how so extraordinary, so acute, so sensitive a creature can impress us, as she does, with the certainty of her benevolence. It seems to me that there were a million chances to one that she would have been a miracle of acidity and bitterness." William Cullen Bryant was likewise among the guests, and Nathaniel noticed his white head and palmer-like beard bent deferentially toward Mrs. Browning as he listened to her "shrill, yet sweet tenuity of voice." He doubted that Bryant had any high appreciation of her poetry or of her husband's, and suspected that the Brownings cared very little for Bryant's verse. Robert Browning circulated about the room, appearing to converse with every one simultaneously, and accompanying the velocity of his talk with vivid gestures. "Browning's nonsense," Nathaniel reflected, "is of very genuine and excellent quality, the true bubble and effervescence of a bright and powerful mind. And he lets it play among his friends with the faith and simplicity of a child." All during the evening there drifted about the room a slender, fragile boy of nine whose long curls and black velvet costume made him seem effeminate; the Brownings' son, Pennini, who served the guests with strawberries, tea and cake, and joined precociously in their conversation.

The conversation had chiefly to do with spirit communication, a subject which Nathaniel now found wearisome and disagreeable. Bryant, who appeared to have no conviction about the matter, told a story of the successful communication between James Fenimore Cooper and his sister, who had been dead for fifty years. Mrs. Browning had been converted to a belief in these manifestations by the American medium Home, who had held séances in Florence. At one of Home's séances Browning and his wife had felt unearthly hands, one of which had placed a laurel wreath on Mrs. Browning's head. Browning declared that Home was a charlatan, that the unearthly hands had been affixed to his feet and manipulated from beneath the table, and although Mrs. Browning gently expostulated, Nathaniel felt the mystery melt away in Browning's hearty grip, and at the sharp touch of his logic. Nathaniel was surprised to find Browning's conversation so clear and so pointed, "since his poetry can seldom proceed far without running into the high grass of latent meanings and obscure allusions." "He must be an amiable man," he said of Browning. "I should like him much, and should make him like me, if opportunities were favorable."

The question of spirit communication was agitating Nathaniel's acquaintances in Florence, all of whom had participated in experiments. Mrs. Browning was a convert to the practice, and a believer in the medium Home. Robert Browning was an angry skeptic; he considered Home an irresponsible charlatan and wrote a poem, *Mr. Sludge the "Medium,"* in which he recorded that opinion with vigorous bitterness. Powers had complete faith in the verity of spiritual communications; he believed Home to be a knave, but a sensitive medium. Nathaniel was taken to visit Seymour Kirkup, an aged antiquarian who was reported to be a necromancer, and held communication, through a medium, with the illustrious dead of all ages. Kirkup lived in gloomy rooms overhanging the Arno, crowded with ancient pictures and books; he had had a mistress, a Florentine girl remarkable for her talents as a medium. This girl had died, leaving Kirkup a small daughter whom he believed to be his own, but who was actually the child of his mistress by a young lover. This child, Imogen, was now four years old and lived with Kirkup, and he had already developed the mediumistic gift in her. To Nathaniel she seemed a romantic figure as she frisked about the shadowy rooms crowded with the trumpery of ages long past, following the old man's footsteps and playing with her Persian kitten; he determined to use the old man and the child as characters in a book which he hoped to write after returning to America.

Sophia's curiosity about spirit-communication thrived upon the experiences of her acquaintances, and she longed to have similar experiences herself. It developed that the children's governess, Miss Shepard, who disbelieved in the possibility of communication, was nevertheless extremely successful in the process of automatic writing. Sophia plunged into experiments, receiving, to her extreme delight, messages purporting to come from her mother, father, brother and a sister who had died in infancy. Nathaniel was unconvinced by these messages, in which he recognized Sophia's sentimental fancies and preconceived ideas. He was amused by the malicious pranks of a spirit named Mary Runnel, who wandered through the séances to the great distress of more respectable ghosts. Nathaniel did not then connect her with the first love of his grandfather Daniel Hawthorne.

Nathaniel felt repugnance to those experiments, and shared Browning's disapproval of a serious reliance upon their authenticity. "What astonishes me," he remarked, "is the indifference with which I listen to these marvels. They throw old ghost-stories quite into the shade; they bring the whole world of spirits down amongst us, visibly and audibly; they are absolutely proved to be sober facts by evidence that would satisfy us of any other alleged realities; and yet I cannot force my mind to interest myself in them. They are facts to my understanding which, it might have been anticipated, would have been the last to acknowledge them, but they seem not to be facts to my intuitions and deeper perceptions. My inner soul does not in the least admit them; there is a mistake somewhere."

(VI)

"It is pleasant to feel at last that I am really away from America," Nathaniel wrote to Fields from the congenial seclusion of Montaüto; "a satisfaction that I never really enjoyed as long as I stayed in Liverpool, where it seemed to me that the quintessence of nasal and hand-shaking Yankeedom was gradually filtered and sublimated through my consulate, on the way outward and homeward. I first got acquainted with my countrymen there. At Rome, too, it was not much better. But here in Florence, and in the summer time, and in this secluded villa, I have escaped out of all my old tracks and am really remote. I like my present residence immensely. The house stands on a hill, overlooking Florence, and is big enough to quarter a regiment, insomuch that each member of the family, including servants, has a separate suite of apartments, and there are vast wildernesses of upper rooms into which we have never yet sent exploring expeditions. At one end of the house there is a moss-grown tower, haunted by owls and by the ghost of a monk who was confined there in the thirteenth century, previous to being burnt at the stake in the principal square of Florence. I hire this villa, tower and all, at twenty-eight dollars a month, but I mean to take it away bodily and clap it into a romance, which I have in my head, ready to be written out."

Nathaniel set to work upon the first sketch for this romance, *The Marble Faun*, spending his mornings in the square writing study he had appropriated; a little salon ornamented in fresco with nymphs, temples, Cupids, peacocks, parrots and sunflowers. As the sketch expanded under his hand he found himself putting into it all the harvest of his Italian life. From page after page of his notebooks he reconstituted the Roman scene of palaces and churches, galleries and gardens; the effect of substantial actuality he attempted to gain by elaboration of detail; but the tone and color of that scene, the brooding melancholy that enveloped it, were properties not of Rome but of his perception. He was wistfully aware of his incapacity, as a resident, to master the city and make it an intelligible element of his experience; the meagerness of a New England environment and the crude brightness of American civilization had inadequately prepared him for more than a tourist's eager but baffled appreciation. He had some conception of the rich rewards that the city might yield to a traveler less incompletely prepared and more fortunately endowed than himself. It was his perception of the discrepancy between these potential rewards and the inconsiderable ones which he had himself acquired, that gave to his representation of Rome a romantic tone of melancholy and mystery. The city, as he builded it into his novel, is felt to be unyielding; it withholds more than it reveals; and it remains in the end incomprehensible and overwhelming to the characters and the reader.

As the immediate environment of his characters he chose that world of the foreign colony of artists in Rome with which he had become acquainted through Story. He thereby hoped to isolate them from the scene in which he placed them, much as he himself had been isolated from Italian life, and to make them free of a world, independent, as he thought, of the conventions by which society is circumscribed. All that he had learned about their art from Powers and Story and Thompson he communicated to his characters, and he furnished their studios with his favorites among the works of his friends.

The theme of his novel was the nature of sin and evil; but in this book, as in no one of its predecessors, he proposed to study their genesis, not their consequences. The plot was to hinge upon a main episode of crime; in developing it he employed only sufficient material to embody his theme in incident and situation, leaving its opening and conclusion vague. The mystery of his heroine's past and the mystery of his faun's future did not concern him; he was indifferent to the personal fortunes of his characters after they had fulfilled their function of illustrating his moral problem. In this book the illustration was to be accomplished chiefly by the faun-like Donatello who, beginning life with natural, almost animal, innocence, gains a soul by the perpetration of a crime. "The entire system of man's affairs, as at present established," Nathaniel believed, "is built up purposely to exclude the careless and happy soul. The very children would upbraid the wretched individual who should endeavor to take life and the world as—what we might naturally suppose them meant for—a place and opportunity for enjoyment." This belief, so foreign to anything that America had taught him, was the lesson of his excursion into Renaissance Italy. And he continued in words that seemed to indicate his critical attitude toward the civilization of his native land: "It is the iron rule in our day to require an object and a purpose in life. It makes us all parts of a complicated scheme of progress, which can only result in our arrival at a colder and drearier region than we were born in. It insists upon everybody's adding somewhat—a mite, perhaps, but earned by incessant effort, to an accumulated pile of usefulness, of which the only use will be to burden our posterity with even heavier thoughts and more inordinate labor than our own. . . . We go all wrong by too strenuous a resolution to go all right."

His story was, once again, to illustrate the evolution of good out of sin, not the repentance of sin; its doctrine was the most optimistic interpretation he had yet given to the theory which Mr. Emerson had announced in *Circles.* But the logical conclusion of this doctrine is, as he saw, a change in the concept of sin itself, and that change he suggested in a question which tentatively expresses his conviction after much brooding upon the problem: "Is sin then,—which we deem such a dreadful blackness in the universe—is it, like sorrow, merely an element of human education, through which we struggle to a higher and purer state than we could otherwise have attained? Did Adam fall, that we might ultimately rise to a far loftier paradise than his?"

(VII)

In October Nathaniel and his family left Florence, and after a ten days' visit with the Storys at Siena, returned to Rome for the winter. Nathaniel liked Siena. "It is a fine old town, with every promise of health and vigor in its atmosphere; and really, if I could take root anywhere, I know not but it could as well be here as in another place. It would only be a kind of despair, however, that would ever make me dream of founding a home in Italy; a sense that I had lost my country through absence or incongruity, and that earth is not

He lives over again in order to repair some great error, or he has done something in his past life, which he fears will be of very bad influence on mankind, & therefore he lives again to grub up this evil by the root. He attaches himself to the family to whom he did the wrong, trying to influence their fortunes to good, but finds that the evil is ineradicable, unless he will pull up great deal more good with it. But some definite thing. He is a poor, simple old gentleman, and has incurred an obligation in very past years—a debt—which weighs upon his mind as he approaches the end of his life. He has the invaluable secret of prolonging or renewing life; he [illegible] till it, to be able, [illegible] his old time; but this is against his conscience; so he determines to live back again and get the money in some other way. Yes,—the debt was to a poor widow [illegible] troubling him; it ought have been discharged by his father, and have grown by interest up to its present amount. The widow was perhaps an infant [illegible]; he lives a [illegible] of him. So they live [illegible]

AN UNPUBLISHED

This manuscript was written by Hawthorne on a letter to him from germinal ideas—the discovery of the elixir of life, and the ineradicability Hawthorne. (Courtesy of George S. Hellman)

HAWTHORNE MANUSCRIPT

James T. Fields. It is the note for the plot of a story containing the of evil—which underly *Doctor Grimshawe's Secret* and other writings of

an abiding-place." But after their arrival in Rome, he remarked, "I had a quiet, gentle, comfortable pleasure, as if, after many wanderings, I was drawing near Rome, for, now that I have known it once, Rome certainly does draw into itself my heart, as I think even London, or even little Concord itself, or old sleepy Salem never did and never will." They had rented an apartment at 68, Piazza Poli, and Nathaniel planned to remain for six months and finish his book.

His anticipations of a pleasant winter met with a rude check. Una, who was in the habit of making sketching expeditions with Miss Shepard, remained late one afternoon at the Palace of the Caesars to complete a drawing. She fell ill with Roman fever, and for four months her father's life centered in her sick-room. He had no heart for writing, abandoned his novel, and even discontinued his journal. A strange helplessness and inertia took possession of him. The physician was pessimistic; Nathaniel himself watched his beloved daughter growing day by day more feeble. Finally she lapsed into a state of coma; the physician told them that unless the fever abated before morning, Una would die. That night, as usual, Nathaniel produced a pack of playing-cards, and the family sat down to whist. One hand was played. Then Nathaniel arose. "We won't play any more," he said, and left the room. As the decisive hour drew near, Sophia, alone in the sick-room with her daughter, bitterly complained of the ways of Providence. Then, unaccountably, a subtle peace quieted her protests. Why should she doubt God's goodness? Let Him take Una if He thought best. She could no longer combat His will. She returned to Una's bedside; the girl's brow was cool, her pulse regular, and she slept quietly. The crisis had passed.

Una's convalescence lasted well into Carnival, in the first week of March. Nathaniel enjoyed watching the spirited throng in the Corso from the balcony of his friend, J. L. Motley, the historian. He resumed his long walks in the Campagna with Motley and Story. He began once again to see the Brownings and other friends; Elizabeth Hoar came to Rome, then Horatio Bridge, and finally Franklin Pierce. Pierce's tenderness and affection helped Nathaniel through the last hideous days of Una's illness. "I think I owe to him, almost, my husband's life. He was divinely tender, sweet, sympathizing and helpful," Sophia wrote. And Nathaniel, after resuming his journal, paid touching tribute to his friend:

"I have found in him, here in Rome, the whole of my early friend, and even better than I used to know him; a heart as true and affectionate, a mind much widened and deepened by his experience of life. We hold just the same relation to one another as of yore, and we have passed all the turning-off places, and may hope to go on together still the same dear friends as long as we live. I do not love him one whit the less for having been President, nor for having done me the greatest good in his power; a fact that speaks eloquently in his favor, and perhaps says a little for myself. If he had been merely a benefactor, perhaps I might not have borne it so well; but each did his best for the other as friend for friend."

With Una's recovery assured, Nathaniel began to plan his return to America. In March, 1859, he wrote to Ticknor from Rome:

"I told you, in my last, that I had written a Romance. It still requires a good deal of revision, trimming off of exuberances, and filling up vacant spaces; but I think it will be all right in a month or two after I arrive. I shall do my best upon it, you may be sure; for I feel that I shall come before the public, after so long an interval, with all the uncertainties of a new author. If I were only rich enough, I do not believe I should ever publish another book, though I might continue to write them for my own occupation and amusement. But with a wing of a house to build, and my girls to educate, and Julian to send to Cambridge, I see little prospect of the *dolce far niente* as long as there shall be any faculty left in me. I have another Romance ready to be written as soon as this one is off the stocks."

Late in May Nathaniel and his family left Rome, and traveling by way of Marseilles, Avignon, Geneva and Paris, arrived in London toward the end of June. It was his intention to sail for home within six weeks. Shortly after arriving in London, however, Nathaniel found it necessary to postpone his return home for another year. He had given ten thousand dollars of his capital to John O'Sullivan to invest in Spanish mines. Instead of producing the fortune which O'Sullivan had optimistically prophesied, the investment had completely disappeared. Upon Nathaniel's arrival in England the publishing firm of Smith and Elder had offered him six hundred pounds for the English copyrights of his new romance, as yet unfinished, and this offer persuaded him to remain in England until he had completed the book. After a few weeks in London he retired to the country, going first to Whitby and thence to Redcar, a watering place on the German ocean, where the family settled for a long stay. Here Nathaniel wrote every day until afternoon, and then walked the brown, dreary sands planning the labor of the following day. In October the family moved to Leamington, where, on November eighth, Nathaniel completed his book. On the last day of February, 1860, the book was published in England under the title *Transformation,* which had been chosen by the publishers, and shortly thereafter it was issued in America under the author's chosen title, as *The Marble Faun: A Romance of Monte Beni.* The reviews were not favorable, on the whole, and there was sufficient complaint about the inconclusive conclusion of the novel to persuade Nathaniel to add, in a second edition, a final chapter purporting to dispose of its mysteries. He was discouraged by what he considered his failure.

The book completed, Nathaniel and his family went to Bath for some weeks, and thence to London for a final holiday before their departure for America. "You would be stricken dumb to see how quietly I accept the whole string of invitations, and what is more, perform my engagements without a murmur," Nathaniel wrote to Fields from London. "The stir of this London life, somehow or other, has done me a wonderful deal of good, and I feel better than for months past. This is strange, for if I had my choice,

I should leave undone almost all the things I do." He was entertained by the Motleys, by Lord Dufferin, by Monckton Milnes, and met Henry Chorley, who had praised him in *The Athenaeum* in the dark days before the publication of *Twice-Told Tales.* As the time for departure drew nearer, he became more and more reluctant to go. America, he anticipated, would now seem alien; The Wayside might no longer seem to be a home. Bennoch and Henry Bright, he thought, were the only two men in England to whom he would feel grieved to say farewell; "but to the island itself," he wrote, "I cannot bear to say that word, as a finality. I shall dreamily hope to come back again at some indefinite time; rather foolishly, perhaps, for it will tend to take the substance out of my life in my own land. But this, I suspect, is apt to be the penalty of those who stay abroad, and stay too long."

THE HOME RETURN

(1)

On a sultry June afternoon in 1860 Nathaniel and his family arrived in Concord. The sun beat down in a hard white glare; the countryside, its fields burned to a dreary brown and its trees powdered with dust, seemed flat and unlovely; even The Wayside, so lovingly remembered, looked small and forlorn. After seven years, home. And home was a disappointment.

For some days even their oldest friends were unaware of their return. Then, as if they had never been away, the lazy, agreeable village life enfolded them. Old friends were their neighbors; Mr. Emerson, graver and more suave, resumed his calls as though they had not been interrupted; Mr. Alcott, their nearest neighbor, still devoted himself to conversation and rustic building; Ellery Channing was fitfully satiric and whimsical; Thoreau's eyes burned feverishly and his whole frame quivered with indignation at the inevitable mention of John Brown. In Boston, Ticknor arranged a banquet in Nathaniel's honor.

During the autumn Nathaniel was engaged in carrying out some long contemplated improvements to his house and grounds. A tower, reminiscent of the ancient tower at Montaüto, was added; this contained Nathaniel's working study, a square room with five windows and closets for books, papered in pale gold, and here he spent his mornings sketching out passages of the romance he intended to write. The alterations which he had made in The Wayside, although not as extensive as those originally planned, had cost more than he had estimated. His capital, depleted by O'Sullivan's financial irresponsibility, he considered scarcely sufficient to provide for the future needs of his family. He took up the task of writing with infinite distaste; his art was no longer a delight but a burden; composition had become so fatiguing to him that he had abandoned, in France, the lifelong habit of keeping a journal. The winter of Una's illness in Rome had drained his energy. He now became aware of a new weariness, a disinclination to all activity, a disappointment with the dullness and meagerness of Concord. He thought of Europe with regret, and at times The Wayside seemed only an ugly reminder that he must forever abandon all dreams of returning abroad. Life itself had suddenly ceased to interest him; the future stretched before him monotonous and empty. At fifty-six old age had come upon him. He became painfully sensible of his feebleness; and when he looked in the mirror he saw the whitening hair and shrunken body of a failing man.

(II)

He spent his mornings in the tower study, feverishly seeking to overcome the obstinate resistance of his mind, impatient of his lassitude and of the reluctance of his imagination. After dinner he walked about the grounds with Sophia, and toward sunset ascended the hill behind the house, usually alone, and slowly paced its summit, gradually treading a footpath between the huckleberry and sweet-fern bushes under the pines. On one such evening walk he was accompanied by a visitor who had brought an introduction from James Russell Lowell; a bashful young man named Howells, some of whose verse Lowell had accepted for *The Atlantic Monthly,* and who, emboldened by this success, had come to Boston from Ohio to engage in the profession of letters. They sat down upon a bench on the hilltop, Howells slightly embarrassed in the presence of America's most distinguished novelist, and had what the visitor afterward described as "a silence of half an hour together." Nathaniel questioned his visitor about the West, and said that he would like to find some part of America "where the cursed shadow of Europe had not fallen." Then, learning that Howells was eager to meet Emerson, he took a card from his pocket, scribbled upon it the words "I find this man worthy," and directed him to Emerson's home.

The times were unfavorable to the peace of mind that Nathaniel had always required when engaged in composition. Shortly after his arrival in America, secession had begun, and for months afterward the atmosphere seemed tense with intimations of impending catastrophe. The winter passed dismally. Despite Nathaniel's detachment from the issue which was now convulsing the nation—and he was sufficiently detached to refuse to read the newspapers—he could not be in-

FIELDS, HAWTHORNE, AND TICKNOR

Courtesy of Houghton Mifflin Company

different to the possibility of war. "I spend two or three hours a day in my sky-parlor," he wrote Ticknor, "and duly spread a quire of paper on my desk; but no very important result has followed thus far. Perhaps, however, I shall have a new Romance ready by the time New England becomes a separate nation—a consummation I rather hope for than otherwise." He had no sympathy with a popular clamor for war, and none with the causes which, throughout the northern states, accented that clamor with bitter passion. A war to preserve the Union seemed to him preposterous; a certain disaster. As the conflict became more and more inevitable, he was able to contemplate only its havoc and waste, its toll in human misery, its hideous futility. He recognized, but owned himself incapable of comprehending, the wave of profound emotion which dominated the national life; and, unmoved by that emotion, he held himself imperturbably aloof from its every manifestation. When at last, in the spring, war was declared and his peaceful neighborhood was transformed overnight into a camp from which regiment after regiment of youths departed for the battlefields to the south, Nathaniel found himself isolated as never before in his experience. His politics were obsolete; his friends considered him perversely oblivious to the most important crisis in his country's history; his profession seemed the most useless of occupations. Events had compelled him to assume a definite position, and mechanically he adopted the view of New England. But his mental reservations outweighed his outward and casual acquiescence. In May, 1861, he wrote to Bridge:

"The war, strange to say, has had a beneficial effect upon my spirits, which were flagging woefully before it broke out. But it was delightful to share in the heroic sentiment of the time, and to feel that I had a country—a consciousness which seemed to make me young again. One thing, as regards this matter, I regret, and one I am glad of. The regrettable thing is that I am too old to shoulder a musket myself, and the joyful thing is that Julian is too young. He drills with a company of lads, and he means to enlist as soon as he reaches the minimum age; but I trust that we shall either be victorious or vanquished before that time. Meantime (though I approve of the war as much as any man) I don't quite understand what we are fighting for, or what definite result can be expected. If we pummel the South ever so hard, they will love us none the better for it; and even if we subjugate them, our next step should be to cut them adrift. If we are fighting for the annihilation of slavery, to be sure, it may be a wise object, and offers a tangible result, and the only one which is consistent with a future reunion between North and South. A continuance of the war would soon make this plain to us, and we should see the expediency of preparing our black brethren for future citizenship by allowing them to fight for their own liberties and educating them through heroic influences.

"Whatever happens next, I must say that I rejoice that the old Union is smashed. We never were one people, and never really had a country since the Constitution was formed."

Six months later he wrote again; his point of view

had not been modified, and the disasters of conflict had but intensified his belief that disunion afforded the only practicable solution:

"I am glad you take such a hopeful view of our national prospects so far as regards the war; but my own opinion is that no nation ever came safe and sound through such a confounded difficulty as this of ours. For my part I don't hope, nor indeed wish, to see the Union restored as it was. Amputation seems to me much the better plan, and all we ought to fight for is the liberty of selecting the point where our diseased members shall be lop't off. I would fight to the death for the Northern Slave States and let the rest go."

He despaired of the Union, and disbelieved in it, and therefore deemed it not worth fighting for; the issue of the conflict scarcely moved him; in these circumstances the war became for him a prolonged desolation of the spirit. In February, 1862, he wrote to Bridge once more:

"Frank Pierce came here and spent a night, a week or two since, and we mingled our tears and condolences for the state of the country. Pierce is truly patriotic, and thinks there is nothing left for us but to fight it out, but I should be sorry to take his opinion implicitly as regards our chances in the future. He is bigoted to the Union, and sees nothing but ruin without it; whereas I (if we can only put the boundary far enough south) should not much regret an ultimate separation. A few weeks will decide how this is to be, for, unless a powerful Union feeling shall be developed by the military successes that seem to be setting in, we ought to turn our attention to the best mode of resolving ourselves into two nations."

(III)

Nathaniel had been working at a romance in which he proposed to employ two themes; that of the elixir of life, suggested by Thoreau's account of an early occupant of The Wayside; and that of the "bloody footstep" which he had seen at Smithell's Hall in England. He had made two drafts of the book, but had been dissatisfied with each in turn, and was engaged somewhat hopelessly upon a third when Ticknor suggested, in March, 1862, a visit to Washington. Nathaniel's depression had increased under the rigors of a New England winter, and largely because Sophia urged upon him the probable benefits of a change of scene, he acceded to Ticknor's invitation. He was restless and ill at ease; even the seclusion of his tower study was not impenetrable to the disturbing influences of war; perhaps by confronting the reality of a conflict which left him unmoved, he would be able to exorcise its paralyzing effect upon his imagination.

The two friends arrived in Washington just too late to witness the impressive departure of the troops for Manassas. But they had a good view of Washington under war conditions, they visited Fort Ellsworth, they saw General McClellan at his headquarters at Fairfax Seminary, they went to Harper's Ferry and Fortress Monroe, and made a trip to Manassas. They also had an opportunity of calling upon President Lincoln with a delegation charged with the presentation to the President of a whip specially made for him by a Massachusetts manufacturer. Nathaniel drew a striking and coldly detached portrait of Lincoln; in his observation of the President he had learned nothing and forgotten nothing:

"He was dressed in a rusty black frock-coat and pantaloons, unbrushed, and worn so faithfully that the suit had adapted itself to the curves and angularities of his figure, and had grown to be an outer skin of the man. He had shabby slippers on his feet. His hair was black, still unmixed with gray, stiff, somewhat bushy, and had apparently been acquainted with neither brush nor comb that morning, after the disarrangement of the pillow; and as to a nightcap, Uncle Abe probably knows nothing of such effeminacies. His complexion is dark and sallow, betokening, I fear, an insalubrious atmosphere around the White House; he has thick black eyebrows and an impending brow; his nose is large, and the lines about his mouth are very strongly defined.

"The whole physiognomy is as coarse a one as you would meet anywhere in the length and breadth of the States; but withal, it is redeemed, illumined, softened and brightened by a kindly though serious look out of his eyes, and an expression of homely sagacity, that seems weighted with rich results of village experience. A great deal of native sense; no bookish cultivation, no refinement; honest at heart, and thoroughly so, and yet, in some sort, sly—at least, endowed with a sort of tact and wisdom that are akin to craft, and would impel him, I think, to take an antagonist in flank, rather than to make a bull-run at him right in front."

After his return to Concord Nathaniel wrote, for *The Atlantic Monthly,* an account of his visit to Washington, entitled "Chiefly About War Matters." His text was sufficiently unsympathetic with the feeling of the times to alarm both Fields and the editor. Fields insisted, despite Nathaniel's protests, upon removing from the article the description of President Lincoln. Nathaniel, to make the situation easier for editor and publisher, added to the article a series of savagely dissenting footnotes purporting to have been written by one of the editorial staff. In this fashion the article was published in July, 1862, and drew a considerable amount of protest from readers of the magazine. As might have been expected, it was completely disengaged from the bitter realities, the no less real passion and prejudices, and the national spirit of the day. It was the work of a detached and cool observer whose lack of sympathy disposed him to minimize what he disliked and to report his impressions with absolute indifference to their effect upon other people.

He returned from Washington refreshed and stimulated, and, besides producing his article on war matters, continued contributing to *The Atlantic Monthly* a series of essays on subjects drawn from his English notebooks, which, in the summer of 1863, were collected into a volume under the title of *Our Old Home.* He undertook this work for pecuniary reasons, realizing that the mass of material yielded by his English notebooks would probably never serve him in the composition of a romance, and being reluctant to lose all the labor that had gone into the preparation of the notebooks. He wished to dedicate the volume to Franklin Pierce, but Fields was doubtful of the public's acceptance of this compliment to the universally unpopular ex-President, and feared that the dedication, in connection with Nathaniel's attitude toward the war, would injure Nathaniel's literary reputation as well as the sale of the book. Nathaniel pondered Fields' advice, but finally informed Fields of his adherence to his original design:

"I thank you for your note of the 15th instant, and have delayed my reply thus long in order to ponder deeply on your advice, smoke cigars over it, and see what it might be possible for me to do towards taking it. I find that it would be a piece of poltroonery in me to withdraw either the dedication or the dedicatory letter. My long and intimate personal relations with Pierce render the dedication altogether proper, especially as regards this book, which would have had no existence without his kindness; and if he is so exceedingly unpopular that his name is enough to sink the volume, there is so much the more need that an old friend should stand by him. I cannot, merely on account of pecuniary profit or literary reputation, go back from what I have deliberately felt and thought it right to do; and if I were to tear out the dedication, I should never look at the volume again without remorse and shame. As for the literary public, it must accept my book precisely as I think fit to give it, or let it alone."

The book was accepted temperately, though cordially, in America, but in England it excited violent indignation. The English reviews were unanimously unfavorable and occasionally sharply sarcastic; Nathaniel's English friends did not spare him their regretful reproaches. He was astonished and distressed by the reception of his book in England. He protested that in his comparison of the two peoples, he had almost invariably cast the balance against his own, and accused the English of being excessively sensitive. "They do me a great injustice in supposing I hate them," he said. "I would as soon hate my own people."

(IV)

Mr. Thoreau had been in ill health for more than a year; a change of climate had been recommended, but a trip to the West had produced no permanent benefit. All during the autumn Nathaniel had watched his old friend gradually wasting away; his eyes growing brighter and more feverish, his body perceptibly shrinking. With the onset of winter Thoreau had taken to his bed. Sophia, with the kindly intention of distracting him, had ransacked the attic of The Wayside and found the old music-box which, in happier days twenty years before, had fascinated him during his first visit to the Manse. When Nathaniel returned from Washington, it was to learn that Thoreau's case had been pronounced hopeless; death was imminent but dilatory. He went to see his friend and found him quietly listening to the aged instrument. The forgotten tunes tinkled softly in the little room, as if the ghosts of ancient memories were dancing there. Nathaniel sat by the bedside and listened to them. What memories they evoked! That first summer of felicity at the Manse . . . Sophia and himself racing up the tree-shaded avenue . . . Sophia dancing on the lawn in the moonlight . . . The sunsets that flooded the little study with liquid gold, and their hearts with an ineffable ecstasy . . . The pain and splendor and enchantment of love . . . He smiled sadly. The music-box had ceased its silvery chatter. Twilight was coming on. The dying man lay quietly on his pillows with eyes closed. . . .

A month later Mr. Thoreau was dead. Nathaniel and Sophia went to the funeral. Mr. Emerson spoke of his friend, and Mr. Alcott read from Thoreau's writings. The coffin, covered with wild-flowers, stood in the vestibule of the church. They followed the coffin to Sleepy Hollow where, in the past years, they had so often walked on spring days soft as this. Upon leaving the cemetery they turned, with one accord, toward the Old Manse, Sophia gently assisting Nathaniel to walk. She saw in his eyes a look of gratitude, but his lips twitched as if her touch had wounded him; she could not know the injury to his pride. She walked slowly, accomodating her pace to his faltering step. They paused at the bottom of the avenue and stood gazing at the Old Manse. Then, in silence, they continued their way home.

(v)

In the autumn of 1862 Una, whom her father idolized, fell ill. She was sent to the seaside, and returned after a month physically improved, but Nathaniel knew that the relapse was ominous; he saw in her deficient strength and too delicate sensibility portents of a peril which he could not bring himself to communicate even to Sophia. During her absence from home he aged and grew more feeble daily. Sophia, in a letter to Una, remarked that "Papa has not a good appetite, and eats no dinner except a little potato. But he is trying to write, and locks himself into the library and pulls down the blinds."

He was, in fact, completing *Our Old Home,* and when the task had been finished, he turned once more to another version of his romance. Writing had now become sheer torture; he realized that he had but little time to live; every dollar that his pen might earn would be useful to his family after his death. Relentlessly he drove his flagging energies in their service, but despite his efforts he made no satisfactory progress. During the long, tedious summer he became more languid every day; he rarely left the house now, and when he did, it was only to walk uncertainly along the paths or stand gazing wistfully across the fields. He seemed to have no definite organic disease, and refused all medical attention, but he manifested no interest whatever in life. It was as though he had relinquished life at last, and was weariedly awaiting death. His friend Richard Henry Stoddard sent him a poem, *The King's Bell,* and in acknowledging it Nathaniel said: "I have been a happy man, and yet I do not remember any one moment of such happy conspiring circumstances that I could have rung a joy-bell at it."

With the advent of autumn he resumed work on his romance. Fields, thinking to spur him on, suggested that the work be published serially in *The Atlantic Monthly*, beginning with the issue for January, 1864. Nathaniel consented to this arrangement, but with reservations. "In this untried experiment of a serial work," he wrote to Fields, "I desire not to pledge myself, or promise the public more than I may confidently expect to achieve. When the work is completed in the Magazine, I can fill up the gaps, and make straight the crookednesses, and christen it with a fresh title." During the following months he wavered between confidence and depression. His assurance that he would soon complete the book would be followed, within a few days, by a helpless assertion of his incapacity to continue the work. "There is something preternatural in my reluctance to begin. I linger at the threshold and have a perception of very disagreeable phantoms to be encountered if I enter. . . . I don't see much probability of my having the first chapter of the Romance ready as soon as you want it. There are two or three chapters ready to be written, but I am not robust enough to begin, and I feel as if I should never carry it through." Shortly thereafter he wrote again: "I am not quite up to writing yet, but shall make an effort as soon as I see any hope of success. You ought to be thankful that (unlike most other broken-down authors) I do not pester you with decrepit pages, and insist upon your accepting them as full of the old spirit and vigor. That trouble, perhaps, still awaits you, after I shall have reached a further stage of decay. Seriously, my mind has, for the present, lost its temper and its fine edge, and I have an instinct that I had better keep quiet. Perhaps I shall have a new spirit of vigor, if I wait quietly for it; perhaps not." And in December, 1863, he wrote, "Those verses entitled *Weariness* in the last magazine seem to me profoundly touching. I, too, am weary, and begin to look ahead for the Wayside Inn."

Finally, in February, 1864, he gave up the struggle, and advised Fields that some notice be given the public that he could not furnish the promised romance, offering, with a grim humor, some model announcements of his final failure:

"I hardly know what to say to the public about this abortive romance, though I know pretty well what the case will be. I shall never finish it. Yet it is not quite pleasant for an author to announce himself, or to be announced, as finally broken down as to his literary faculty. . . . I cannot finish it unless a great change comes over me; and if I make too great an effort to do so, it will be my death; not that I should care much for that, if I could fight the battle through and win it, thus ending a life of much smolder and a scanty fire in a blaze of glory. But I should smother myself in mud of my own making. . . . I am not low-spirited, nor fanciful, nor freakish, but look what seem to me to be realities in the face, and am ready to take whatever may come. If I could but go to England now, I think the sea voyage and the 'Old Home' might set me all right."

(VI)

In March Sophia suggested that a change of scene might be beneficial to Nathaniel's health. She was incapable of abandoning hope, and a journey southward seemed to her to offer some slight chance for the improvement of Nathaniel's condition. Nathaniel no longer deceived himself about its gravity. He knew that death was imminent, and had no desire to postpone it, but he wished above all to occasion Sophia no vain regrets. So with ready docility he assented to the projected journey. Arrangements were made that he be accompanied by Ticknor and Pierce, but at the last moment Pierce was forced to withdraw. He set off with Ticknor alone in the last days of March on a journey of indefinite duration without any rigorous itinerary.

A few days after their departure a letter came to The Wayside from Bridge, and in Nathaniel's absence Sophia replied to it:

"Alas! it was no 'author's excuse' which was published in *The Atlantic,* but a most sad and serious truth. Mr. Hawthorne has really been very ill all winter, and not well, by any means, for a much longer time; not ill in bed, but miserable on a lounge or sofa, and quite unable to write a word, even a letter, and lately unable to read. I have felt the wildest anxiety about him, because he is a person who has been immaculately well all his life, and this illness has seemed to me an awful dream which could not be true. But he has wasted away very much, and the suns in his eyes are collapsed, and he has had no spirits, no appetite and very little sleep. Richard was not himself, and his absolute repugnance to see a physician, or to have any scientific investigation of his indisposition, has weighed me down like a millstone. I have felt such a terrible oppression in thinking that all was not doing for his relief that might be done, that sometimes I have scarcely been able to endure it—at moments hardly able to fetch my breath in apprehension of the possible danger."

Meanwhile, Nathaniel and Ticknor had proceeded as far as New York, where they put up at the Astor House. Ticknor had left Boston suffering from a heavy chest cold, and a week of bitter, inclement weather in New York added to his discomfort. He contemplated undertaking the journey from New York to Cuba, in search of sunlight and warmth, but the continuance of violent storms caused the abandonment of that project. At the end of a week it was decided to move on to Philadelphia. Storms mercilessly pursued them here also, like an inexorable destiny. Nathaniel insisted upon taking advantage of the first sunny day to go about the city, and the two friends went for a carriage-ride through Fairmount Park. But the belated sunshine was deceptive. The air proved to be chillier than they had anticipated and, when they were riding through the park, Ticknor slipped off his overcoat and wrapped it about Nathaniel. On the following morning Ticknor complained of his cold; the next day he took to his bed, and the physicians summoned by Nathaniel pronounced his malady to be congestion of the lungs. Within another day, and before his family could be summoned, Ticknor had died. Nathaniel had never before seen death. . . .

"He came back unlooked for that day;" Sophia informed Fields after Nathaniel's lonely return to The Wayside, "and when I heard a step on the piazza, I was lying on a couch and feeling quite indisposed. But as soon as I saw him, I was frightened out of all knowledge of myself,—so haggard, so white, so deeply scored with pain and fatigue was the face, so much more ill he looked than I ever saw him before. He had walked from the station because he saw no carriage there, and his brow was streaming with a perfect rain, so great had been the effort to walk so far. . . . He needed much to get home to me, where he could fling off all care of himself and give way to his feelings, pent up and kept back for so long, especially since his watch and ward of most excellent Mr. Ticknor.

"It relieved him to break down as he spoke of that scene. . . . He has more than lost all he gained by the journey, by the sad event. From being the nursed and cared for,—early to bed and late to rise,—led as it were, by the ever-ready hand of Mr. Ticknor, to become the nurse and nightwatcher, with all the responsibilities, with his mighty power of sympathy, and his vast apprehension of suffering in others, and to see death for the first time in a state so weak as his,—the death also of so valued a friend—there are lines plowed on his brow which were never there before."

(VII)

After Ticknor's funeral Nathaniel sank into a condition approaching stupor. He could not forget Ticknor's death; the last agonizing hours during which Ticknor pleaded for his family; the moment before death when he dreamed that they stood about his bedside, and gasped a blessing upon the merciful hallucination that brought him final peace. The grim, ironical futility of Ticknor's death possessed Nathaniel; he could only reiterate, over and over again, that death should have come to him and not to Ticknor.

Instinctively, Sophia realized that Nathaniel must be taken away from Concord immediately. In the emergency she appealed to Franklin Pierce, who proposed taking Nathaniel on a carriage-tour in the New Hampshire mountains. To this Nathaniel consented, less in the belief that it might result in any profit to his health, however temporary, than in the hope that it might hasten the inevitable end. A premonition that he was never to return obsessed him, and he accepted it with a melancholy pleasure. To leave Sophia and the children would be painful; but it was kind to suffer pain himself and spare her the anguish of watching him sink into death before her eyes. He could not endure the thought of the lingering days that precede death; the waiting and watching and helpless grief, the long hours during which the heart is full but cannot utter its passion. No; it was better that the blow come without warning, better for them all that Sophia should not know that he was going, but should learn only that he

NATHANIEL HAWTHORNE

After a Crayon Drawing by Samuel Rowse

had gone. If death would but take him as he slept, without his knowing . . .

On a warm bright day in May the station wagon drove up to The Wayside. Nathaniel feebly walked out of the house, supported by Sophia's arm. Before painfully climbing into the carriage he stood for a moment gazing at his two daughters; then his eyes moved over the familiar scene, the buff-colored house with its tower and terraced hill, the lawn with its acacia trees in blossom, the quiet green meadows across the road dappled with sunlight. His daughters remarked that he held himself erect, but that he seemed an old, old man. Sophia assisted him into the carriage, quietly sobbing. They said little to one another on the way to the railway station, but Nathaniel gently stroked her hand. From the window of the railway coach he looked back at her, bravely waving and blowing him kisses, a shrunken, suffering figure, unspeakably desolate in her loneliness. . . .

He met Pierce in Boston, and they began their journey, stopping a week at Concord, New Hampshire, and then proceeding to Franklin, Laconia, Centre Harbor and Plymouth. Pierce was shocked by the change that had come over Nathaniel since he had last seen him. Nathaniel was deathly pale and shrunken, he walked with extreme difficulty, and the use of his hands was impaired. They arrived at Plymouth late on the afternoon of May 18, and secured adjoining rooms at the Pemigewasset House, a vast white structure adjacent to the railway station. Nathaniel ordered some tea and toast in his room, slept for an hour upon the sofa, and then told Pierce that he would retire for the night. The door between their rooms stood ajar and Pierce left the light burning in his room, that he might see Nathaniel without moving from his bed. Nathaniel fell asleep very quickly. Between one and two in the morning, Pierce arose and crept to Nathaniel's bedside. Nathaniel was sleeping soundly.

Perhaps that sleep was not dreamless. Perhaps once again he saw Powers, as together they stood on the terrace at Montaüto, watching the twilight enfold Florence; and Bright, walking with him across English fields splashed by watery sunshine; and Macaulay and Browning at breakfast in Brook Street; and the Marquis of Lansdowne stepping aside that Nathaniel might precede him up the stairs; and the Yankee captains at whist in Mrs. Blodgett's cosy smoke-room; and Herman Melville riding up to the little red house at Lenox for a long evening of talk; and Fields, in the dingy upstairs room in Mall Street, insistently asking for the first draft of *The Scarlet Letter;* and Sophia surprising him with her little hoard of gold on the day of his removal from the Custom House; and Emerson coming up the avenue toward the Old Manse, bringing Thoreau with him; and the fantastic evenings at Brook Farm when Margaret Fuller held conversations; and the interminable succession of coal ships awaiting his inspection in Boston Harbor; and Sophia in her simple white wrapper, coming down from her studio to greet him on the evening when he had fallen in love with her; and himself in the solitude of "Castle Dismal" in Salem; and Bridge affectionately encouraging him on many a moonlit walk at Bowdoin; and Sebago Lake at Raymond as he skated alone on wintry nights; and perhaps he heard the tremors of spring in an old Salem garden, and his mother's voice bidding him come to her. . . .

When Pierce came once more to his bedside, life had ceased.

EPILOGUE

. . . Emerson took his pen from the pen-tray, carefully wiped it clean, and began to write, slowly and deliberately, on the fresh white page of his journal:

"Yesterday, May 23, we buried Hawthorne in Sleepy Hollow, in a pomp of sunshine and verdure and gentle winds. James Freeman Clarke read the service in the church and at the grave. Longfellow, Lowell, Holmes, Agassiz, Hoar, Dwight, Whipple, Norton, Alcott, Hillard, Judge Thomas and I attended the hearse as pall-bearers. Franklin Pierce was with the family. The church was copiously decorated with white flowers delicately arranged. The corpse was unwillingly shown—only a few moments to this company of friends. But it was noble and serene in its aspect—nothing amiss—a calm and powerful head. All was so bright and quiet that pain or mourning was hardly suggested, and Holmes said to me that it looked like a happy meeting.

"Clarke in the church said that Hawthorne had done more justice than any other to all shades of life, shown a sympathy with the crime in our nature, and, like Jesus, was the friend of sinners.

"I thought there was a tragic element in the event that might be more fully rendered,—in the painful solitude of the man, which, I suppose, could not longer be endured, and he died of it.

"I have found in his death a surprise and disappointment. I thought him a greater man than any of his works betray, that there was still a great deal of work in him, and that he might some day show a purer power. Moreover, I have felt sure of him in his neighborhood, and in his necessities of sympathy and intelligence —that I could well wait his time—his unwillingness and caprice—and might one day conquer a friendship. It would have been a happiness, doubtless, to both of us, to have come into habits of unreserved intercourse. It was easy to talk with him—there were no barriers—only he said so little that I talked too much, and stopped only because, as he gave no indication, I feared to exceed. He showed no egotism or self-assertion, rather a humility, and, at one time, a fear that he had written himself out. One day when I found him on the top of his hill, in the woods, he paced back the path to his house, and said, 'This path is the only remembrance of me that will remain.' Now it appears that I waited too long."

New York City, October, 1925—
Cap d'Antibes, July, 1926.

INDEX

INDEX

INDEX

INDEX

INDEX

175

813H399X M876r
The rebellious Puritan
3 1144 00161315 6